Talking the Walk & Walking the Talk

VERBAL ARTS :: STUDIES IN POETICS

SERIES EDITORS :: Lazar Fleishman & Haun Saussy

Talking the Walk
& Walking the Talk

A RHETORIC OF RHYTHM

Marc Shell

FORDHAM UNIVERSITY PRESS   *New York*   2015

Copyright © 2015 Fordham University Press

All rights reserved. No part of this publication may be reproduced, stored in a retrieval system, or transmitted in any form or by any means—electronic, mechanical, photocopy, recording, or any other—except for brief quotations in printed reviews, without the prior permission of the publisher.

Fordham University Press has no responsibility for the persistence or accuracy of URLs for external or third-party Internet websites referred to in this publication and does not guarantee that any content on such websites is, or will remain, accurate or appropriate.

Fordham University Press also publishes its books in a variety of electronic formats. Some content that appears in print may not be available in electronic books.

Visit us online at www.fordhampress.com.

Library of Congress Cataloging-in-Publication Data

Shell, Marc.
  Talking the walk & walking the talk : a rhetoric of rhythm / Marc Shell. — First edition.
     pages cm. — (Verbal arts: studies in poetics)
  Includes bibliographical references and index.
  ISBN 978-0-8232-5682-2 (hardback)
  ISBN 978-0-8232-5683-9 (paper)
   1. Poetics. 2. Rhythm in literature. 3. Walking in literature. 4. English language—Versification. I. Title.
PN1059.R53S44 2015
808.1—dc23
                       2015013308

17 16 15   5 4 3 2 1

First edition

What justification is there for comparing a poem with a walk rather than with something else?
—A. R. Ammons, "A Poem Is a Walk"

CONTENTS

1. Starting Out: Prologue and Preamble   1
2. Walking Voices   41
3. Trips of the Tongue in *Hamlet* (1600)   57
4. Talking Cures   72
5. Walkie Talkies   88
6. Marching and Heiling in *The Great Dictator* (1940)   100
7. Knock-Kneed and Tongue-Tied in *The King's Speech* (2010)   116
8. Sign Languages   123
9. Postamble and Epilogue   133

Notes   149
Index   205

Talking the Walk & Walking the Talk

CHAPTER ONE

Starting Out

Prologue and Preamble

I will . . . talk with you, walk with you . .
—SHYLOCK, *The Merchant of Venice*[1]

Concerning the apparent similitude of talking and walking, or voice and attitude, Ralph Waldo Emerson cites authority in his essay "The Conduct of Life" (1860). Emerson remarks that the French novelist Honoré de Balzac "left in manuscript form a chapter, which he called *Theory of Walking* [Théorie de la demarche] (1833). In that essay, reports Emerson, Balzac put forth the argument that "the look, the voice, the respiration, and the attitude or walk, are identical."[2] In this work, I hope to contribute to understanding an intellectual requirement to regard walking and talking in a single rhythm vision. In so doing, I will contribute also to theory of prosody, understanding of respiration and look, and, in sum, to particular links, across the board, between the human characteristic of biped walking and meaningful talk.

The first three sections of this opening chapter introduce a few philosophical, neurological, anthropological, and aesthetic aspects of the subject in historical perspective. The following sections focus on rhetoric and introduce a tension between the small and large issues of rhythm. The fourth section considers the roles of breathing in poetry as a life-and-death matter, with attention to beats and walking poems. In this way, we begin to introduce relevant technical concepts from the classical traditions, usually originally ancient Greek and Roman, of rhetoric and philology. The fifth section involves the relationship between prosody and motion, including in its purview both animals and human beings as well as both ostensibly able-bodied creatures and presumptively disabled ones. Finally, the sixth section focuses on dancing and writing as aspects of walking and talking, with special attention to motion in Arabic and Chinese calligraphy.

Chapters 3 through 7 provide a select series of interrelated representative case studies that both expand upon problems raised in the first chapter and take off from them. The order of "case studies" is roughly chronological, as the chapter and section titles indicate. The obvious exception is the first case study, which takes place, at least according to the Bible, when worldly or fallen time has not quite begun. All chapters here group texts by theme, rhetorical terminology, or artistic medium. Each chapter deals with different issues surrounding the prosody and psychology of walking as talking: talking animals, verbally or pedally disabled creatures, dancing and singing, and what some psychiatrists call "the vertigo of walking." The various works discussed in the latter parts of this book shed light on the issues introduced in earlier chapters, while at the same time illuminating the texts under discussion. These parts of *Talking the Walk & Walking the Talk* walk the talk and crisscross the paths.

As we amble toward the Postamble and Epilogue, we come to consider uniquely reduplicative aspects of the English language that inform *Talking the Walk & Walking the Talk*. We also return then to the neurology of walking and talking understood as a single activity, to the anthropology of people from different cultures walking as well as talking in different ways, and to the politics of crowds and herds on the march. This "rhetoric of rhythm" then moves to the question of how human thinkers have often been distracted from the question of what constitutes acceptable argumentation in rhetoric and prosody. There follows the topic of ability or disability in walking and talking and, at the finish line, a reconsideration of what remains to do.

Talking the Walk & Walking the Talk originates from two of my lately published books. One of these, *Polio and Its Aftermath,* is partly about the more-or-less permanently paralyzed ability to walk. The other book, *Stutter,* is about the more-or-less temporarily paralyzed ability to talk. "What does talking have to do with walking?" "What do the vocal and the pedal have in common?"[3] In what way can we say that "Talking the walk" matches up with "Walking the talk"? Those are questions students at Harvard have asked me while attending seminars of mine on the subject of motional ability and disability. This book, in which lameness and frailty are integral aspects of the subject matter, is an elaboration of one way to answer their broad-based questions.[4]

TALKING AND WALKING

Only thoughts reached by walking have value.
—FRIEDRICH NIETZSCHE, *Twilight of the Idols*[5]

Let me begin with something seriously meant—that is, philosophically intending—to be funny. In the Marilyn Monroe movie called *Let's Make Love* (1960)—ghostwritten by her husband, the playwright Arthur Miller—Milton Berle, the then much celebrated vaudeville and television comedian, plays himself as the funniest man in the world. Berle tries to teach the richest man in the world—played by Marilyn Monroe's on-screen paramour and off-screen adulterous lover, Yves Montand—to *walk* spastically like a stumbling "dodo" while simultaneously to *talk* stutteringly like a real "d-duh." The funniest man in the world (Berle) tells the richest man in the world (Montand) that that's what cracks them up—makes people laugh—every single time he does it. The vaudeville comedian's practiced pratfalls on a slippery banana peel (a favorite act), from this point of view, matches his careful slips of the tongue (likewise a favored act).

Like it or not, Milton Berle was no fool. The stumbling, stuttering walky-talky on stage was funny. At least in "The West." It works every time.

Yet, at the same time, there are legendary figures who aren't so funny when they talk or walk haltingly. Among these would be the oh-so-serious Greek, staff-bearing, crippled punster, tyrant Oedipus and the utterly foundational Jewish/Egyptian staff-bearing stutterer Prince Moses. They too walk and talk crookedly, even to the point where they are entirely stoppered. (Moses's need for his staff, a prosthetic leg, matches his need for his brother Aaron, a prosthetic mouth.) What gives there? One seems almost to require a theory of walk-dance and/or stutter-talk.

For one thing, these presumably disabled talky-walkies at the font of Western civilization—the Jewish Moses and the Greek Oedipus—are not "orthodox" philosophers, at least not in the usual exoteric sense of *philosophy*. Moreover, in fact, in traditional philosophy at least, walking and talking well go together. The Western languages, at the least, often suggest as much. Consider the case of English. "To be straight," or *orthos*, in English, means, among other things, both "talk the talk" and at the same time "walk the walk." Thinkers have long insisted that talking philosophically requires walking meditatively.

Plato's little joke is that Thales of Miletus fell down into a hole in the earth because he was meditating linguistically on the stars above while walking. The Greek Aristotle has his conversational philosophical academy in a peripatetic grove intended for walking while talking. Walking meditation (*cankama*) has been one of the popular methods for mind development in Buddhism ever since the Buddha's time. The French Rousseau writes in his *Confessions*, "I am unable to reflect when I am not walking: the moment I stop, I think no more, and as soon as I am again in motion my head resumes its workings"; he almost proves as much, *solvitur ambulando*, in his *Reveries of a Solitary Walker.* Just as Saint John claims (in his Gospel), "In the beginning was the *word* [*logos*]," so cultural anthropologist Marvin Harris declares (in his *Our Kind*), "In the beginning was the *foot*."[6]

The Huguenot-American Thoreau says that, in order to enter into oneself, or *s'entrer*—or to enter into the Mosaic Holy Land, or *Saint Terre*—one must *saunter*, or walk about. (The OED rejects Thoreau's etymology of *saunter* as coming from *s'auntrer*, "to venture into oneself.")[7] It seems almost to follow for Thoreau that one born without "walking legs," so called, cannot be a philosopher: "It requires a direct dispensation from heaven to become a walker. You must be born into the family of the Walkers. "*Ambulator nascitur, non fit* [The walker is born, not made]."

Wallace Stevens, who claimed to keep his insurance work and poetry writing separate, composed his poems while walking to and from work. The young German dialectician—and stutterer[8]—Hegel, whose first publication was a sort of tourist's walking-guide to part of Switzerland, would have hiked with the great geologist and walker Horace-Bénédict de Saussure in the Swiss Alps in order to produce his first publications. (Saussure was the first to promote the idea of climbing Mount Blanc and of the greater "Alpine walking tour.") The so-called Philosophers' Path in Kyoto (Japan) derives its name because the philosopher Kitaro Nishida used to walk the path to meditate. Heidelberg (Germany) has its *Philosophenweg*. The twentieth-century Martin Heidegger likewise had his Black Forest walks before and during his philosophical lectures. How come this widespread coincidence of vocal and pedal?

I am hesitant to follow the lead of such writers as Rebecca Solnit in her popularizing *Wanderlust: A History of Walking* (2000), who suggests more than argues that "the rhythm of walking generates a kind of rhythm of thinking."[9] (Gretel Ehrlich likewise writes, "Walking is also an ambulation of mind.")[10] We will return to this notion. Maybe, though, human beings are, by nature or convention, talking biped walkers.[11] (In this line of reasoning, there are arguments, like that of Amato in *On Foot*, that "in the beginning was the foot," so that "the origin of bipedal man" is key to understanding basic human nature.[12] One might want as well to recall that, when a blind man sees for the first time, he may see men—not improperly—as walking trees.)[13] Further, therefore, philosophy requires less to "talk the talk" and "walk the walk"—which is what I have called "being straight," or, *orthos*, than real philosophy actually requires something like "walking on talk" or "talking the walk." It is as if walking on talking (see Figure 1.1) were the same as talking on walking.

I am therefore also hesitant to deride the notion *ambulo ergo sum* (I walk, therefore I am) in the way that much scientific philosophy has done in the past. The philosophers Pierre Gassendi and Thomas Hobbes, for example, use the saying, *ambulo ergo sum*, which they take to be absurd on the face of it, as a means to mock René Descartes's most famous dictum, namely *"Je pense donc je suis* [I think, therefore I am]"[14] or *"Cogito ergo sum* [I think, therefore I am]."[15] Gassendi and Hobbes claim that Descartes might as well be deriving existence from any activity, even from "mere ambulation." The joke on Descartes is supposed to reside partly in the fact that ambulation in Hobbes's English usage applies only to the locomotion of walking; nonhuman animals,[16] human beings riding on animals,[17] or human beings walking *like* animals[18]—not to human beings walking like human beings—and Descartes, of course, argued that nonhuman animals do not cogitate. The Hobbesian critique of the Cartesian *cogito* does not depend entirely on the activity of ambulation ("walking") in particular in order to make its point about consciousness and language ("talking").[19] The Cartesian *cogito*, moreover, has other difficulties besides that on which Gassendi and Hobbes focus their attention. What if it turns out, however, that there is a way of walking, specifically human, that goes the same as human talking? Or, as Horace Walpole puts it, that human thoughts amble?[20]

Figure 1.1. Liliane Dardot. Museum installation, 2006. Popular plant names, listed in a footnote in "Cara de Bronze" (1956), itemize the plants and the people of the distinctive Brazilian backcountry called *sertão*. The list is transcribed in cursive handwriting using white sand on a black plane. In order to access the installation, people removed their shoes, each person thus defining a new and different reading of printed text. "Por fundo de todos os matos, Amém!" Work of Liliane Dardot at Museu Mineiro, Belo Horizonte, Brazil, 2006. Based on a footnote of the short story "Cara de Bronze," by João Guimarães Rosa, from the book *No Urubuquaquá, no Pinhém*, which is part of the *Corpo de Baile*. Photograph by Luiz Henrique Vieira.

RHYTHM AND METER

There is as it were an oscillating rhythm in the life of organisms.
—FREUD, *Beyond the Pleasure Principle*[21]

Talking the Walk & Walking the Talk does not offer a full theory of rhythm, a whole explanation of the origin of rhythm, a definitive proof of a thesis about language and corporeality, a total psychoanalytic overview, or a perfected rhetorical theory about the near-ubiquity of inadvertent and calculated irregularity in verbal and ambulatory practices. Instead, it focuses on a particular linkage of rhythm understood in a larger cultural aspect with rhythm understood in a smaller facet, suggesting thus phenomenological aspects of a political and biological notion about rhythm that human beings have known or intuited for centuries but rarely, if ever, brought out even in preliminary fashion.

The "macro" focus partly engages many aspects of the rhythms of biological life, a field one of whose originators in modern times was Sigmund Freud's confidante and nose surgeon, Wilhelm Fliess.[22] By the same token, the large view engages aspects of human political life (imperialism, urbanization, rapid social change, and globalization) and human communication (dance and film, art and architecture, as well as *talking*) as large fields devoted to inanimate movement (geology and hydrology). Relevant works about the role of rhythm and culture and the development of civilization[23] would include Gaston Bachelard's *La dialectique de la durée* (1936),[24] Mary Elizabeth Hallock Greenewalt's *Pulse in Verbal Rhythm* (1905),[25] Ludwig Klages's *Vom Wesen des Rhythmus* (1934),[26] and Henri Lefebvre's sociologically oriented *Rhythmanalysis: Space, Time, and Everyday Life* (2004).[27] There is also Hans Mayer's *Rhythmus: über die rhythmische Prägung des Menschen und ihre kulturellen Erscheinungsformen* (1991),[28] Matila Costiescu Ghyka's *Essai sur le rythme* (1938),[29] and all those works discussed by Pascal Michon in "*Rythme, pouvoir, mondialisation* (2005) and *Les Rythmes du politique: Démocratie et capitalisme mondialisé* (2007).[30] Referenced later in *Talking the Walk & Walking the Talk* are many other such works, ranging from anthropology and neurology to musicology and mathematics. As we shall see, however, most all such works, no matter how brilliant, tiptoe around the tighter relationships, often bordering on identification, specifically between talking with walking, while at the same time they are, of course, thanks partly to the quiet influence of variants of an old definition of a *human being* as "a *talking* featherless bi-*ped*."

By contrast, then, there is rhythm understood variously in the narrower terms of linguistic meter. In prosody, *rhythm* refers to "the measured flow of words or phrases in verse, forming various patterns of sound as determined by the relation of long and short or stressed and unstressed syllables in a metrical foot..."[31] *Rhythm in this context often involves* the phonetic realization of *meter* within a particular line of verse; *meter* is the form of periodicity. "There can be no rhythm without meter," writes a formalist Victor Zhirmunsky (1925).[32] Émile Benveniste's essay "The Notion of 'Rhythm' in its Linguistic Expression" (1966)[33] puts forward the traditional view concerning rhythm and rheology: "One can derive ρυθμος [rhythm] *from* the Greek ρειν [to flow]," meaning something like "the repetitive breaking of waves onto the shore." Rhythm indicates *"form in the instant that it is assumed by what is moving, mobile and fluid, the form of that which does not have organic consistency; it fits the pattern of a fluid element, of a letter arbitrarily shaped,* of a robe which one arranges at one's will, of a particular state of character or mood. It is the form as improvised, momentary, changeable."[34]

Henri Meschonnic, who tries to blend the micro and macro viewpoints on rhythm, however much he passes over the sciences (where rheology means the "science that deals with the deformation and flow of matter"),[35] argues that rhythm brings out "the continuous movement of significance constructed by the historical activity of a subject."[36] Meschonnic's interest includes verse and language, as in his essays *Critique du rythme: Anthropologie historique du langage* (1982)[37] and *Traité du rythme: Des vers et des proses* (1998),[38] as well as the more broadly cultural subjects treated by the authors listed in the paragraph above, as in his *Politique du rythme, politique du sujet,* (1995).[39] Meschonnic's poetry, at the least, sometimes links walking with talking, as if he intuits a definite way to link the two foci. There is, for example, his *Je marche mon infini* (2007)[40] and his *De Monde en monde* (From World to World, 2009): *"chaque moment je recommence / le désert / je marche chaque douleur un pas / et j'avance / de monde en monde."*[41] The title of his *Puisque je suis ce buisson* (Since I am this Bush, 2001) refers partly to the biblical burning bush that Moses, the lame stutterer, encounters at Sinai.

J'avance avec
le silence des arbres
je marche avec
le rond du ciel

je ne parle pas
mes mots
je les marche
et je marche mon silence
ça ne commence pas
et ça ne finit pas.[42]

The case of Moses helps to define an entire civilization. Moses is, for a good part of so-called Western civilization, a quintessential example (though by no means the only one or, for many, even the main one) of the pedal-vocal communicator.

Much as the biblical god breathes life into a lump of clay by way of its nostrils and thus creates a living Adam, even so he kisses the lame stutterer Moses—it is an inhalational kiss on the mouth (*al pee hashem*)—and thus sucks the life out of him.[43] The breathing is all; the talking is ideal as the walking is real.

SCANSION AND BREATHING

The resemblance of the motion of a person in walking has given to syllables when they form poetical lines, the name of feet.
—BARRETT, *The Principles of Grammar*[44]

Walking the mind, walking the prosody.
—RILEY, *Noon Provence et autres poèmes*[45]

There are many walkers who think of walking in terms of prosody (and, as the epigraph from Riley suggests, others think of prosody in terms of walking). Tim Miller writes in his review of Brian Boudlrey's *Honorable Bandit: A Walk Across Corsica*, "Walking has a prosody: when I walk downhill, the legs do dactyls (for the unschooled: one long stride, two doorstop jambs, a stressed syllable and two unstressed: 'dithering,' 'wearying'—'Corsica')."[46] George Saintsbury, who wrote the *History of English Prosody from the Twelfth Century to the Present* (1908)—one of the great studies of English prosody—as well as editing the first English-language edition of Balzac's *Comédie humaine* (1895–98), believes much the same. As Dorothy Jones writes, Saintsbury "more than once refers to prosody as akin to dancing and also says he did much of his thinking about prosody while walking, the two 'modes of motion,' physically or metaphysical, suggesting each other."[47] Daalder writes about Joshua Steele's *An Essay Towards Establishing the Melody and Measure of Speech*

(1775), where there is the belief "that there must be a close connection between supposed movement of speech and that of our pulse, or our feet in walking." On the analogy of the distinction between "the walk of a sound or perfect man" and "the halting of a lame man," Steele claims that "speech is either in common or triple time, or a combination of the two."[48]

If walking is a kind of talking, talking is a kind of walking. Authors often claim, with more-or-less precision, that talking is walking but do not get down to the brass tacks of exactly how that is true (literally) or even how it seems likely to be the case (metaphorically).[49] Any good coach for talking and walking, though, will tell you to watch out for rhythm and breathing. In popular music, certainly, the twin theme of walking and talking is common. The Velvet Underground has their hortatory song, "You better walk it, talk it / You better walk it as you talk it or you lose that beat."[50]

In poetics, that is the business of scansion and prosody. The editors of the *OED* point out that *to scan* means "to analyse (verse) by determining the nature and number of the component feet or the number and prosodic value of the syllables." Likewise, it means "to indicate the structure or test the correctness of (a verse) by reciting it with metrical emphasis and pauses, or by counting on the fingers the feet as they occur in recitation." Hamlet suggests that scansion of the talk (the idea) is a way to understand also the walk (what is really meant). ("That would be scanned," says Hamlet.) I intend to follow out some of the consequences of this way of thinking about walking, talking human beings.

Not all languages use *feet* to describe scansion. Almost all do, however. Where a particular language seems not to use *feet* to describe prosodic meter—Old English, say—the case is usually debatable both ways.[51] All languages treat their rhythms in terms of some pulsing rhythm organ (for example, the heart)[52] or potentially tempo-marking limb (for example, the hand) of the human body. (The traditional view that the hands are instruments of rational skill whereas the feet are instruments of bipedal locomotion overlooks how evolutionary biology links hands and feet.[53] In prosody, by analogy, *daktylos* ["finger"]—names the pedal long-short-short—as suggested in the index finger's sections, beginning from the palm.[54] Finger-hexameter is the standard rhythm of national epic: the Greek Homer's *Iliad* and *Odyssey*, for example, and the Roman Virgil's *Aeneid*.) Relevant is the field of "comparative national metrics," including such broad-based studies as Mikhail Leonovich Gasparov's *History of European Versification.*[55]

Thoreau wrote much about strolling. He published his lectures or essays "A Walk to Wachusett" and "A Winter Walk" early on in 1843; he ended his publishing career, when he would have been forty-five years old, with the posthumously published "Walking" (1862). Emerson said, in his "Eulogy" (1862) on Thoreau, "The length of his walk uniformly made the length of his writing." (*Length* here means, among other things, both, in calculation, "the measure of a boat, a horse, etc., engaged in a race, taken as a unit in measuring the amount by which the race is won"[56] and, in prosody, the "quantity [of a sound or syllable].")[57]

The "feet" of prose and those of the walker seem sometimes to match up. In his eulogy for Thoreau, Emerson goes on: "If shut up in the house he did not write at all."[58]

Relevant—to this conjunction of hand/foot and tongue—is the way in which we speak of (or, as it is often called, "scan") the beat or rhythm of speaking poetry and prose in terms of feet. It is as if poetry and prose had a cadence—in much the way that a walker's footfall or musician's foot-beat or foot-tap does, when it "beats" (to) the music.

CAESURA

The first time he opened his mouth and was just going to spread himself, his breath took a walk.
—MARK TWAIN, *Sketches New & Old*[59]

For human beings, breathing through the windpipe—inspiration and expiration taken together—is a life and death matter. Therefore oral poetry—meant to be recited aloud by a single speaker who does not die in the process of recitation—needs to take into account the breathing stop. Michel Mourgues thus writes in "De la Cesure" (1697), "It would be rather awkward to sustain one's voice for ten or twelve consecutive syllables without breathing (sans respirer) especially when a Pronunciation is grave and majestic, as when one recites or declaims poetry. For this reason our two longest poetic lines [the Alexandrine line, which has twelve syllables, and the decasyllable line, which has ten] are marked by a specific repose, which divide them into two halves [hemi-stiches] and this is called 'the caesura.'"[60] There's no way around this requirement to breathe. Breathing and the timing of breathing come to define the rhythm and prosody of poetry—no matter what.[61] The "pause" in poetic rhythm is central to works like Shakespeare's *Hamlet*, where it assumes vital status.[62] The person who stutters fears terminal exhaustion: "A brusque question," writes Conrad in *The Secret Agent*, "caused him to stutter to the point of suffocation."[63]

Musical notation sheds light on the various sorts of pauses that one encounters in the rhetoric of rhythm. Igor Stravinsky wrote that "the subject of [his] ballet [*Apollon Musagetes* (1927–28), in which the Greek of music Apollo is visited by three different muses with rhythmic concerns. These are Terpsichore, muse of dance and song, Polyhymnia, muse of mime, and Calliope, muse of poetry] is versification." The published score has the following Alexandrine about the repose or caesura, quoted from a didactic poem by Nicholas Boileau-Despréaux in *The Art of Poetry* (1674):

Que toujours, dans vos vers, || le sens coupant les mots
Suspende l'hémistiche, || en marque le repos.

[that always, in your verses, the half line, which cuts the words, suspend the sense, and mark its pause.][64]

No matter the many variants among languages and literary traditions, even those where the caesura is understood peculiarly as a hyphen ("hyphens of silence between each two syllables"),[65] the vitals remain nearly the same: a suspension of breath.[66]

In this arena, one might want to draw an analogy with music and musical notation. Consider three sorts of pause signals. The fermata, indicated by "⌒", and the grand pause, indicated by "G.P.," do not require breathing. The caesura, indicated by the double-pipe at oblique angle, "//", allows for it. The breathing stop, indicated by " ' ", calls for breathing by the players of those wind instruments, including recorder-pipes and human voice-box, that require human beings directly to pass breath out of their own lungs and through the windpipe. Both recorder and voice require breathing stops in the same way. Says Hamlet to Rosencrantz and Guildenstern, "Sblood, do you think I am easier to be played on than a pipe? . . . Look you, these are the stops."

In poetry, the sign for the caesura is often the double-pipe at a vertical axis (||), as in the Boileau passage quoted above. Even where the meaning of *caesura* is so apparently straightforward as "the division of a metrical foot between two words,"[67] however, there are debates; George Puttenham thus argues in his *The Arte of English Poesie* (1589) that "caesura must never be made in the midst of any word, if it be well appointed."[68] Not every caesura is a breathing stop and not every breathing stop is a caesura, but every breathing stop, meant for breathing in, affects sound and rhythm by presence and absence, and all wind performers need to breathe just as much as any other human being. The sound of inspiration usually has no semantic content—although some words, like *tsk*, can be spoken on the in-breath. Whether the in-breath itself has a meaning, the silence or sound of the pause it presents is part of the metrical structure and score of the work. *Caesura*, understood now in terms of the breathing stop, is what Philip Sidney has in mind when he writes in his *Defence of Poetry* (1595), "That Caesura, or breathing place in the midst of the Verse [especially, for Sidney, English]." Many people suggest that, for some kinds of verse, including "free verse,"[69] the caesura is "optional," but for all human beings, breathing is involuntary.

The caesura has a special place in modern thinking thanks partly to the mostly figural usage of *caesura* by the poet Friedrich Hölderlin, especially in his own writing (1804) about Sophocles's *Antigone* and *Oedipus*,[70] and in the series of essays and books that followed from it, among them Walter Benjamin's essay on the subject of caesural rupture and representation (1922). The musicologist Michael Spitzer argues that "the heroic style changes the paradigm of the caesura [as Hölderlin presents it] from the poetic [realm of discourse] to the anthropomorphic [realm]: in Hegel's words [from his 'Preface' in *The Phenomenology of Mind* (1807)], 'the child's first breath.'"[71]

The Hegelian notion is that a caesura makes a Janus-like turn (revolution) in history, which is well enough (so far as it goes), but *Talking the Walk & Walking the Talk* has, as well as a phenomenological angle, a physiological one, concerned with such events as "oscillations of heart rate and respiration synchronization during poetry recitation," especially Greek dactylic hexameter.[72] Such hexameter is often split in two parts by a break (caesura), which in the most archetypal form (for example, Homer's *Iliad*) takes place after the long part of the third dactyl.[73] The conveniently paced asymmetrical breathing patterns of the hexameter help the would-be talking stutterer and support the ambling walker's gait, generally bracing human memory. Consider the "therapeutic" usefulness of "Anthroposophic Therapeutic Speech"[74] exercises based on the ideas of the Austrian thinker Rudolf Steiner. For him, the German term *eurhythmy* meant not only "regularity in beat"[75] but also, as for the ancient Greek *eurythmia*, "graceful proportion and carriage of the body"[76]—ultimately, "visible speech."[77] Rhythm exercise "enable[s] the individual to feel and express music corporally."[78] "The rhythmic function of the caesura," understood in terms of breathing stop with life-and-death consequences, informs poetry as a medium to keep one alive.

A therapist and theorist *might* think now of those survivors of bulbar polio who have lived in iron lungs to regard the regular rhythms or "raps exhalative" in Vergilian and Shakespearean poetry as well as about the breathing stops that allow for life. Robert Mauro, who was paralyzed and lived in an iron lung for decades, writes, "When I was but a boy of five,/ an iron lung did breathe for me./ . . . / and now when lovers with me lay,/ I happily take their breath away."[79] Likewise the poet Mark O'Brien, in his poem "The Man in the Iron Lung," alludes to how even a scream is controlled by enforced caesura, or breathing stop, mandated by his iron lung: "I scream / The Body electric / This Yellow, metal pulsing cylinder / Whooshing all day, all night / In its repetitive dumb mechanical rhythm."[80] The breathing, rhythmic, determines all.

Equally important is the poetry of swimming, which, properly speaking, *must* heed the need to breathe, even as Cleopatra observes the swimming patterns of the dolphin, when she describes Mark Antony: His delights / Were dolphin-like, they showed his back above / The element they lived in."[81] Not to breathe is to die. One old etymology of *walking* thus connects it with Anglo-Saxon *wealcan*, meaning "roll[ing] about and toss[ing], like the sea."[82]

BEAT

Knock, knock, knock! Who's there?
—THE PORTER, in *Macbeth*

In Samuel Taylor Coleridge's "Metrical Feet: Lesson for a Boy" (1806–7),[83] written for his son, the first lines of the poem describe the meter in which they themselves are written.

> Trochee | trips from| long to | short;
> From long | to long | in sol | emn sort
> Slow spon | dee stalks; | strong foot! | yet ill | able
> Ever to | come up with | dactyl tri | syllable.[84]

The verse trips on to the end. The walk talks or the talk walks trippingly throughout.

Starting Out

What, then, are the ways to describe rhythmic feet in these terms? A few examples will help.

On the one hand, a spondee, for example, is a metrical foot that consists of two long syllables (for example, *knick-knack*). In similar terms, a dactyl is a metrical foot that consists of a long syllable followed by two short (for example, *blueberry*). Just so, an iambus, supposedly the natural gait of English as well as (modified) Greek language, is a metrical foot consisting of a short followed by a long syllable (*today*). In this same vein, a dipody (from Greek *pous,* meaning "foot") is a series of two feet. There are also tripodies (three feet): one remembers the riddle of the Sphinx to which Oedi-*pus* ("swollen foot") supplied one possible answer. There are also tetrapodies, pentapodies, and hexapodies.

However, in poetic prosody, *foot* is, as OED points out, "commonly taken to refer to the movement of the foot in beating time. A division of a verse, consisting of a number of syllables one of which has the ictus or principal stress."

In English, *baston*—related to beat—means both "a staff or stick" and "a stanza or verse." *Staff* itself means either "a stick carried in the hand as an aid in walking" (as by Moses, say), and "A set of horizontal lines (now five in number) on which, and in the spaces between, notes are placed so as to indicate pitch" (and timing). In this context, *beat* refers to the motion of the hand or foot used by musical performers or conductors to mark and regulate the measure of the movements.

Some musical historians like to report that the French composer Jean-Baptiste Lully, while conducting a *Te Deum* in honor of King Louis XIV's recovery from illness, struck his own foot with his *baton*-staff—used as a metronome to beat out loud the proper rhythm. He beat himself so violently that the blow caused an abscess on the foot. The abscess developed into an Oedipus-like pedal lameness and Lully refused toe amputation; the baton-inflicted wound finally led to Lully's death (1687).[85] (It is doubtful the composer foresaw this end when he wrote his Interlude for the revival of Pierre Corneille's play *Oedipe* in 1664.)

With the baton, dance historians sometimes compare what the ancient Romans wore, a *scabella,* and the ancient Greeks, a *kroupezai.* These were hinged clapper- or clog-like sandals worn on the right foot of choir leaders to tap out the time.[86] One might think of them as "tapper's shoes."

On the one hand, the tapper's shoe is a sort of musical instrument in its own right, as Morton Gould demonstrates in his *Tap Dance Concerto* (1952). Movies easily clarify the role of the shoe: John Baxter's *Talking Feet* (1937) focuses on a young tap dancer so grateful to a doctor for having helped her that she organizes a tap-dancing concert to raise money to save his clinic, and Mike Seeger's documentary *Talking Feet* (1987) features solo flatfoot, buck, hoedown, and rural tap-dancing styles of the South. On the other hand, the taps mark off singing as well as dancing, as in Gene Kelly's song-and-dance routines in *Singing in the Rain* (1952). The rhythm of the rain matters for talking and walking at once.

Consider here the sound of painting, which is often figured as a frozen (nonkinetic) discipline. The post-impressionist Brittany-based paintings of Paul Gauguin, like *The Clog-maker* (1888)[87] and *Breton Boy Adjusting His Clogs* (1888),[88] derive nonetheless from the sound of walking.[89] "I love Brittany which I find savage and primitive," writes Gauguin. "When my clogs [*sabots*] ring [*resonnent*] on the granite ground [*ce sol de granite*] I hear the dull and powerful sound [*le ton sourd mat et puissant*] that I am looking for in painting." Gauguin sculpted his own *sabots* as if they were musical instruments that played upon the Earth (see Figure 1.2). His friend, the Dutch painter Vincent Van Gogh, wanted to be a shoemaker—a producer of pedal prosthetics in musical perspective. To his brother Theo, Vincent wrote, "I think, I think, that I would still rather be a shoemaker than a musician in colors."[90]

From this viewpoint, then, foot-scansion is everything in talking as in walking. Consider the famous riddle Sphinx that Oedipus solved or seemed to solve: "'What is it that is at the same time a biped [two-footed], a triped [sic] [three-footed], and a quadraped [sic] [four-footed]?' And while all the rest were perplexed, *Oidipous* declared that the animal proposed in the riddle was "man," since as an infant he is a quadruped, when grown a biped, and in old age a triped, using, because of his infirmity, a staff [or baton]."[91]

What triggers the action in Sophocles's *Oedipus Tyrannos* is not only the lameness of Oedipus's grandfather and that of his father (to both of which the structuralist Claude Lévi-Strauss emphasize),[92] but also the tri-podal lame aspect of staff-bearing Oedipus himself (the subject of the riddle of the Sphinx). Both figuratively and literally—and much in the fashion of the biblical Moses—Oedipus both stumbles and stutters. Both wittingly and unwittingly punning, Oedipus

Starting Out 17

Figure 1.2. Paul Gauguin. "Pair of Wooden Shoes" (*Sabots*). 1889–90. His own worn, wooden shoes. The National Gallery of Art, Chester Dale Collection, Washington, DC. 1963.10.239.a.

sometimes puts his foot into his mouth.[93] The crippled beat of his talking matches the beat of his lame walking.

WALKING POEMS

As duple Time has its basis in the act of walking and marching, triple Time is practiced every time a girl performs side-skipping
—WILLIAM THOMSON, *The Rhythm of Speech*[94]

Susan Stewart points out, in her book *Poetry and the Fate of the Senses*, that much "poetry of walking," which is a genre in its own right, involves a contrast between two kinds of walking marked by two kinds of metrics.[95] One of her examples of walking poems comes from a favorite child's game, a sort of hopscotch. The poem conveys the notion that bad luck comes from stepping on the seams of a concrete sidewalk.

> Step on a crack [spondee-pyrrhic-spondee]
> You'll break your mother's back [iambic trimeter][96]

The first line suggests the poetic "stop," and the second line suggests the "go." The nursery rhyme suggests an obsessive compulsive "disorder" involving walking and talking. (Sometimes, in fact, it actually helps to give rise to the disorder.) The disorder is the subject of Hesser's children's novel, *Kissing Doorknobs* (1998), about a young girl who believes that she cannot step on cracks or it will break her mother's back, so she counts all the cracks on the walk to school.[97] One expects a third line in *ischiorrhopgic* (back-broken) verse.[98]

Other such stop-and-go walking poems include Friedrich Hölderlin's "Der Spaziergang" ("The Walk," 1795–96) and W. H. Auden's "As I Walked Out One Evening" (1940). Both of these poems define things in terms of—and in polar opposition to—the feminine amphibrachic.

In fact, many poets have walked in order to derive their poetic metrics. Coleridge and Wordsworth used the metrics of walking to help them compose their poetry.[99] Coleridge's autobiographer William Hazlitt writes, "Coleridge has told me that he himself liked to compose in walking over uneven ground, or breaking through the struggling branches of a copse-wood, whereas Wordsworth always wrote (if he could) walking up and down a straight gravel-walk, or on some sport where the continuity of his verse met no collateral interruption."[100] In his "Something about Shakespeare" (1815–16), the German translator and interpreter of Shakespeare, August Wilhelm Schlegel, "likens prose-poetry to the ostrich, which has a gait half flying, half running, and wholly awkward."[101]

Many people learn to imitate a talk by imitating a walk. The American poet and critic Barry Schwabsky, allying talking with walking, comments thus on a review of his work: "Tom Beckett has written in a review of my books that 'voices carry the weight of the work,' and he's right in that I'm sort of a ventriloquist, manipulating my dummy self into saying just about anything, in any accent. I start mimicking the locals as soon as I get off the plane. I'd ape the locals' gait and pace of walking."[102] Patrick Dorn, in telling the reader how acting is sometimes taught in Great Britain, recounts how "members of the Royal Shakespeare Company . . . worked with us, teaching us basic textual analysis and how to walk and talk iambic pentameter."[103] The British actress Gill Stoker, also referencing the process of teaching poetry, reports, "In the verse speaking workshop, Tom Cornford [the acting teacher] got us all up onto our feet, 'walking' a speech in iambic pentameter, with instructions to change direction at every line ending and punctuation mark."[104] When Marcel Mauss says, in his "Techniques of the Body" (1935),[105] that Parisians learned the American "walk" from Hollywood films, he is concerned also with Parisian patterns of "talk."

In these same terms, consider this dialogue between the poets Annie Finch and Marilyn Hacker. Both women are teachers of poetry as well as poets.

> *Finch*: Do you have any advice for students or teachers or poets who want to train their ear, who don't really know how to hear the meter and want to learn how to hear it?
>
> *Hacker*: Reading and reading out loud: find five poems in sapphics, or five poems in dactylic meters, by different writers, read them out loud, move your body while you read them.
>
> *Finch*: Sometimes I tell my students to dance meters because they don't know how physical it is.
>
> *Hacker*: I know. When I'm composing something longish, especially in a non-iambic meter, I find myself walking a lot. Walking in alcaics is hard. Sapphics are easier: DAda DAda Dadada . . .
>
> *Finch*: It took me a long time to get those alcaics. I learned them from you. I noticed that in this poem, "The River Merchant's Wife," you do a lot of trochees in the second foot, which gives it very much of that stop-and-start quality.
>
> *Hacker*: Some of that is, not unconscious exactly, but happening on a physical rather than a conscious level. You feel in your body that it's time to push down on the pedals or change the gears.

Hacker uses *pedal* to mean not only "either of two foot-operated levers used for powering a bicycle or other vehicle propelled by the legs"[106] but also the foot itself[107]—even Oedipus's.

In this context, one might revisit the long history of "walking songs," especially as developed in American blues. The genre of the "walking song" as such would include *Walking the Blues* (1955), by Champion Jack Dupree, which is a meditation on walking deliberately. "Man, slow down, don't walk so fast," Dupree begins. "All you got to do is put one foot in front of the other one and just keep on walkin', / Walkin' them blues."[108] In a similar tradition there is Louis Armstrong's *Walkin' My Baby Back Home* (1931),[109] Robert Johnson's *Walking Blues* (1936),[110] and The Soul Stirrer's *Walk Around* (1939).[111] There is also Muddy Waters's *Walkin' Blues* (1950),[112] the Solitaires's *Walking Along* (1956),[113] Benny Carter's *A Walkin' Thing* (1957),[114] Fats Domino's *Walking to New Orleans* (1960),[115] the

Ronettes's *Walking in the Rain* 1964),[116] Little Milton's *Walking the Back Streets and Crying* (1972),[117] and more.[118]

KINESIOLOGY AND PROSODY

If we could walk with the animals, talk with the animals . . .
—LESLIE BRICUSSE, *Dr. Doolittle* (the musical film)

Since earliest literate times, thinkers in the area of gait analysis have recognized the link between kinesiology and prosody. In later chapters, we shall consider this link in terms of several kinds of case studies. At the same time, we will deliberate on works that have informed the study of motion, among them the Athenian Aristotle's classical *On the Gait of Animals* (fifth century BC),[119] the Neapolitan mathematician Giovanni Alfonso Borelli's Renaissance *On the Gait of Animals* (1680),[120] and the German biomechanical-scientist Christian Wilhelm Braune and physiologist Otto Fischer's *The Human Gait* (1895).[121] Here we want mainly to introduce an enduring pedal association: the similarity—sometimes seeming to border on a distinct identity—of animal-feet (what we *walk* on) with verse-feet (what we *speak* on).[122]

One can understand this association even without a general theory of bodily gesture or motion. After all, the prosodic "foot" (an Anglo-Saxon translation of Latin *pes*) is ordinarily thought to refer to the motion of the foot in beating time. This sort of thinking is usually considered "mere" metaphorization, but it is more than that in Ovid's *Amores* (16 BC).[123]

English writers were much affected by the way that Roman writers, including Ovid, absorbed Greek prosody's relationship to the Latin language. They too were seeking to develop a prosody of their own. In so doing, English writers relied on the "metaphor" of the foot poetical and ambulatory. The poet and historian Samuel Daniel—author of the rhyming dialogue *Musophilus* (1599) and the son of a music master—disliked how Latin poets took license with modifiers, claiming in his *A Defence of Rhyme* (1603) that they were too often "disjoyn[ed] such as naturally should . . . *march* together."[124] (Compare Joshua Poole's *English Parnassus* [1657]: "To this head [of practices to condemn] may be added a certain licentiousness, which some *English* Poets have in imitation of the *Greekes* and *Latine*, presumed to *dismember*, and *disjoyn* things that should naturally march together.")[125] Thomas Nashe also had reservations concerning the hypallage, or verbal interchange, at work in English thanks to foreign prosody. Latin "Hexamiter," he proclaimed in *Strange Newes* (1592), is the meter which "goes twitching and hopping in our language like a man running vpon quagmiers, vp the hill in one Syllable, and down the dale in another, retaining no part of that stately smooth gate."[126]

Three questions arise now from the association of verse metrics with walking beats.

First:—Do verse metrics and concomitant walking beats always accompany human language? One would think so, from reading many of the theorists of walking and poetry. George Puttenham in his *English Poesie* (1589) describes verse feet in terms of literal human feet. He states, "A foote by his sence naturall is a member of office and function, and serueth to three purposes, that is to say, to go, to runne, & to stand still; so as he sometimes must be swift, sometimes slow, sometime unegally marching or peradventure steddy."[127] Puttenham continues with what he deems the best metrical analogy:

> Nothing can better shew the qualitie [of meter] then these runners at common games, who setting forth from the first goale, one giueth the start speedely & perhaps before he come half way to th'other goale, decayeth his pace, as a man weary & fainting: another is slow at the start, but by amending his pace keepes euen with his fellow or perchance gets before him; another one while gets ground, another while loseth it again, either in the beginning or middle of his race, and so proceedes unegally, sometimes swift sometimes slow, as his breath or forces serue him: another sort there be that plod on, & will never change their pace, whether they win or lose the game.[128]

Second:—Do *particular* verse metrics or walking beats vary according to particular languages? Consider Samuel Daniel's *A Defence of Rime* (1603), a work that he had written in answer to Thomas Campion's *Observations in the Art of English Poesie* (1602). Campion had argued first that the English tongue had its particular characteristics (his subtitle is: "wherein it is demonstratively proved, and by example confirmed, that the English tongue will receive eight several kinds of numbers, proper to itself") and then "that rhyme was unsuited to the genius of the English language." Daniel, in his effort to prove "that Ryme is the fittest harmonie of words that comportes with our Language," adopted the imagery of "running": English trochaic verse "runnes" similar to ancient verse, no verses "runne" free from disgrace if they are "idle," and some "bare numbers" that are forced to "runne" in "our slow language" will never be popular.

It is worth asking, in the context of this debate about English, whether the scansion of one language differs "naturally" from that of other languages. About the English language in particular George Puttenham writes the following in his *English Poesie* (1589): "Of all your words bissillables the most part naturally do make the foote Iambus, many the Trocheus, fewer the Spondeus, fewest of all the Pirrichius."[129] We will return later to this term *Pyrrhic*.

Third:—When human verse metrics do not match up appropriately with human walking beats, are we to characterize the mismatch as "nonhuman" (say, canine or equine), or as "lame" (though also human)? If the former, then the subject of the present section, gaits, involves how humans make animals talk (as in animated cartoons) as well as how they see animals walk.

CANINE WALKIES

Thus, we have the line "I Prefer the Walkies," with its last word coined to rhyme with "talkies."

—HART, "Jazz Jargon"[130]

Walkies is a term that refers to "a childish or jocular form of walk used chiefly with reference to dogs."[131] *Walkies* as such is often contrasted or set beside *talkies*, as in the epigraph above from Hart's "Jazz Jargon."

In the same way, writers compare a lame dog's gait with poetic metrics that they dislike. Edmund Spenser (1580), for example, writes, "Heaven being used shorte as one sillable, when it is in verse stretched out with a Diastole, is like a lame dogge that holdes up one legge."[132] (To the question, "What walks on three legs?" the response might as well be "A dog with one-leg-less" as "A human being with one-leg-more.") By way of contrast, however, there is the justly celebrated Chinese representation of the great calligraphers standing on one leg.

The English *dog* often already means "bad." (*Dog* can also mean "mongrel," "mixed," bastard"—the same terms sometimes used to describe the English-French hybrid that became the language of England following the Norman conquest.) The translator John Florio (1611) thus refers to "dog-rimes, filthy verses."[133] A manuscript of 1625 refers likewise to "dogrime verse."[134] There is also the English-language name for such mixed languages: "dog-Latin."[135] *Dog-Latin* still informs the spoken and written English of our own times;[136] just so one reads in the New *York Times Book Review* (1961), "They have been translated into a kind of academic dog-English."[137]

We often call poor verse "doggerel." Puttenham writes, "A rymer that will be tyed to no rules at all . . . such maner of Poesie is called in our vulgar, ryme dogrell."[138] There is no warrant to presume a tight or "scientifically proven" etymological link between *dog* and *doggerel*, but in the case of other such terms, among them *galloping verse*, there is clear linkage between animal gait and human beat.

GALLOPING VERSE

The not unsolemn rhythm of the regular trot of the horses.
—ROBERT PLUMER WARD, Tremaine[139]

Peter Watt, in an essay on Ibsen's *Peer Gynt* (1867), refers to that drama's "galloping verse, with rhythms often double or triple."[140] Stopford Brooke refers to Tennyson's poem "The May Queen" (1832) and its "galloping verse."[141] Writers tend to mean many different things by *galloping*, but oftentimes, as the editors of one popular encyclopædia remark, they come to rest with an *ottava rima* like that of the English swimmer-poet Byron's poem "Beppo" (1818).[142] In dance music, it is the Dominican *meringue*, with its 2/4 rhythm, that is associated with the gallop.[143] (Not everyone has in mind the apparently "off-natural" rhythms of the dancing horses of the Vienna *Reitschule* or even the equine gallop than informs the gallopade rhythm of John Ashbery's "Grand Galop" [1974].)[144]

The standard equine "clippety-clop" of poetry occurs famously in Shakespeare's *As You Like It*. Touchstone belittles Orlando's attempts at poetry. "This is the very false gallop of verses. Why do you infect yourself with them?"[145] Touchstone's idea is that there is a metrics proper to each one of the animal kinds—and that they all differ from that for humankind. Thomas Nashe writes similarly in his *Strange Newes* (1593): "I would trot a false gallop through the rest of his Verses, but that if I should retort his rime dogrell aright, I must make my verses (as he doth his) run hobling like a Brewers cart vpon the stones."[146]

In Shakespeare's *Henry IV, Part 1*, the English-speaker Hotspur disparages the bilingual English-and-Welsh-speaker Glendower. The latter has "framèd to the harp / Many an English ditty lovely well,"[147] but Hotspur says he would rather hear a kitten's mew or a brass candlestick grating on an axle tree as the Welshman's "mincing poetry."[148] "'Tis like," says he, "the forced gait of a shuffling nag."[149]

Compare the correspondence of Edmund Spenser and Gabriel Harvey on the equine (nag's) gait and prosody. Harvey, seeming to favor the canter or gallop, wrote to Spenser that good quantitative verse in English is like "a good horse, that trippeth not once in a journey."[150] Spenser replied by shifting the equestrian focus to other animals—and, just as importantly, changing the central dialectic of the metaphor about verse from that of "animal (whether dog or horse—or gosling) versus human" to that of "lame creature versus able-bodied creature." The "chiefest hardnesse," writes Spenser, of composing quantitative hexameters in English is . . .

> in the Accente . . . and sometime the measure of the Number, as in Carpenter the middle sillable, being vsed shorte in speache, when it shall be read long in Verse, seemeth like a lame Gosling that draweth one legge after hir: and Heauen, beeing vsed shorte as one sillable, when it is in Verse stretched out with a Diastole, is like a lame Dogge that holdes vp one legge.[151]

The study of accent, a variant of beat, always has to do with feet. Dorothy Leigh Sayers's *Gaudy Night* (1935): "How *dared* he pick up her word 'sleep' and use it four times in as many lines, and each time in a different foot, as though juggling with the accent-shift were child's play?"[152]

How do horses move? In what way do they move differently from "able-bodied" humans? In his sequential still-photography studies of equine and canine animal location, which he made at around the period when still-photography was being developed into cinematography, Eadweard Muybridge was especially attracted to the predictably varied gaits—and the footfall sequences—of horses, which are unguligrade mammals,[153] in walking, ambling, trotting, pacing, cantering, and galloping at speed, and jumping. He was also attracted to the gait(s) of heavy dogs like mastiffs in single suspension gallop and light dogs like whippets in a double-suspension gallop.[154] Apollinaire, in his way, can do no better. (See Figure 1.3.)

Muybridge studies also the movement of lame human beings.

LAME METRICS

I tried to walk but I was lame
I tried to talk but I just stuttered
—THE BEATLES, "Young Blood"[155]

In his *English Poesie* (1589), Puttenham associates catalexis, normally defined as the "absence of a syllable in the last foot of a verse,"[156] with

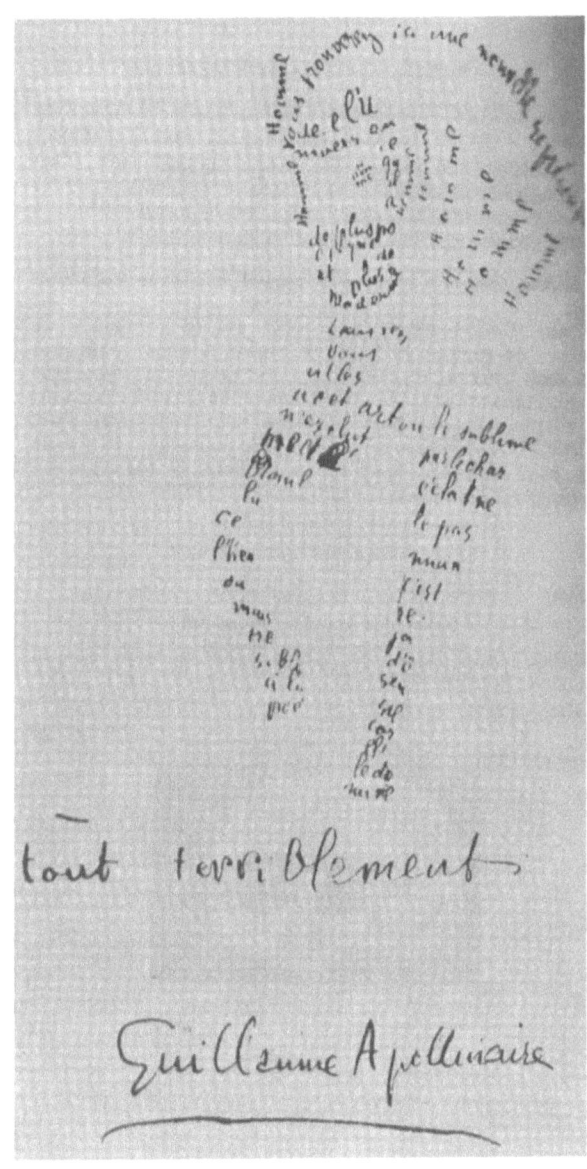

Figure 1.3. Guillaume Apollinaire. "Horse Calligram." In *Les Peintres Cubistes* (1918). The raised foreleg of the bridled horse is about to hit the earth (*pietener*). Apollinaire probably composed this work for the exposition of works by Leopold Survage and Irène Lagut (1917). By means of *rhythmes colorés*, Survage had planned to animate abstract compositions using color and movement. The handwriting reads: "Homme Vous trouverez ici une nouvelle représentation de l'univers … [Mankind, you will find here a new representation of the universe …]."

maiming. "The Greekes and Latines," he writes, "vsed verses in the odde sillable of two sortes, which they called Catalecticke and Acatalecticke ... the catalectik or maymed verse."[157] On the earliest catalectic versifiers was himself apparently lame. Hipponax of Ephesus, exiled from his native town in the sixth century BC was both ugly[158] and physically deformed (probably due to of chilblains).[159] He is said to have invented the *scazon*, or *choliamb* (lame metre). Herondas writes about him thus: "O stranger, stay clear of the horrible tomb of Hipponax.... You might wake the sleeping wasp whose bile would not rest even in Hades, but launches shafts of song in lame measure."[160] The verse brings the reader down on the "'wrong' foot" by reversing the stresses of the last beats.[161] Karl Otfried Müller writes in his *History of the Literature of Ancient Greece*, "[Hipponax] crippled the rapid agile gait of the iambic by transforming the last foot from a pure iambus to a spondee, contrary to the fundamental principle of the whole mode of versification."

Müller explains that "metre ... maimed and stripped of its beauty and regularity, and technically made *arruthmos,* was a perfectly appropriate rhythmical form for the delineation of such pictures of intellectual deformity as Hipponax delighted in."[162] Hipponax used a great many Lydian (non-Greek) words in his verse.

Ananius, a contemporary of Hipponax, invented the even edgier *ischiorrhopgic* (back-broken) verse.[163] Compare such other prosodic terms as *brachycatalectic* (wanting one foot, or two syllables).[164] Obadiah Walker, author of *Some Instructions Concerning the Art of Oratory* (1659), writes, "Archilochus and Hipponax, two very bad Poets,... invented those doggrel sorts of Verses, Iambics and Scazons."[165] The most hobbled line would be, in this context, acephalous verse, "headless" in the sense that an unstressed syllable is dropped from the beginning.

The English language, like the Greek, often allies irregular talk, bodily irregularity, and, in particular, irregular walk: "stammering" tongue, for example, with "staggering" gait. Thomas Parnell writes in his "Anacreontic" (1727), "Cupid mock'd his stammring Tongue."[166] That "the tongue walks" is an English conceit from before the time of Edmund Spenser,[167] so it should not surprise us that *stumble* or *stutter* are cognate and that *falter, shamble, shrench, stacher, titubate,* and *totter* all mean both "stutter" and "stumble." The same association of disabled or impeded walking and talking obtains in most of the other languages that I have been able to consult.

The lame body metaphors in prosody are otherwise also palpable. A hexameter beginning with a short syllable, for example, is *acephalous* (without a head).[168] An iambic verse with a spondee or trochee instead of an iambus in the last (sixth) foot is the aforesaid *choliamb* (from Greek *chōlós*, meaning "lame"). The lengthening of a naturally short syllable is a *diastole*. (This Latin term provides the English *dilation*. There is the dilation of the heart when it rhythmically alternates with a *systole*, or contraction, the two movements together constituting the *pulse*, as when one speaks of the dilatation of the lungs as the combination of inspiration and expiration. As we shall see below, there is also the pedal and verbal poetic movement of romantic poets, among them William Wordsworth.)[169] Prosody often contrasts "smooth-pac'd verse" to "hobbling prose."[170] Thus one person says, "If blank verse be not tumid and gorgeous, it is crippled prose,"[171] another complains about a "rough construction and the poltfoot [clubfoot] metre, lame sense and limping verse," and yet another will claim that a verse may be "lame for want of half a foot."[172]

Roger Ascham, in "Of Imitation" (in his *Scholemaster* [1570]), thinking about prosthetics for lame persons, writes, "And as a foote of wood is a plaine shew of a manifest maime, euen so feete in our English versifing without quantitie and ioyntes be sure signes that the verse is verie vnseemlie."[173] Ascham writes likewise that "their feete: be feete without ioyntes, that is to say, not distinct by trew quantitie of sillabes: And so, soch feete, be but numme feete" (my emphasis).[174] In this view, poetry can be numb, that is, "deprived of ... the power of movement."[175] Its feet can be paralyzed. Hence they become "as unfitted for a verse to turn and run roundly withal, as feet of brass or wood be unwieldy to go well withal."[176] Just so, Robinson Jeffer's poem "The Loving Shepherdess" (1929) describes a girl—named "[Clare] *Walker*"—as "walking with numbed and cut feet / Along the last ridge of migration."[177]

On the one hand, a person one can have a half a foot too few. John Dryden writes, "Some thousands of his verses ... are lame for want of half a foot."[178] On the other hand, one can have a foot too many. Shakespeare's Touchstone in *As You Like It* scoffs thus about poor verse:

Celia: Didst thou hear these verses?

Rosalind: O, yes, I heard them all, and more too; for some of them had in them more feet than the verses would bear.

Celia: That's no matter: the feet might bear the verses.

Rosalind: Ay, but the feet were lame and could not bear themselves without the verse and therefore stood lamely in the verse.[179]

When Shakespeare's Aufidius in *Coriolanus* says, "Unless by using means I lame the foot / Of our design,"[180] the reference is partly to issues of prosody.

When Rosalind in *As You like It* mocks the feet of Orlando's verses ("the feet were lame") and Touchstone does the same ("This is the very false gallop of verses"),[181] they seem to jest about the metrics of only English-language poem, Orlando's.[182] What they say about Orlando's poem, however, might well be true of rhyming poetry in English. John Milton thus notes about the verse of his *Paradise Lost* (1667) that his English metrics flouts the "wretched matter and lame Meeter" of most (English-language) rhyming poetry.[183] Shakespeare's narrator "John Gower" in *Pericles of Tyre* actually apologizes for "carry[ing] wingèd Time . . . on the lame feet of my rhyme."[184] The English composer and songwriter Thomas Campion, grandson of an Irishman, disparages native English rhyming in his *Observation in the Art of English Poesie* (1602), describing especially nonsensical ballads as "lame halting rhymes."[185]

The debate about whether some languages, at least, ought *not* to rhyme at all brings to mind how, in his *Scholemaster* (1570), Roger Ascham regarded two works of interlinguistic conversion or translation: the Earl of Surrey's English-language translation of Vergil's Latin-language *Aeneid*; and Gonsaluo Periz's Spanish-language translation of Homer's Greek-language *Odyssey*. Even though the two Moderns (Surrey and Periz) wisely avoided "the fault of Ryming," says Ascham, their verse was not yet "perfite and trew versifying."[186]

> As a foot of wood is a plain shew of a manifest maim, euen so feet in our English versifing without quantitie and ioyntes be sure signs that the verse is very unseemly.[187]

The question as to whether perfect translation between such languages is ever possible bears comparison with the question as to whether a lame person can ever write true verse and also with the question raised earlier in *Talking the Walk & Walking the Talk* as to whether a person who cannot walk ever be a philosopher. If the metrics of poetry can transcend crippled feet, the answer would seem to be Yes. If, however, "a sound mind" *requires* "a sound body"—as goes the old saw—the answer might well be No.

Shown next is the polio-survivor Frida Kahlo's extraordinary "Feet what do I need them for / If I have wings to fly. / 1953," from her diary. (See Figure 1.4.) *Does* she have wings to fly?

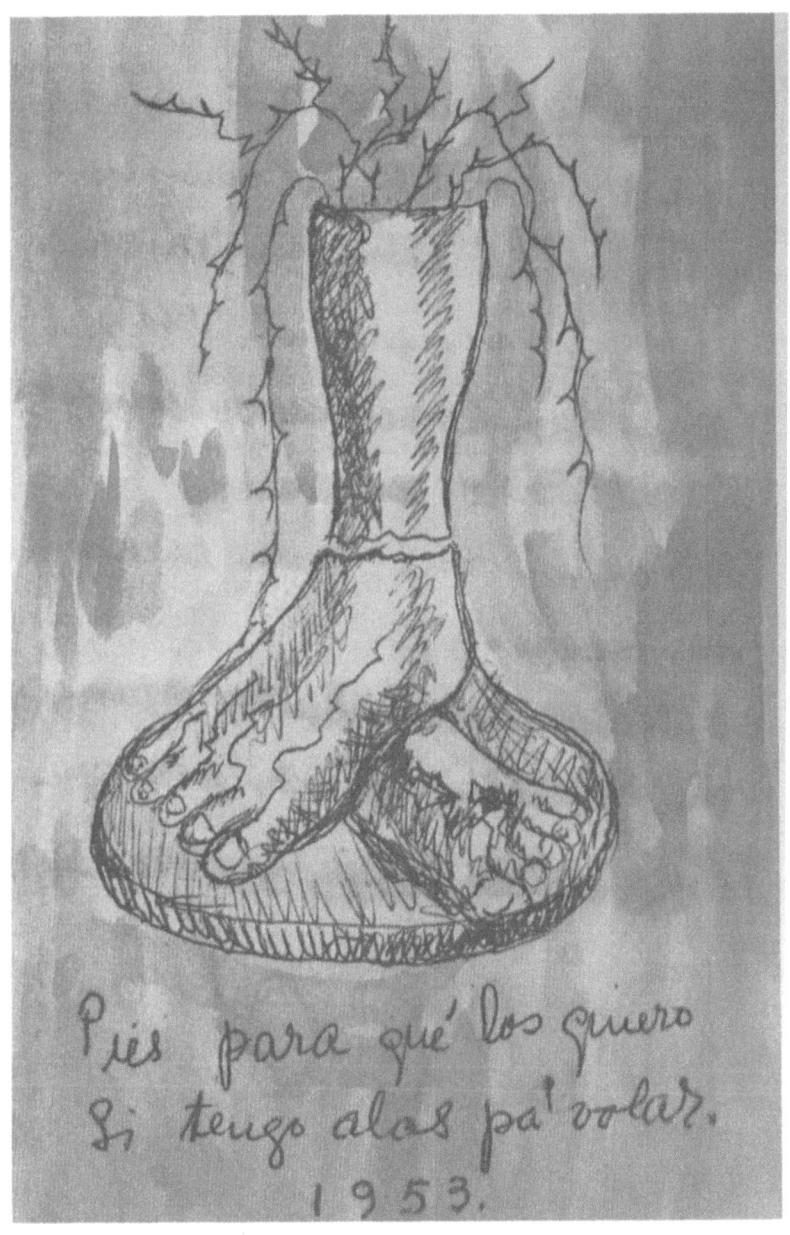

Figure 1.4. Frida Kahlo. "Feet, what do I need them for?" In *The Diary of Frida Kahlo: An Intimate Self-Portrait*, Translation. Ed. Sarah M. Lowe, intro. Carlos Fuentes, essay and commentaries Sarah M. Lowe (Mexico City: Abrams and La Vaca Independiente, 1995), 233.

In human history in general, there had been, until the twentieth century in which Kahlo lived, an extraordinary absence in theory of talking well without walking well. Balzac had pointed this out already in his *Theory of Walking* (La demarche, 1833). He writes, "Isn't it really quite extraordinary to see that, since man took his first steps, no one has asked himself why he walks, how he walks, if he has ever walked, if he could walk better, what he achieves in walking ... questions that are tied to all the philosophical, psychological, and political systems which preoccupy the world?" In his *On the Philosopher's Medicine of the Body* (De Medicina Corporis, quae Philosphorum est, 1780s), Immanuel Kant argues, "We must see to it that we have a sound mind in a sound body." (The Roman poet Juvenal had said merely that a sound mind in a sound body is "devoutly to be wished for.")[188] Kant's view is that philosophers can and must cure the body in something like the way that good physicians "assist the afflicted body by a mental régime."[189] The language impedance and pedal difficulty that Kant was experiencing in the 1780s, possibly symptoms of "Lewy Body Dementia,"[190] encouraged his interest in a philosophical talking cure. In any case, his daily strolls were linked inextricably with his corporeal and spiritual character. People in Königsberg would set their clocks by him when he passed their house, and it is said, he failed to take his walk on only two days: the day he read a work by Rousseau (1760s), and the one when he read about a key victory during the French Revolution (1790s). The poet Heinrich Heine reports that the lane where Kant walked was called "the philosopher's walk" in his day.[191] Philippe Collin's French-language movie *The Last Days of Immanuel Kant* (1994), partly inspired by Thomas de Quincy's work (1827), is based on these walks.[192] Kant also developed a concomitant breathing procedure. De Quincy had explained that Kant walked alone because "he wished to breathe exclusively through his nostrils; which he could not do if he were obliged continually to open his mouth in conversation."[193] In summer, Kant walked slowly so as not to perspire because he thought that his constitution required that he should avoid perspiration.[194] "In order to walk more firmly, he adopted a peculiar method of stepping: he carried his foot to the ground, not forward, and obliquely, but perpendicularly, and with a kind of stamp, so as to secure a larger basis, by setting down the entire sole at once."[195] Kant's walk was, in its way, a philosophical dance of the body.

WRITING AND DANCING

Dancing in all its forms cannot be excluded from the curriculum of all noble education; dancing with the feet, with ideas, with words, and, need I add that one must also be able to dance with the pen?
—NIETZSCHE, *Twilight of the Idols*[196]

A pen I handled for a fan,
And learnt not how to dance by scan.
—JOSEPH WARTON, "Sappho's Advice"[197]

Two typical foci of the field of comparative arts are (1) how the affiliation of *dancing* with walking, which some dance theorists claim that dance typifies and fulfills, relates to the affiliation of singing, or *poetry*, with talking, which some poetry theorists claim that poetry fulfills and typifies, and hence how dancing is related to poetry. T. S. C. Hans, looking to the Mundari language of the Chota Nagpur Plateau region in eastern India, puts it this way: "Walking is dancing, talking is singing."[198] The French poet Paul Valéry, in his "Philosophy of the Dance" (1936), argues "poetry is to prose as dancing is to walking,"[199] even as, for the Enlightenment encyclopædist Denis Diderot, "dance is to pantomime what poetry is to prose."[200] Hansgörj Bittner writes in *The Metrical Structure of Free Verse* (1997): "To dance is to perform rhythm. If walking were to be a rhythmic experience, one would have to walk dancingly. This would involve a conscious effort to perceive the movement of walking as rhythmical."[201]

In the English language, the suggestions at play are expressed by how the term *poetry* raises up phrases like *poetry of motion* (as in Jonathan Richardson)[202] and *poetry of the foot* (as in John Dryden).[203] Both phrases refer to dancing.[204] *Poetry in motion* refers moreover to "(the motions) of a person or thing regarded as beautiful or excellent."[205] Thus Balzac essays to unify "le regard, la voix, la respiration, la démarche"[206] under the rubric of movement; he calls the body's gestural language "perpetual hieroglyphs of human gaits [*les hiéroglyphes perpétuels de la démarche humaine*]."[207]

Questions that arise now are: Can human poem/song *depict* movement? Can it *be* a dance? Can talking walk? (Can walking talk?) A tentative answer to these linked questions is essayed by Burt Bacharach in his popular dance piece *Walk the Way You Talk* (1970). His Brazilian-style beat (for dancing with the feet) works against the lyrics, whose lines variably contain what seems to be one too many, or one too few, prosodic feet per line.[208] The message of the song is conveyed in the line, "You are only what you do." A couple of years after its first appearance, the song was adapted by the US Air Force for recruiting young men who wanted to "walk the walk" by acting out an ideal talk of courage.

One might *visually* depict talking or walking, or both talking and walking, at the same time, by means of a motionless (still) poetic calligram. That would be a sort of Egyptian hieroglyphic—ambiguously "representational" of the sort of walking commonly referenced in the romantic period.[209] Thus does the poem "Boxeur" by Apollinaire.

Consider also the moving or mobile (that is, kinetic or cinematic) calligram created by the Belgian artist Hugo Heyrman. This work provides something like a serial cinematic medium for walking and talking at once.

Some forms of ballet express writing systems—as for Liu Qi's *Beyond Calligraphy*, which the Guangdong Modern Dance Company first performed in 2005. The five dances in this work demonstrate the five different script styles in Chinese calligraphy. Each of these dances would seem, in its own way, to make the written word flesh.

Moses, the stumbling stutterer, brought the Jewish people two interrelated prohibitions: that on graven images (hence, a god whose name could not be spoken) and alphabetic writing (hence, scribbles without potentially idolatrous aspect). And, in fact, some forms of writing better retain—or dance out—the mobile quality of talking than others. On the one hand, "print" handwriting moves, if one can say it moves at all, jerkily, from individual "block" letter unconnectedly to the next "block" letter. It walks foot by foot in an unfluid manner. On the other hand, and by analogy, "cursive" (literally, "running") handwriting, as opposed to "uncial" writing[210]—sometimes called "real writing" during my school days in Montréal in the 1950s—moves fluidly, even to the point where one might say it dances. Many manuals for teaching cursive writing claim to educate students to dance with the pen.[211] "A dance of the pen" is how British calligrapher Alfred Fairbank described italic handwriting.[212] (The origin of this phrase *real writing* is worth pursuing.)

Again, a cross-cultural perspective is useful. The statue in the Confucius Temple in Nanjing, China—standing, or dancing, meditatively on one foot and holding his calligraphic brush to the head—is helpful in this regard insofar as it recalls popular figuration of the "god of literature" and/or "lesser god of scholars": K'uei Hsing. One ink

Starting Out 33

rubbing depicts the figure "standing on the head of the turtle" (鰲) and "pointing the dipper" (斗), suggesting expressions that mean "coming first in the imperial civil service examinations."

Nevertheless, Chinese writing, and the highly developed art of Chinese brush calligraphy in particular, is regarded as, or in terms of, various styles with telling names: standing, walking, running, and "crazy cursive." In this tradition, as Lin Yutang writes, "calligraphic strokes [which to some extent represent talk] are ... appreciated for their pure 'beauty of momentum' [as Liu Yutang puts it],[213] written in a confident, powerful way, defying any correction or touching up."[214] (It is as though "the hand hath writ, and having writ, moves on.") Beyond this specific requirement for movement in stillness there is the specific analogy to that form of walking we call dance. Chiang Yee, in pursuing this viewpoint, argues first, "The [calligraphic brush] stroke responds to the slightest movement of the wrist and fingers or of the right elbow and arm."[215] The argument moves from the movement of the region of the hand (calligraphy) toward its further explanation as, or in terms of, the movement of the region of the foot (dance). "The sensation," argues Chiang Yee, "is really very like that aroused by a ballerina balancing upon one toe."[216] By the same token, the movement of the sword in Taijiquan sword form is much like that of the pen in calligraphy. (Consider both the *Dian* [点] dot and *Ti* [提] upward character strokes.)[217]

The affiliation of artful, martial footwork with brushwork helps to explain why celebrated Taijiquan (Tai chi chuan) teachers have often been master calligraphers. It may also suggest that the one old Western saw, that "The pen is mightier than the sword,"[218] might well be rewritten as something like "Brushing is swordplay and/or Swordplay is Brushing." (We are partly introduced to the Players in *Hamlet* by means of Rosencrantz's statement about the child-players that "that many wearing rapiers are afraid of goose-quills."[219] Hamlet's use of the *goose-quill*, in order to write a few lines that bring out Claudius's guiltiness, turns out to be as useful to Hamlet as a detective trying to demonstrate publicly Claudius's guiltiness and guilt as Hamlet's sword, in the final act of *Hamlet*, turns out to be useful to him in actually killing Claudius.)

The following reproduction compares dancing (as suggested by the sketch of a dancing girl) with writing (as suggested by the character *sui* [to follow] in the calligraphic running style of Wang Xizhi [321–379]),[220] often called "the sage of calligraphy." (See Figure 1.5.) The

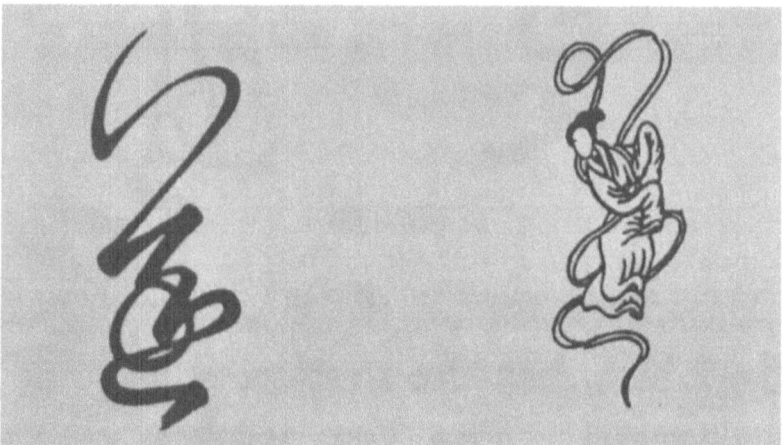

Figure 1.5. Chinese calligraphic character and dancer. The twentieth-century sketch of the dancing girl is by Chiang Yee. In Yang Haocheng, Zhongguo shu fa lan sheng (Nanjing, China: Jiangsu jiao yu chu ban she [jing xiao Jiangsu sheng Xin hua shu dian], 1998). Permission: Yang Haocheng.

character *sui* (随) ("to follow") is in the running style.[221] The calligrapher Wen Zhengming (1470–1559) had a cursive style that has been called "The Dance of the Brush."[222]

The Japanese Zen teacher Soen Nakagawa (1907–84), who was born in Taiwan, produces an interesting calligraphic poem, "Into the Twilight—maple leaves—come dancing."[223] (See Figure 1.6.)

The rhythmic speech and walk appropriate to such a three-legged man as Sophocles's aged man relates here to the rhythmic calligraphy of the six-fingered man the remarkable hexa-dactylic writer Zhu Yunming (祝允明), as for his *kuang cao* (crazy-cursive style). Zhu Yunming, who was already producing one-foot-long (Chinese scale) characters at age five, had a special interest in appropriate "walking" as the distinction of proper humankind: "The remote peoples of the lands encircling our seas, and all our furred and feathered neighbors, though they walk somewhat erect like men," said he, "are not our kind."[224]

The end (*telos*) of human dance, for him, is the crazy cursive—or vice versa.

Yasin Safadi remarks in *Islamic Calligraphy* (1978)[225] that three Arabic scripts—Thuluth, Naskh, and Nasta'liq—were employed to create calligraphic zoomorphic compositions. (See Figures 1.7 and 1.8.) The other major Arabic scripts were generally not used

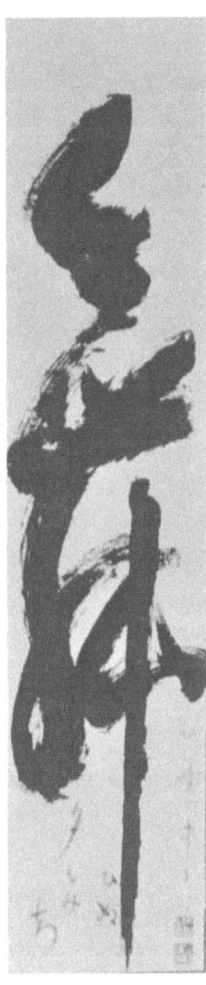

Figure 1.6. Soen Nakagawa. "In autumn, maple leaves from the mountain forests surrounding Ryutaku-ji sailed in the wind, dancing. Some of them flew into the serene *zendō*." A *zendō* is the room where people practice zazen, which is group-centered, breathing-focused, sitting-zen.

for such compositions. Relevant here are the variously monotheist doctrines that outlaw representational art even when employing a presumably nonrepresentational alphabet (as opposed to an ostensibly representational writing system like the Chinese or Egyptian). In some branches of Islam, zoomorphic calligraphy was therefore not much practiced until the late fifteenth century—and then, usually, only in a few places, like Ottoman Turkey, India, and Iran at the time of the Qajar dynasty.

The contemporary Sudanese Hassan Musa's work most distinctly reveals the linkage between the movement of talking (its

Figure 1.7. Ahmed Hilmi. Calligraphic composition in the form of a lion. Ink and watercolor on paper. Ottoman Turkey, 1913. Image: © Nour Foundation, Courtesy of the Khalili Family Trust.

general way of being written down) and walking (its particular mode of representation in writing).

LETTING THE DUCKS OUT

... and then she remembered that human beings could not live in the water...

—HANS CHRISTIAN ANDERSEN, *The Little Mermaid*

Harry Levin and I first met, entirely by accident, in 1973, in the sea water just off the Wellfleet Bay Wildlife Sanctuary on Cape Cod. I was then a graduate student writing my dissertation at Yale University. Harry was the first holder of the Irving Babbitt Chair in Comparative Literature at Harvard University and the influential chairperson of Harvard's program in comparative literature.

Harry and I were both doing the Australian front-crawl, but in opposite directions. The crawl is a rhythmic "high-speed swimming stroke [a variation of the Trudgen crawl stroke]—both above and below the surface of the water—in which the swimmer, lying

Figure 1.8. Arabic calligraphy. "Bird Running" (the Arabic word *bismillah* [in the name of god] created in the form of an ostrich), by Hassan Musa (b. Sudan, 1951). 2004. Courtesy of Grandir Editions.

face-downwards, usually with the face submerged, makes alternate overhand arm-strokes assisted by the quick movement of the legs."[226] It's a powerful means of locomotion for human beings alone in the water. Harry and I collided, full force. We were both bloodied. We retreated to Boundbrook Island and then walked, talking, along the footpath to Harry's summer home. There we bandaged up our wounds—and spoke for a few hours about the aesthetic and rhythmic aspects of swimming.

Gliding in the water and walking on earth, as Harry and I did that day, are comparable activities. In *Paradise Lost* (1667), John Milton thus addresses, "Ye that in Waters glide, and ye that walk / The Earth...."[227] I knew that line from having repeated it hundreds of times in Mrs. Cardozza's elocution class for stutterers at Montreal's Royal Victoria Hospital the mid-1950s. Mrs. Cardozza was following the recommendation of Professor Alexander Melville Bell. Bell was the coauthor with his son, David Charles Bell, of *Standard Elocutionist* (1878), who pinpointed that very line.[228] (Professor Alexander Melville Bell was *son* of Alexander Bell, author of *Stammering and Other Impediments of Speech*

[1836].²²⁹ He was also the *father* of Alexander Graham Bell—the inventor of the telephone.)

That day, when Harry and I met, our conversation focused on the relationship between two kinds of bodily rhythm and exercise. First was the alternating beat of pedal and manual limbs. Second was the measured tempo of life-giving inspiration and expiration punctuated by the life-preserving caesura, or breathing stop. These two kinds of rhythm, taken together, help to explain the Australian crawl. Our discussion that day about *natational* inspiration (the drawing of breath into the lungs while swimming) led to dialogue about of the rheology of *poetic* inspiration.

Swimming, as Harry and I agreed, was always a partly submerged activity. For that reason we did not discuss walking on water (as Jesus does in the fourth watch of the night),²³⁰ surfing (frequently called "walking on water"),²³¹ or water-skiing (sometimes discussed as "walking on water with skis").²³² Likewise, swimming usually gets someone elsewhere than where he started. For that reason, we did not discuss treading water, in the sense of "mov[ing] the feet [while in the water] as in walking upstairs, while the body is kept erect and the head [always] above water."²³³ After all, "men treading water in their careers tend to check out earliest of all."²³⁴

Similarly, we passed in silence the question whether fish-tailed mermaids and mermen were human beings who suffered from Sirenomelia, or fusion of the legs. I did not, however, recall that the witch in Hans Christian Andersen's story *The Little Mermaid* (1836) requires that, in order that the mermaid be transformed into a more fully human form, she must lose her old ability to locomote and to vocalize. First, she must lose her ability to dance painlessly as a mermaid dances. "You will still have the same floating gracefulness of movement, and no dancer will ever tread so lightly," says the witch, "but at every step you take it will feel as if you were treading upon sharp knives, and that the blood must flow." Second, she must lose her merperson's ability to sing, which is the apex of humanoid vocalizing. "No one on earth," says the narrator, "has such a lovely voice as [the mermen and mermaids]. The little mermaid sang more sweetly than them all. . . . [S]he knew she had the loveliest voice of any on earth or in the sea." For that reason, the witch cuts off the mermaid's tongue as recompense for the metamorphosis: "Put out your little tongue [*lille Tunge*] that I may cut it off as my payment."²³⁵

For Harry and I, the issues at hand were life-and-death as well as locomotion-and-breath. Swimming, we agreed, involves rhythmic movement of the limbs (the legs flutter kick for the front crawl) synchronized with rhythmic exhalation below the water surface and inhalation above the water surface. Without that rhythmic synchronization, the poetic justice would be a death by drowning. The Scottish poet Robert Sempill put it thus in his broadside "Ane Ballat declaring the Nobill and Gude Inclination of our King" (1567):

> He swoumit in the fluidis of Poetrie,
> And did exerse the science liberall;
> The facund Phrase did vse of oratrie.[236]

Harry and I discussed the prosody of swimming. He mentioned John Cheever's "The Swimmer" (1964). I brought up "Written After Swimming from Sestos to Abydos" (1810) by the club-footed Lord who became a swimmer at the Harrow School. I asked Harry whether the *arrhythmia* of Byron's walking and the *rhythm* of his swimming may not have affected the poet's experiments with rhythm and verse metrics. Edward Munk's *Greek and Roman Metres* (1844), I recalled, wrote about *arrhythmy* in verse as opposed to its *eurythmy*.[237] Harry pointed out that, decades later, *arrhythmia* came to be used in relationship to the heart and pulse.[238] Rhetoric, we decided, precedes neurology.

After tea, we touched on Gaston Bachelard's *L'eau et les rêves* (Water and Dreams, 1942), in particular his comparison of lyric rhythm with river rheology and his focus on the swimmer as fighter in Algernon Charles Swinburne's "A Swimmer's Dream" (1889). (Swinburne, we noted, played an important a role in the third volume of George Saintsbury's History of English Prosody.)

Might the metrics of physics assist poetics? Here we discussed the art and science of skipping stones. The Hungarian term for "skipping stones" is kacsáztatás, meaning literally "making it walk like a duck."[239] The English game "ducks and drakes"[240] and its concomitant nursery rhyme[241] likewise involve stone skipping.

The metrics of skipping stones has long interested specialists in fluid mechanics, sometimes also called rheology.[242] Lazzaro Spallanzani's *De lapidibus ab aqua resilientibus* (1766)[243] was the first of many treatises in the field,[244] some with distinct military application.[245] The rhythmic rheology of stone skipping involves the intersection of two kinds of speed: acceleration, as the stone hits the water more and more quickly, and deceleration, as the stone covers less and less distance per hit).[246] That is where hydrodynamics meets poetic rhythm:

poetic metrics understood as a continuing beat and stone-skipping metrics conceived as a continual skipping ending with "that dying fall"—the rhetorical term that Shakespeare's Duke of Ilyria employs in the first speech of *Twelfth Night*.[247] In that speech, the acceleratingly fading cadence—a sort of musical decrescendo—sinks utterly. The once-skipping stone becomes a still-moving sinking stone.

At the end of our conversation our wounds seemed entirely healed. We were refreshed.

A few weeks after our encounter, I sent Harry a copy of Dorothy Dow Rogers's thesis, "A Study of the Relationship Between Certain Measures of Swimming Achievement, Fear, Motor Ability and Rhythm Among College Women" (1934).[248] He sent me a note about the importance of learning to swim according to the rules of "a regular Harvard College education."[249]

Two decades later, by accident, I become the second holder of the Irving Babbitt Chair in Comparative Literature.

CHAPTER TWO

Walking Voices

And they heard the voice [*kol*] of the LORD God walking in the garden.... And the LORD God called unto Adam, and said unto him, WHERE ART THOU?
—GN 3:8 (KJV)

Shema Yisroel [Hear, O Israel!]
—DT 6

"AND GOD WENT, 'WHERE ARE YOU'?" IN THE BIBLE'S "IN THE BEGINNING"

The present chapter is the first of a sequence of mostly chronologically ordered "case studies." The series begins with a reconsideration of the beginning of human history as the Bible describes it: the so-called Fall of Man. It proceeds to the Renaissance and concludes with the modern era. The case studies further the implications of the ideas introduced in the first chapter and reveal their workings in major literary, musical, dramatic, poetic, medical, and cinematic texts. At the same time, they pay special attention to cultural and political analysis, the relations among the arts, and the present need for reexamining classical linkages between the terminologies and methods of rhetoric and neurology.

The Book of Genesis. The Beginning. In the Garden of Eden, we are told that Adam and Eve were footloose and fancy-free. They were at liberty to move about on both real and unreal planes. At least within a certain boundary. God had told them, after all, not to eat of the fruit. The slippery words of a whispering being (what the Latin Vulgate calls a "serpent") follow: "Yea, hath God said, 'Ye shall not eat of every tree of the garden?'" (Gn 3:1). These words trip up Eve. She eats of forbidden fruit. Then her voice (*kol*) convinces Adam to eat of the same fruit. That is when God makes his most famous call. "WHERE ART THOU?" (Gn 3:8). Soon afterward, Adam and Eve are banished from the Garden.

What happened, pedal-wise, in the Garden? For blind English poet John Milton, any answer to this question would involve the walk and talk of God. The first speech in Milton's *Comus* (1634) ends with the words, "But I hear the tread / Of hateful steps; I must be viewless now."[1] One hears the dancing measures of "Other trippings to be trod / Of lighter toes."[2] Milton, who was a great walker, has Adam and Eve leaving the garden slow-footedly. "They hand in hand with wandering steps and slow"[3] depart the Garden—that is the penultimate line of his *Paradise Lost* (1667). Andrea del Migna's late sixteenth-century painting The *Expulsion of Adam and Eve*[4] shows Adam and Eve in contorted (*contrapposto*) posture as the angel directs them out of the Garden and points to their feet.

God's words, "WHERE ART THOU?" (Gn 3:8), make up the second question in the Bible. Theologically momentous, they are thus the central pivot of a divine economy, counterpoising the beguiling *kol* of Eve (Gn 3:17), beguiled by the words of the serpent (Gn 3:1, 4–5). Moreover, they are, in themselves, God's first real intervention in human history: the first time that the biblical narrator presents God as a fully anthropomorphic being. God, notes one commentator, seems now to be "presented so casually, strolling about, seemingly incidentally, like a man of leisure on an afternoon walk."[5] Milton reports in *Paradise Lost* that "the voice of God they heard / Now walking in the Garden,"[6] and when God asks Adam, "Where art thou ADAM[?]," God remembers, almost nostalgically, that the clay (*adam*) into which he had breathed life had hitherto been "wont with joy to meet / My coming seen far off."[7]

God's new anthropomorphism can be attractive: (the verbal ideal made into the pedal real, the divine word made human flesh, but the plot summary I have offered so far presents only part of the dialectic at play in this foundational myth. It ignores a definite ambiguity in the tale that the European tradition that one can, in this context, almost define by the way it presents—or, more frequently, forgets— the talking and walking of God in dramatic works and vocal musical. There is, after all, some theologically consequential disagreement, usually overlooked by the Christian commentators partly for theological reasons, as to whether it is a God that strolls about the garden or the Voice that strolls. If the latter, then the answer to some such question as "What is the voice of the Fall?" would be "The foot-fall of God"[8]—the rhythm of His talking and walking.

Some scholars say that it is a god, or God himself, that talks or that Adam hears. That God himself is walking (*holeich*) is a position variably taken by Rashi,[9] Moshe ben Nahman,[10] and Rabbi Abba bar Kahana.[11] ("I heard thee in the garden," says the noncommittal John Milton's Adam.)[12] Others, however, say that the voice (*kol*) walks in the garden; among these thinkers are David Kimchi,[13] Maimonides,[14] Ibn Ezra,[15] Levi ben Gershon,[16] and Sa'adia Gaon.[17] (The extraordinary Wycliffe translation of Gn 3:8 goes along with this tradition, when it has "And when they heard the sound of the Lord God walking in the garden.") Different understandings about what sort of being (walking) or Being (God) walks the talk and/or talks the walk arise from syntactic and lexical ambiguities in the Hebrew as well as theological predilections. Hebrew-language scholars addressed themselves to these issues for millennia,[18] along with the European Christian translators. A few of the latter manage to convey the crucial ambiguity as to whether it is "a walking *voice* (belonging to God)" that asks the question or instead "(a voice that belongs to) a walking god."

The Douay Rheims Bible, for example, has "the voice of the Lord God walking in paradise." The Darby Bible has "the voice of Jehovah Elohim, walking in the garden." The English Revised Version has "the voice of the LORD God walking in the garden." The Webster's Bible has "the voice of the LORD God walking in the garden." Martin Luther's translation of the Bible has the relevant phrase as "die *Stimme* Gottes des Herrn, der im Garten *ging*." Saint Jerome's Latin has "*vocem* Domini Dei *deambulantis* in paradise" (my emphasis). These translations are accurate enough, so far as the English language allows. However, the English language, among others, is limited in the present context, since the verb "to go" in that language rarely means "to say" (although, as we shall see, sometimes it does). What is more, the Christian translators of Gn 3:8, having an anthropomorphizing "christophanic" or "theophanic" ax to grind about the talking Word made walking Flesh, are prepped to ignore altogether or be entirely ignorant of a poetic conjunction of walking and talking, or going and sounding, that informs many similar passages in the Bible. Before God passes along the Ten Commandments to Moses, for example, the *talk* of a trumpet *walks*: "And when the voice [*kol*] of the trumpet walked [*holeich*], Moses spake, and God answered him by a voice [*kol*]" (Ex 19:19).[19] The rabbinical commentators note the repetition of *kol* (talk) and the use of *halak* (walk),[20] relating it to the earlier passage about God or God's voice going (Gn 3:8).

Holeich means "go" rather than "walk" insofar as it references sounding as well as moving. In that sense, it would be better to translate GN 3:8 not as "And the Lord God called" (Gn 3:8) but instead as, "And the Lord God went, 'Where are you?'" This translation would better go along with usages of the verb *went* that pertain to sounding and speaking. Such usages are many: *Go* means "to discuss ad nauseam,"[21] to sound in accord with a particular rhythm,[22] rhyme,[23] theme,[24] melody,[25] or rouse text.[26] It indicates "circumlocution"[27] or verbal repetition, as when President Ronald Reagan said, "There you go again," during his 1980 American presidential debate with Jimmy Carter.[28] The sentence "*That goes without saying* [Çela va sans dire]" no more means "Going precedes saying" as "Going replaces saying" or, at the extreme, "Going is saying." Dialectal slang is pertinent here when, as in California's "Valley[-Girl] Speak," people are said not to "speak" but instead to "go."[29] The *Urban Dictionary* thus has this instance for the use of *went*: "And so I went, 'You'll never get this thing running,' and he went, 'Then I'll push it off a cliff.'"[30] In the Swiss Protestant Jacob Ruff's play *Adam und Heva* (1550), Adam is confused after hearing God's voice talking—or was it the divine voice that was walking?—and so he does not know how things went down: "*Ich Weiss nit wies zügangen ist.*"[31]

Most European translators of Genesis 3:8 usually miss this way of thinking where talking and speaking merge on being one and the same. Concomitantly, they fail to link the "walking voice" in Genesis 3:8 with sounding, or walking, of the shofar, that musical horn (trumpet) fashioned from a ram's horn. The shofar blasts at key moments in subsequent biblical history. Before Mount Sinai the granting of the Ten Commandments, for example: "And mount Sinai was altogether on a smoke, because the LORD descended upon it in fire: and the smoke thereof ascended as the smoke of a furnace, and the whole mount quaked greatly. And when the voice [*kol*] of the trumpet sounded [*holeich*] long, and waxed louder and louder, Moses spake, and God answered him by a voice" (Ex 19:18–19). A more accurate translation would be: "The voice of the shofar walked." The link with God or God's voice walking in the Garden of Eden, obvious in the Hebrew, is gone in the English, not so much because the European translators really dislike the term shofar, but because they do not catch the relationship between going and sounding, or walking and talking. The same misprision informs European translations of many other key passages. Among these is that where the prophet Ahijah the Shilonite hears "the voice of the walking" of Jeroboam's wife (1 Kgs 14:6) and that where the prophet Elisha, disciple of Elijah, refers to "the voice of walking" by the master of a messenger (2 Kgs 6:32).

Is it a realized God or an idealized voice of god that stalks the garden? The Apostle John's beginning, "In the beginning was the Word," almost suggests an embodied voice, yet the depiction of God's talking in Gn 3:8 has remained a vexing problem in Christendom. One solution for stage productions has been a megaphone or speaking tube. God speaks to earthlings through that instrument; He is the music, the rhythm. There are thus speaking tubes in medieval drama.[32] One might consider here the *Sprachrohr* or *Hörrohr* (speaker-ear or hearer-ear) thanks to which his audience can perceive the voice of the *Wurm* (serpent) Fafnir in Richard Wagner's opera *Siegfried* (1870).[33] Likewise, there is the logo of the Victor Talking Machine Company, Francis Barraud's painting "His Master's Voice" (1899).[34] In German, the label reads, "Die Stimme seines *Herrn*," a lexical recall of the voice of God (Luther's *Herr*) walking in the garden.[35] The gramophone horn shown in the advertisement is at once a broadcaster and a receiver: a "speaking tube" for the recorded voice of the unearthly master; and a "hearing trumpet" for the dog, who he is listening to his master's voice. (The master here is not divine; he is dead.) How else, but by means of a speaking trumpet, might a masterful God (*Herr*) speak to a man? How else, but by means of a hearing trumpet, might a man be enabled really to hear a god? In his poem "Die Posaunestelle" (The shofar place, 1969),[36] the Jewish poet Paul Celan thus writes:

| hör dich ein | [listen (your way) in |
| mit dem Mund. | with the mouth]. |

Unlike the *Posaune* understood as "trombone," the shofar has no detachable mouth- or earpiece. The Italian composer Luciano Berio set "Die Posaunestelle" to music as the Prologue, "Hör" (*shema*) for his *Requiem der Versöhnung* (Requiem of atonement, 1995). One not only speaks *into* a shofar but also hears *out* of one.

God exhales life into Man: His breathing life *into adam* (clay) is, according to Genesis, the human creation. God also inhales life *out of* Man: Moses dies *al pi adonai* (at the mouth of a kissing God).[37] God both breathes life into human beings and takes the breath away. The association of vital beginning and end with enabling and disabling umbicular caesura is explicitly distinct with Jewish thinkers.[38] When European Christian translators miss how God takes away the breath even as European Christian organists essay to extend forever the *tekiah gedolah*, they get it wrong in translation, most saying that Moses died "as the Lord had said,"[39] "according to the word of the Lord,"[40] "*iubente Domino*,"[41] "*nach dem Wort des HERRN*,"[42] and so on. In like manner they overlook how the shofar or Ghostly trombone suggests the Fall and the human relationship, at once pedal and oral, with God, as set from the beginning, not only in the Garden, with its walking voice, but also in the relationship between God and the distinctly impeded Moses.[43]

Consider here the Jewish tribes' several "circumambulations"[44] of the walls of Jericho following the death of Moses, when Joshua becomes the leader of the Jewish people. In particular, there is the blowing of the shofar that triggers the fall of the city walls. Handel tells the story of this "fall"[45] in his oratorio *Joshua* (1747).[46] After we hear "Sound the shrill trumpets, shout, and blow the horns,"[47] there follows a presumably onomatopoeic musical tott'ring, trembling. The end of the second act reiterates the great power of God, this time in the natural realm. The sun and moon stand still in their course (literally, runway).[48] A sustained high A note, coming from string instruments, long continues, for many bars. (A similarly exhausting pedal-point occurs in William Crotch's oratorio *Palestine* [1812].)[49] (The orchestral tradition using the shofar call to assemble troops continues to the twentieth century: the three whistling tritones that open the overture of Leonard Bernstein's *West Side Story* are precise, shofar-type calls.)[50]

How long can a human musician sustain a single note? The long note of the shofar, the *tekiah gedolah*—a single unbroken blast of the shofar held as long as possible, meaning almost to the point of mortal expiration—ends with the priest entirely exhausted, almost to the point of death. The human breath can't last long without a caesura for breathing. The string musician can last longer, of course. A keyboard instrument, in particular the church organ, is the preferred instrument in many Christian places of worship due partly to its ability to extend the pedal point. With such an organ, there is only the down-to-earth trembling of the alternating *shevarim* that Handel conveys in Joshua. His ground-base (*basso ostinato*) for *Joshua*'s "Almighty Ruler of the Skies" suggests the sort of walking bass that American jazz musicians, like William Turk, represented on the left side of the piano: Turk, they say on this account, had "a left hand like God."

Handel's attraction to the shofar is no stretch: he knew the biblical instruments,[51] had Jewish subscribers and friends,[52] heard the shofar in Hamburg and Venice and perhaps also London, and introduced trombones to England from his native Germany partly as a substitute for the Hebrew trumpet. The biblical King David, he knew, included the shofar in his orchestra as an instrument for praising God.[53]

As Anthony Cuthbert Baines points out, Handel made the trombone parts a centerpiece of his music, as for the oratorio *Saul* (1739),[54] one of whose "symphonies"[55] has opening bars that imitate the notes of the shofar.[56] The trombones suggest there the shofar notes—*tekiah*, *teruah*, and *shevarim*—and the shofar's *teruah* in particular, as its rhythm especially would seem to allow for walking with God. As King David writes, "Blessed [is] the people that know the joyful *teruah*: they shall walk [*holeich*], God, in the light of thy countenance."[57]

In Handel's work, it is only in *Joshua* that we hear the exhausting *tekiah gedolah*. Thanks to God, Joshua makes the sun and moon stand still: the heavenly bodies pause in their paths. It is much as when Abraham, on his way to killing Isaac, is halted from doing so by some better angel and a ram caught by the shofar in a thicket. For the Jews, the shofar represents not only the divine speaking tube but also the divine ear trumpet, as when shofar is a ram's horn is employed as a "hearing aid."[58] The starkly rhythmic command to the auditor, "Hear [*shema*] O Israel, the Lord Our God, the Lord is One"[59]—the core of the twice daily rhythmical Jewish prayers and directly endorsed by Jesus[60]—leads to an equally powerful direction to the speaker. The speaker is directed to recite the command to hear (*shema*), among other ways, "when thou [the human being] walkest [*holeich*] by the way."[61] Saint Jerome has "*ambulaveris* in via" and Martin Luther has "auf dem *Wege* gehst." The specific blessing for blowing the shofar concludes with the words reminding the auditors that said God commanded "to hear of the shofar [*li-shmoah kol shofar*]."

In the twentieth century, trombonists carry forth Handel's orchestral radical experiment with the trombone, as in Meira Warshauer's concerto *Tekeeyah: A Call*: Concerto for Shofar and Trombone (2009). The horn-player Haim Avitur, who performed *Tekeeyah* at its opening night, says that "the sound [of the shofar] is alive," whereas "the same note on the trombone has a constructed, cultivated sound, man-shaped and manipulated."[62] No matter this reversion to notions of a polar opposition between human "domesticity" and divine "wilderness," there is the more pertinent work by the composer Arnold Schoenberg. Some thinkers believe that in Schoenberg's *shema*, the music theorist Arno Nadel's "criteria for a genuinely Jewish musical intonation combine in a dodecaphonic public exhortation" was fulfilled.[63] To some extent, this is accurate enough for *A Survivor from Warsaw* (1947), which includes variants of the shofar call.[64] Already in 1933, however, Schoenberg claimed explicitly to be breaking spiritually with the European German tradition.[65] He had in mind only partly his prose drama *Der biblische Weg* (1926) and work on his opera *Moses und Aron* (1954), which concern issues of "ineffability" and Moses's speech impedance. Schoenberg's turn also revises the *basso continuo* tradition. Schoenberg had done many *basso continuo* arrangements and cadences[66] based on works of contrapuntal baroque composers like Matthias Georg Monn, Johann Christoph Mann, and František Tůma—works of the sort we will consider in the next two sections. "For the first time," writes Theodor Adorno, "a break is made in [Schoenberg's] *Chamber Symphony* [Number 1, 1907[67]] with what had been a basic stratum of music since the age of the *basso continuo* [*Generalbasszeitalter*], from the *stile rappresentativo*, from the adjustment of musical language to the significative aspect of human language."[68] Remarkable here is Schoenberg's variably tonal *Concerto for String Quartet and Orchestra in B flat major* (1933), the atonal composer's "re-composition" of work by Handel (1739). That work's first movement[69] is a largo leading into an allegro fugue on only a single note, proceeding thence by repeating identical notes for three bars each—2 half-notes, 4 quarter notes, and 8 eighth notes ("quavers")—matters more than all else, as when the quivering staccato of the *teruah*.

The above-going considerations tend to reinforce a relatively full archaic link between talking and walking, or dancing and singing, and many Christian adaptations and translations of Genesis 3:8 have tended to limit this fullness. For them it often seems that the walking voice, insofar as it involves a shofar's tritones, are feared along with the voice of the devil. The tritone is a principal interval of dissonance, even restlessness, in much Christian music. Known as the *diabolus in musica* (the devil in music), the tritone was sometimes even banned.[70]

Consider, for example, the long-standing Christian interpretation, sometimes bordering on a purposeful misreading, of even the noun that names the particular talking being that tricks Eve. The Hebrew term for this creature involves breathing: *nachash*. The being is, in this view, a hiss or whisper. Most Christian interpreters, however, follow Jerome in calling it a "serpent" from the get-go. (The Latin *serpens* means "one who crawls.")[71] So the precise linkage between talking (what the being does craftily) and walking (how the being will be punished, by leg amputation), between the clever talker (forked-tongued) and the lame walker (cloven-hoofed).

Only with the Expulsion does the being go "crawling between heaven and earth"—as Hamlet says of himself.[72] Human beings after the Fall might well hope that the devil has been sufficiently disabled— "thou shalt bruise his heel [*eikev*]," says God to Eve[73]—that he no longer so craftily walk the talk or talk the walk.[74] In later days, however, we encounter trickster Jacob, whose name (*yakov*) means "crafty heel-grabber" as "crafty." His defeat of the "angel" maims him, and now renamed *Yisroel* (he who struggles with God) carries the staff, or baton, that will pass down to Moses himself.

THE WALKING BASS IN MONTEVERDI'S *MY FOOT SLIPS AGAIN* (1624)

The Basso continuo became the main hallmark distinguishing Baroque styles from earlier periods, as well as from the following Classical era. The rhythmic concomitant of the basso continuo, the so-called walking-bass texture—although it is inseparably associated with the bass line, hence with harmony in general—also governs an entire durational stratum. . . . The walking bass persisted from Monteverdi's time to Bach, but still often occurs in compositions of later generations as well. As we shall see, the walking-bass element was also used in Baroque stile antico as an additional modernizing factor, whereas in the next generation, the late 18th century, it represented a retrospective element. In other words, it is the same stylistic component signaling musical modernism in early Baroque, and conservatism in the Classical period.
—IDO ABRAVAYA, *On Bach's Rhythm and Tempo*[75]

Formerly the use of the fundamental harmony had been theoretically regulated through recognition of the effects of root progressions [as in *basso continuo*]. This practice had grown into a subconsciously functioning sense of form which gave a real composer an almost somnambulistic sense of security in creating, with utmost precision, the most delicate distinctions of formal elements.
—ARNOLD SCHOENBERG, *Composition with Twelve Tones*[76]

Claudio Monteverdi's *L'Orfeo* (1607), arguably the first definitive "opera" written anywhere,[77] has a "walking bass" that walks, or almost walks: Orpheus, as he leads Eurydice out of the Underworld.

When paedagogue Orpheus looks back, the bass stops, and tragedy ensures. The term *walking bass* is a staple in the musicology of the baroque period. It figures the steady rhythm of symmetrical ambulation, often "in 4/4 time, suggestive of the rhythm of walking,"[78] generally including two or four bass notes per bar on a "walking" (melodic) bass. Earlier metrical instances would include dance terms: the *chaconne*, in the tradition of Claudio Merulo,[79] for example, and the *passacaglia* (literally, "walking the streets") in the influential tradition of Girolamo Frescobaldi.[80] Oftentimes, for the walking bass, "broken octaves . . . go up and down the scale in steps [of equal value] or small intervals,"[81] the speed varying from "coursing" to "ambling"[82] and so forth. The double-bass player usually plays *pizzicato*, "often plucked or slapped," with "scale tones, arpeggios, chromatic runs, and passing tones."[83] The organist, by contrast, may extend a walking bass out to a *pedal point*, or long sustained note,[84] comparable to that suggested, in the last section, for the *tekiah gedolah* imitated in Handel's *Joshua*. The trend-setting Monteverdi took up the walking bass as a thematic issue a few years after *Orfeo*, in his brilliant setting of the biblical Psalm, an "introit," that begins *Laetatus Sum* (I rejoiced, 1610).[85] His music now "puns" when it yokes together the pedal rhythm of music and language:

Laetatus sum in his quae dicta sunt mihi: In domum Domini ibimus. Stantes erant *pedes* nostri, in atriis tuis Jerusalem.	I rejoiced with those who said to me, Let us go to the house of the LORD. Our feet are standing in your gates, Jerusalem.

Monteverdi's madrigal, *My Foot Slips Again* (1624) goes further, as it begins "self-referentially" with a reference to the "foot." To its jazzy aspect we will turn below.

Ohimè, ch'io cado ohimè, ch'inciampo ancora il *piè* come pria.	Alas for me, I tumble down, alas for me, my *foot* slips again just as it did before.[86]

Walking Bass applies to hundreds of works, including many by Arcangelo Corelli, among them his *Sonata in C Major* (1694),[87] and its comprehension helps much to understand the works of George Frideric Handel.[88] The chorus *"Let None Despair"* from his musical *Hercules* (1744) is a case in point.[89] There Dejanira of Trachis fears that her husband Hercules has been killed, and the Chorus of Trachinians consoles her thus:

> Let none despair; relief may come though late,
> And Heav'n can snatch us from the verge of fate.[90]

Beneath this rhyming couplet, provided by the librettist and religious universalist Thomas Broughton,[91] is the walking bass referenced in the epigraph above, with and also against which the chorus sings. The organist fingers' keyboarding and feet pedaling produce this walking bass.

In *Hercules*, the aesthetic effect of the walking bass in relationship to the choral voice is spectacular. The affirmative promise of the chorus ("Do not despair"—provided by the universalist Divine Broughton) seems to mark a steady progress toward affirmation (Hercules is yet alive), but it turns out to be a way station along the path to tragedy (Dejanira will kill Hercules). A second example would be the *Messiah*'s "O death where is thy victory?"[92]

An example of a less ambiguously affirmative walking bass, likewise concerned with the vocal and pedal, would be Johann Sebastian Bach's organ work *Wachet Auf, Ruft Uns Die Stimme* (Wake arise the voices call us, 1731),[93] based on the Lutheran hymn by Phillip Nicolai (1599), particularly as transcribed for organ.[94] The opening two lines of each of the hymn's three stanzas, as employed in Bach's cantata of the same name,[95] refers to voice or song (*Stimme, singen, gesungen*),[96] even as the organ's walking bass marches toward Jerusalem; the baseline marks God's steady and forceful approach to the gentiles (*Heiden*): "Now come, thou precious crown, / Lord Jesus, God's own Son! [Nun komm, du werte Kron, / Herr Jesu, Gottes Sohn!]"

Another well-known example of God's bass walk (approach) in Bach's works would be the magnificent pedal component of his G-minor organ music version of *Nun komm' der Heiden Heiland* (Now come, Savior of the gentiles),[97] for which Martin Luther's hymn of the same name (1524) elsewhere provides the text. There is also Bach's *Credo in Unum Deum* (I believe in one God) in Bach's *Mass in B Minor* (1749),[98] completed just a year before he died.

The presumably Godlike quality of the steadily progressive walking bass is often noted by musicologists. "The basso continuo is a *walking bass*, with regular beat marking the eternal time of God," writes the musicologist Alexandra Amati-Camperi about the *Suscepit Israel* (God has received Israel) in *Bach's Magnificat in D Major* (1723).[99] The divine walk of baroque music, with all its slips, attracted twentieth-century American jazzmen. When boogie-woogie, ragtime composer James "Eubie" Blake wanted to praise piano-player William Turk, he said that Turk had "a left hand like God."[100] Many jazzman and rock-n-roll musicians incorporate this aspect of baroque music into their work: the British Jethro Tull's instrumental *Bourée* (1969),[101] for example, is based on Bach's *Suite in E Minor for Lute*.[102] More importantly, many expert players of baroque music bring out the walk elements of early music: Claudio Monteverdi's *My Foot Slips Again* (1624), for example, is the basis for the early music group Arpeggiata's brilliant performance with countertenor Philippe Jaroussky.[103] The Handel scholar Ben Finane rightly calls this version a suitably "jazzy *basso continuo* cum *walking bass*" of the bass-walking seventeenth century.[104]

The string player "walks the strings and even sings," as the thumb-style guitarist Eddie Pennington puts it,[105] and the double-bassist who walks sets aside the bow and let's his fingers do the walking, and in that sense sings.[106] Henry Alexander's clever jingle for Ma Bell, "Let your fingers do the walking," has its presumed origin. "An American jazzman speaks bass like this," says the francophone voice-over in jazz bass-walker John Lindberg's movie *Bass Walk* (2007),[107] where the fingers do the talking. In fact, the jazz walker's digital ambulation is the punning subject of the cover art for bassist Leroy ("The Walker") Vinnegar's album *Leroy Walks Again!!* (1962). Vinnegar's plainer pedal ambulation was the punning subject for the cover art for his earlier album *Leroy Walks!* (1957), in which six of the seven cuts are walking numbers.[108] The history of jazz is filled with great walkers. In addition to those mentioned above there is Blind Willie McTell's "Mr McTell Got the Blues" (1927: "Gonna walk these blocks, honey, gotta buy me some shoes. / That's the reason why Mr McTell got the blues.") "Walking Blues," first recorded by Eddie James "Son" House Jr. (1930), which may still be the best-known example of jazzy walking-bass: "Woke up this morning I looked 'round for my shoes / You know I had those mean old walking blues."[109] Other figures would include Albert Ammons (*Boogie Woogie Stomp*, 1936–38),[110] Ray Brown ("Cool Walk," 1959),[111] Percy Heath of the "Modern Jazz Quartet," Paul Chambers of the "Miles Davis Quintet," Ron Carter of the "Miles Davis Quartet," and Sam Jones.

Relevant to the conjunction of vocal with pedal ability and disability is the bass work of Charlie Haden. Haden had been an able professional vocalist until age fifteen when bulbar polio disabled him in such a way that he was no longer able to sing or even easily to talk.[112] "It was scary," he reports. "I couldn't sing anymore."[113] What could he do now by way of rhythmic communication? The chordal walking bass became the polio's vocal-chords. "After losing his voice to polio as a teenager, [Haden] found a new voice by picking up the bass."[114] His musician's fingers now did the talking.

The rock-and-roll singer Roy Orbison focused a good part of the subject matter of his work onstage on issues of singing or talking and walking or dancing. (His Texas childhood was marked by a removal from Fort Worth to Vernon occasioned by a polio scare.) Orbison's performances during the 1960s are replete with references to the halts of walking and the pauses of talking. In "Running Scared" (1961), based loosely on Maurice Ravel's semiballetic *Boléro* (1928), the girl finally walks off with the singer.[115] Orbison's "In Dreams" (1963) includes the lines, "In dreams I walk with you / In dreams I talk to you" as it walks and talks through three octaves and a powerful falsetto. The singer's "Pretty Woman" (1964) includes the plea, "Pretty woman, talk a while" and ends shortly after the rhetorical question, "Is she walking back to me?" His "Walk On" (1968) recalls of the lament "Remember Me" in Henry Purcell's aria *Dido and Aeneas* (1688), which likewise rises on a fixed ostinato walking bass, proceeding from *pianissimo* (softly) to *fortissimo possible* (as loud as possible).

It is not the dream-like aspect of Orbison's songs that alone explains psychoanalysts' interest in his work;[116] nor is it the extraordinary octaval range of Orbison's voice, taken alone, that explains music lovers' interest in his work.[117] There is also the marked contrast between Orbison's mobile vocal performances and his immobile pedal presentation. On the one hand is the *mobility* of his voice—its octaval range and voluminal power. (His whisper-singing, says Bono, "was the loudest whisper I've ever heard.")[118] On the other hand is the *immobility* of his body. Especially in the 1960s, he performs standing still almost as if he were frozen. Such presentation is much unlike that of his peers,[119] for example, the animated "theatrics" of Johnny Ray. The pedal immobility also has a labial aspect. "He hardly moved his lips," reports Bono—as if Orbison were a ventriloquist, most starkly represented by Terry Fator's prize-winning, ventriloquist-singing cover of Orbison's "Crying" (1962) on the television show *America's Got Talent*.[120] By comparison there is the lip-synched performance of "In Dreams" by Ben in Peter Lynch's movie *Blue Velvet* (1986).[121] The effect of pedal and labial paralysis and vocal mobility, taken together, makes for a fine expression of what one music critic calls "the Orbison persona's passivity and paralysis,"[122] a "paralysis of fright"[123] of an "hysterical" sort much in the newspapers and popular psychoanalytic literature of the 1950s and 1960s.

Orbison's major works were like "art songs." His "Only the Lonely" (1960) is sometimes called the "first operatic rock ballad." (Its success encouraged Elvis Presley to do a cover of the "Neapolitan song" "O Sole Mio" [My own sun, 1898]: "It's Now or Never" [1960].)[124] Bob Dylan, who performed with Orbison in the Travelling Wilburys, said, "Roy was an opera singer but didn't know it."[125] In his obituary of Orbison, David Gates said that Orbison's music was that of "art song."[126] Rock-and-roll's walking roots were much in the thawing out of the classical composer Henry Purcell's frozen-walking compositions.

"I CAN SCARCELY MOVE OR DRAW MY BREATH" IN PURCELL'S *KING ARTHUR* (1691)

Because real stutterers do not stutter when they sing, realistic presentation of stuttering in song is tricky, yet stuttering is often represented as a sort of chattering, the kind of shivering that one might experience, in trying to walk, when one is "half-frozen," perhaps because one is freezing up in the cold or thawing out in the warmth. Thawing as such involves a passage from silence to sound, as from stillness to motion, and freezing up involves the passage from sound to silence, as motion to stillness. The action of freezing up informs the main motifs of the chorus of *trembleurs* in Jean-Baptiste Lully's operatic *Isis* (1677):[127] the members of the chorus cannot speak without chattering ("Nous ne sçaurions parler / Qu'avec une voix tremblante"). Hoarfrost invades the body and numbs the legs.[128] The action of thawing out informs a later English work that well captures the disability of talking and walking so conceived in terms of trembling than the celebrated Cold Genius's aria in Henry Purcell's *King Arthur or, The British Worthy* (1691), with libretto by John Dryden and various political aspects.[129]

Purcell's Cold Genius, as presented in *King Arthur*, is "the genius of this isle [Britain]."[130] Cupid, who calls him thus in "the frost scene," seeks to thaw out the Genius from his frozen state and raise him up. The Genius is thus a recall of Old Hamlet rising up at the "dead hour" (1.1.68).[131] Tortured by the change from silent stillness to vocal pedalism, half-risen Genius sings words that, together with their music, ally walking with breathing difficulty in talking. He begs to be refrozen.

> What power art thou, who from below
> Hast made me rise unwillingly and slow
> From beds of everlasting snow?
> See'st thou not how stiff and wondrous old
> Far unfit to bear the bitter cold
> I can scarcely move or draw my breath?
> Let me, let me freeze again to death."[132]

The ground in T. S. Eliot's England never quite fully freezes: in his *Wasteland* (1922), "Winter kept us warm."[133] In Purcell's *King Arthur*, however, the flesh really does freeze up. If "April is the cruellest month,"[134] for Purcell, it is because Spring relives the silent stillness of Winter only to bring stumbling and stuttering: the partial inability of the thawing-out Cold Genius to walk ("I can scarcely move . . . ") matches his partial inability to talk (" . . . or draw my breath").

And yet, walk and talk he does. The disabled Genius is enabled to walk, albeit haltingly, thanks to people who push him along—as in Nikolaus Hamoncourt's production of *King Arthur* (2004).[135] He is enabled to talk, albeit stutteringly, by music that provides the walking bass and shivering strings[136]—as for Oliver Widmer's vocal chords chattering out the words along with the trembling strings, also in Hamancourt's production. Other performances of King Arthur bring out the same conjunction of quasi-walking with quasi-talking. The countertenor Klaus Nomi,[137] in the last performance (1982) before his death, matched his pedal and manual movements to his stuttering.[138] Michael Nyman's *Memorial* (1984), with stuttering saxophones, was based on the Cold Genius's aria and soon found its way into Peter Greenaway's movie *The Cook, the Thief, His Wife & Her Lover* (1989).[139] Nyman also did the score for Greenaway's *Walk Through H* (1978) and *Drowning by Number* (1988), with its Mozart-based "Wheelbarrow Walk," and wrote the quasi-ballet, *Taking a Line for a Second Walk* (1986).

The bass baritone Petteri Salomaa, in his performance in William Christie's production of *King Arthur* (1995),[140] delivered "the required hiccupping . . . without hyperventilating."[141] That was not surprising: a few months earlier, Salomaa had played the role of the mouth-locked, stuttering Papageno in Wolfgang Amadeus Mozart's *Magic Flute* (1791),[142] in the first production of which the stuttering librettist Emanuel Schikaneder played this same role.

When Sting,[143] bassist for the British rock band The Police, sang out the words, "I can scarcely move or draw my breath" (2009)[144] in his cover of the Cold Genius aria, a chorus of voices breathed *for* him. It was as if he could not breathe without them, and they thus interrupted, if only for a while, the mortal danger of cæsura.

CHAPTER THREE

Trips of the Tongue in *Hamlet* (1600)

Speak the speech, I pray you, trippingly on the tongue
—HAMLET, *Hamlet*, 3.2.1883

I must hold my tongue
—HAMLET, *Hamlet*, 1.2.333

This chapter concerns mostly the Players in Shakespeare's *Hamlet*. Thousands of persons have written about the Player's speeches and the play within the play, among them my predecessor at Harvard, Harry Levin. (See my discussion at the end of Chapter 1 about swimming with Harry.) Here, though, we focus on those aspects of the play within the play, and Hamlet in general, that pertain to walking and talking, and especially to that of Hamlet himself. To begin, we note the onetime predilection (little noted nowadays, to our interpretative peril) for directors of the play to have Hamlet crawl. He walks about the world with leg shackles, "down down-gyved to his ankle . . . his knees knocking each other." At the same time we mark what it means to speak trippingly, or for Hamlet, to talk in stammering triplets.

Most spectators want to say to the stumbling, stuttering Hamlet, "Your bumbling 'Well, well, well' is all very well, but just DO it!" (H, 3.1.1786). As if we did not, every one of us, know already that, because "the human gait is a continuously arrested falling," as the psychiatrist Erwin W. Strauss puts it in his "The Upright Posture," "man has to find a hold within himself."[1]

CRAWL

What should such fellows as I do crawling between heaven and earth?
—HAMLET, *Hamlet*, 3.1.1814

In many productions of *Hamlet*, the lead character crawls on stage during the play within the play and often at other times as well. On the one hand, Prince Hamlet has a "forked tongue," so maybe it makes sense that, like a would-be regicidal snake, he should slither serpent-like toward King Claudius. Claudius, after all, brought down the Edenic garden, or orchard of Old Denmark, which has now "gone to seed" (H) and Claudius was its regicide. So the Ghost of Old Hamlet:

> Now, Hamlet, hear.
> 'Tis given out that, sleeping in my orchard,
> A serpent stung me; so the whole ear of Denmark
> Is by a forged process of my death
> Rankly abus'd; but know, thou noble youth,
> The serpent that did sting thy father's life
> Now wears his crown. (*Hamlet*, 1.5.768)

Hamlet would seem to want to do the same to his uncle-father Claudius. There is, however, more to Hamlet's condition of *serpentine* crawling (serpentine means literally, "one who crawls"). For one thing, the "crawling Hamlet stage tradition" is largely a product of the romantic and Victorian periods, as we will consider in the next paragraphs. Those periods, as we shall see in later discussions of ambulation in poetry (Wordsworth) and hysterical leg paralysis (Freud), are already relevantly concerned with issues of more-or-less involuntary walking disabilities.

Famously in the nineteenth century, the actor Edmund Kean (1814)[2] crawled when he acted Hamlet. Reviewers call his performance snake-like.[3] Similarly serpentine were William Charles Macready (1823) and Edwin Forrest (1829). Artist Daniel Maclise's painting "The Play Scene in *Hamlet*" (1842)[4]—a depiction of Edmund Kean's performance influenced by German Moritz Retzch's engraving (1827)—was often imitated throughout the century.[5]

Lewis Carroll, after attending (1856) a performance of Hamlet by actor Charles Kean (Edmund Kean's son), wrote, "Kean was best in the play scene (evidently [says Carroll] grouped from [Daniel] Maclise's picture)."[6] Edwin Booth's Hamlet (1870) and Henry Irving's Hamlet (1874) both crawled in the central scene. The actor Wilson Barrett seemed almost to crawl in his performances: "rubbing his hands upon his knees, rocking himself to and fro, drumming with his fingers."[7] (*Ham*, he knew, indicates "the back of the knees.") Actor Beerbohm Tree's Hamlet crawled in the traditional way of his century (1892).[8] The "crawling Hamlet tradition" involves more places than England and includes women actors as well as male.[9] When the French actor Jean Mounet-Sully presented a crawling Hamlet (1893), he was already famous for his stage portrayal of Oedipus in Jules Lacroix's literal translation of Sophocles's *Oedipus the King* (1881). The French woman Sarah Bernhardt likewise presented a crawling Hamlet (1899).[10] For Germany, there is the silent-movie *Hamlet* (1921) in which the Danish actress Asta Nielsen crawls.[11] Examples extend well into the twentieth century and include Richard Burton's performance as directed by Michael Bentall (1953).

The theater-going public approved the crawling-Hamlet tradition. Most theater critics, however, did not. Frank Albert Marshall, for example, wrote in 1875: "Most of the actors, that I have seen in the part of 'Hamlet', are wont to execute what I must venture to call the most vulgar piece of melodramatic absurdity which can be conceived. They crawl on their hands and knees from the feet of Ophelia to the King."[12] John Dover Wilson, author of *What Happens in Hamlet* (1935), called the "Hamlet crawl" a cheap trick.

The serpentine Hamlet, though, is more than that. The crafty Ghost delivers to Young Hamlet, for whom the world will soon become "an unweary garden grown to seed" (H), the serpentine words I have already quoted above. The biblical story of the Fall, to which the words of the Ghost allude ("an unweary garden grown to seed"), includes the crafty words of the serpent, which the biblical narrator calls "subtil"[13] and Eve calls "beguiling."[14] Thanks to his talking, as we have seen, the snake becomes serpentine ("one who crawls"). God tells him that, from now on, "upon thy belly shalt thou go."[15] The King James translation ("go") misses how the Latin Vulgate (*gradieris*) implies that will now *step* differently. The Hebrew *telech* is, in fact, the same word that the biblical narrator uses to describe the walking voice (*kol*) of God—the sound that Adam hears calling, "Where art thou?",[16] after he eats the fruit. If Hamlet talks oddly, as we shall see he does, then one might expect his walking to follow suit.

The rest of this chapter essays to provide an answer to Hamlet's serpentine (crawling) question, "What should I do . . . crawling . . . ?" (H) The answers, as we will see in later chapters, portends for later thinkers a notion of "hysteria" connected with walking disability and talking cure.

PAUSE

Answeres and oracles as touching . . . the tripping and stumbling of the foot.
—PHILEMON HOLLAND, trans., Plutarch's *Morals*[17]

Throughout *Hamlet*, there are comparisons between the impending fall of the old Danish regime in *Hamlet* and the fall of Troy in Vergil's

Aeneid. Hamlet's apparent hesitation to kill Claudius in *Hamlet* is like that of Pyrrhus, the son of Achilles, to kill Priam, the father of Hector, in the play within the play—the famous "Mousetrap" in *Hamlet* as a whole Hamlet and Pyrrhus are alike stoppered. In the Vergil-inspired Player's speech about the Fall of Troy, we learn how the son Pyrrhus is about to kill the father Priam when suddenly he is stilled or paralyzed.

> So as a painted tyrant Pyrrhus stood,
> And, like a neutral to his will and matter,
> Did ... nothing. (*Hamlet*, 2.2.1542)

Hamlet himself has chosen this speech on purpose, and he delivers its initial recitation with fine accent. Pyrrhus is frozen, paralyzed, midstream in action, vocal and pedal. ("My tongue is tied and my hand is stayed," writes Richard Grant White in his *Every-Day English* [1880].)[18]

This temporary paralysis, or staying, does not happen in the *Aeneid*.[19] In *Hamlet*, the idiosyncratic ellipsis (...) appearing before the Player's *nothing* is thus idiosyncratic: ("I must hold my tongue" [H, 1.2.333]). The silence and the *nothing* already suggest the central "pause" or "comma" (H) of the play. The Player in *Hamlet* so impedes his usual iambic pentameter—his cadence—that a full line becomes: "Did ... nothing." The old Walt Whitman wrote counterpart lines in "A Carol Closing Sixty-Nine" (1888): "Of me myself—the jocund heart yet beating in my breast/ The body wreck'd, old, poor, and paralyzed."

Should the Player's *nothing* be accented in the "monotonous" fashion that Puttenham calls "the Pyrrhic foot"? The Pyrrhic foot, also called "dibrach" (two unaccented short syllables), is a metrical unit with unstressed-unstressed syllables: the "foote *Pirrichius* ... beares in maner no sharper accent vpon the one then the other sillable, but he is in effect egall in time and tune, as is also the *Spondeus*."[20] The effect is monotone. The *pes pyrrhichius* (Pyrrhic foot), by contrast, pertains to the Pyrrhic dance, named after its presumed inventor Pyrrichus. In this "walking dance" English-language words like *dithyramb* and *iambic* may derive from the Greek *amb* (dance or step), referring to the raising and lowering of the foot, from the ground, in beating the rhythmic time.[21] The actors in the *pes pyrrhichius* are dressed in armor head to foot—like the presumed Ghost of Old Hamlet. They go through the motions (merely) of actual warfare but do not engage in warfare itself.

Few two-syllable words in the English language exemplify the Pyrrhic foot. John Mason writes in *An Essay on the Power of Numbers ... in Poetical Compositions* (1749), "I have exemplified the Pyrrhic, which contains two short Times, by two short Monosyllables, because every Word of two Syllables hath in the Pronunciation an Accent upon one of them, and in English Metre every accented Syllable is long; and therefore no English Word of two Syllables can properly exemplify a Pyrrhic Foot, which consists of two short ones."[22] What stops Hamlet—for whom Pyrrhus is the foil—from action, what impedes his pentameter, "scansion." It is not only his neurotic love for such as Ophelia, who reports of Hamlet's perusal of her, "Long stay'd he so" (H). It is, as he confirms, his own improperly "scanned" metrics:

> Now might I do it pat, now he is praying;
> And now I'll do't. And so he goes to heaven;
> And so am I revenged. That would be scanned:
> A villain kills my father; and for that,
> I, his sole son, do this same villain send
> To heaven. (*Hamlet*, 3.3.2356)

It is consequently also an inability or unwillingness to provide the hearer with the expected rhyme.

> For thou dost know, O Damon dear,
> This realm dismantled was
> Of Jove himself; and now reigns here
> A very, very——pajock. (*Hamlet*, 3.2.2167)

In these lines, the caesura-like pause after "very, very" (H)—indicated by the em-dash or mutton quad (—)—is as memorable as Pyrrhus's elliptical pause in the Player's Speech ("——nothing" [H]). (Compare Hamlet's several triple repetitions elsewhere.) Hamlet seems to stumble here in much the same way that the stutterer Porky Pig seeks word substitutions because he cannot pronounce the first word that comes into his mind. *Pajock* hardly rhymes with *ass*—the word that we might have expected but might also have experienced as probably inappropriate. (Claudius is worse than an ass!) *Pajock* itself lacks determinate meaning, and in any case, this is its *only* actual occurrence in the English language up to that point. *Pajock* is all sound—a mere "slip" of the tongue. Hamlet speaks "trippingly" (H, 3.2.1883) on the tongue—according to the advice that he himself would give to the Player.

Richard Huloet, in his *Abcedarium Anglico Latinum* (1552), might seem to summarize the plot of *Hamlet*, on the diacritical level, when he defines the dash as striking with a pen: "Dashe or stryke with a penne, litura." It is a *comma*, then, that stands between Prince Hamlet and King Claudius:

> As peace should still her wheaten garland wear
> And stand a comma 'tween their amities. (*Hamlet*, 5.2.3690)

Comma here would indicate partly the life-and-death problem breathing, as in prosody the term indicates the breathing periods of reading poetry aloud.[23] As we shall now see, however, it is also a *commere* (H), or comother, that stands between amities in *Hamlet*: the queen.

MOBILITY

> whilst they distill'd
> Almost to jelly with the act of fear,
> Stand dumb
> —HORATIO, *Hamlet*, 1.2.405

> The lady shall say her mind freely, or the blank verse shall halt for't.
> —HAMLET, *Hamlet*, 2.2.1409

After Pyrrhus's pause comes his killing of Priam and the sudden mobility of widowed Hecuba: she "run[s] barefoot up and down" (H). In this bare-footed mobility, Queen Hecuba the mother-wife now opposes the paralytic apoplexy (H) that Young Hamlet in the "bedroom scene" (H) attributes to Queen Gertrude the mother who has been fickle, or "mobile," in her spousal loyalty to Old Hamlet. *La donna è mobile*—as the Duke of Mantua has it in Giuseppe Verdi's opera *Rigoletto* (1851).[24] No wonder he asks that the player speak his speech, "trippingly on the tongue" (H) in other words, using a tripping, gamboling motion of the tongue.[25] This opposition between mobility and immobility in walking and talking sheds some light an old unsolved "puzzle" in Hamlet scholarship: the meaning of *mobled*, thrice-repeated in relationship to Queen Hecuba.

> *Hamlet*: ... say on: come to Hecuba.
> *First Player*: "But who, O, who had seen the mobled queen—"
> *Hamlet*: The mobled queen?
> *Lord Polonius*: That's good; *mobled queen* is good. (*Hamlet*, 2.2.1576)

There have been many answers to the question of what *mobled* means.²⁶ One of these concerns mobility. The nineteenth-century Shakespeare scholar Andrew Becket—himself the author of such plays about disabled persons like the limbless and tongueless heroine of his *Lavinia* (1838)²⁷—points out that Hamlet is remarking on the difference between the unmoved (apoplectic) Gertrude and the "mobiled" Hecuba. As Becket understands it, his view depends on Shakespeare's having "new-coined" *mobile*. Becket errs here: *mobile* was already an English-language adjective a hundred years before. Nevertheless, his intuition about the term is correct. The word *mobled* appears, in fact, in William Caxton's translation of Vergil's *Aeneid* (1490)²⁸— precisely in relationship to Dido, the quintessential "widow." (Compare Shakespeare's *The Tempest*, where the phrase "widow Dido" is repeated.)²⁹ Vergil's narrator speaks thus: "Dydo ... or euer that she coude saye ony thyng, as rauysshed helde her sighte all *mobyle*, wythout to areste it vpon one thynge of a long while." And soon thereafter, "Her fayre eyen ... were incontynent tourned in-to a right hidouse lokynge *mobyle*, & sangwynouse to see."³⁰

The Player in *Hamlet* probably mispronounces the word *mobled* in such a way that it is ambiguous whether the queen is genuinely "moved" or is just *muffling*—a term meaning "hiding," a term that is cognate with *mobling*. Determining whether Gertrude's grief is seeming or being—that is one purpose of the "play within the play." It was partly in order to determine that that would-be playwright Hamlet ("If she should break it now ... [H]) decided to write up his addition to "The Mousetrap" in the first place. He needs to apply the Hecuba test.³¹

CLAUDICATION

"Any actor would give twenty years of his life to play the part." ... "I thought if I told you what it was you'd ham it."
—THOMAS STERLING, *The Evil of the Day*³²

Hamlet taunts Polonius with being hamstrung, or hammed:³³ "Yourself, sir, should be old as I am, if like a crab you could go backward" (H). He refers to two conditions. The first condition is the "retrograde" (literally, backward "stepping, walking")³⁴ movement of certain heavenly constellations, first in one orbital direction and then in another—such heavenly groups of bodies as the Crab (Cancer) constellation.³⁵ (The moment of reversal here—the verse—recalls the stillness of the sun and moon occasioned at Jericho.) The second condition is paralytic or limping gait, often associated with the "crab walk."³⁶

Hamlet's very name, *Hamlet*, suggests (among other things) "little ham"—leg muscles underdeveloped like those of an infant (literally, of "one who does not talk and/or cannot talk").³⁷ *Ham* specifically means "the part of the knee that bends."³⁸ Young Hamlet, after all, was wont to be carried about so very often: "[Yorick] hath borne me on his back a thousand times" (H, 5.1.3515). Günther Grass's novel *Crabwalk* (*Im Krebsgang*, 2002)³⁹ picks up on the fact that how one depicts Hamlet limping on stage—crablike—is just as important as how one depicts him talking—stutteringly.⁴⁰ Ophelia describes Prince Hamlet as knock-kneed: "his knees knocking together" (H, 2.1.103). Prince Hamlet is concerned that his sinews not fail him when he meets the Ghost of Old Hamlet: " . . . you, my sinews, grow not instant old, / But bear me stiffly up" (H, 1.5.830).

"Little ham" (small leg) is one sense of the sound *ham-let*. *Pork*, meanwhile, is the sound made by the creature, the raven.⁴¹ This black-feathered bird is the device of the Danish Vikings, as in Saxo Grammaticus's *History of the Danes*, and when black-clothed Hamlet—crawling serpentine toward Claudius—bellows, "The croaking raven doth bellow for revenge (H, 3.2.2144)," he identifies himself as raven.⁴² The raven's croaking is, to English ears, precisely called *pork-porking*.⁴³ The Shakespearean actor Benjamin Griffin, in his farce *Love in a Sack* (1715), thus has a Hamlet-like "verbal triplicate" mocking the croaking raven that bellows for revenge: "I heard the Ravens last night cry *Pork, Pork, Pork*."⁴⁴ To be a pork, in English, means to be stupid, in the sense that Hamlet is or pretends to be.⁴⁵ In John Milton's *Colasterion* (1645), for example, the philosopher is contrasted with the pork.

Whenever Shakespeare uses *ham*, it is to indicate a weakness at once moral and physical. In *Pericles of Tyre*, he refers to a knight with cowering weak hams and in *Romeo and Juliet* there is the man with a bow in the hams. In *Hamlet*, Hamlet is disabled much as leg-lamed Claudius, with whom the prince compares and contrasts himself in terms of a lamed horse. "Our withers are unwrung" (H, 3.2.2131), Hamlet tells Claudius, ironically, referring to how wringing the withers of a horse disables it.⁴⁶

Claudius's very name, in fact, means "one who is lame." *Claudicant*, meaning "a person who limps intermittently,"⁴⁷ is regular Renaissance vocabulary, as in Waterman's *Fardle of Facions* (1555).⁴⁸ In the particular case of Claudius, his knees don't work well. His would-be prayerful speech, "Make assay: / Bow, stubborn knees" (H, 3.3.2316), does not succeed. He cannot pray: "My words fly up, my thoughts remain below" (H, 3.3.2380). He cannot pray because his knees fail: his claudicant "sinews" (H, 1.5.830)—the "nerves [as linked with the brain]"[49]—do not connect. The king suffers from spiritual apoplexy and/or paralysis.

Here is where one of the Roman stories that underlie *Hamlet* comes to the fore. *Hamlet's* Danish King Claudius is modeled partly on the Roman Emperor Claudius, a famously lame stutterer and verbal claudicant. Hamlet identifies and contrasts himself both with the Emperor Claudius (who is able to pretend to be "mad north northwest" thanks partly to how he talks and walks) and with his nephew Nero (who both kills his uncle Claudius and has sexual intercourse with his mother, Agrippina):[50] "Let not ever the heart of Nero enter this firm bosom" (H, 3.2.2262). The novelist Robert Graves, working from texts by the Roman historian Suetonius, reports that the Roman Claudius said of himself: "I l-l-limp with my tongue and st-st-stutter with my leg! Nature never quite finished me."

Claudication in *Hamlet* has both a walking and a talking aspect. General meanings of *halting* go with *claudicare*.[51] *Halting* means not only the general "hesitating . . . faltering"[52]—that is the main psychological characteristic of Hamlet but also involves the halt in verse. So, in the decades before Shakespeare was writing, John Frith says "that halting verse shall run merrily . . . upon his right feet" (1533)[53] and Abraham Fleming writes, "That usuall verse, althoughe it hault in one syllable" (1576).[54] *Hamlet*, we have seen, contains the warning, "The Lady shall say her minde freely; or the blanke Verse shall halt for't" (H, 2.2.1409).[55] The *Passionate Pilgrim* (1599) contains the Shakespearian line "A cripple soon can find a halt—,"[56] with its em-dash, and there is the like use of *halt* in *Much Ado About Nothing*: "A halting sonnet of his own pure brain, / Fashion'd to Beatrice." Physical laming in Shakespeare is, moreover, not always distinguishable from metric laming. Shakespeare's "*Sonnet 89*" reads: "Speak of my lameness and I straight will halt."[57] The "first person" of the sonnets, in this count, must have been a lame "halter," willy-nilly.

WILL HE, NILL HE

will he, nill he, he goes—mark you that
—HAMLET, *Hamlet*, 5.1.3359

In the Player's Speech in *Hamlet*, both father and son are halted (H), or apoplex'd (H, 3.4.2445). There is the paralysis of the young killer

Pyrrhus the son: "his sword / . . . / . . . seem'd i' the air to stick" (H, 2.2.1542). There is the silent stillness of the old killer Priam the father: "the unnerved father," whose "antique sword / [is] Rebellious to his arm" (H, 2.2.1542). Pyrrhus can or does do nothing: like Tin Man in *The Wizard of Oz*, he can't walk and he can't talk. For a while, "as a painted tyrant Pyrrhus stood," and "like a neutral to his will and matter, / Did . . . nothing" (H, 2.2.1542). Is Pyrrhus's "doing nothing"— his pause—*his* own willful doing? Or was it the doing of something else (a poison, for example, or a trap, or a work of music)? Or was that "doing nothing" the will of someone else (a god)?

These questions, like those that concern Hamlet's holding his tongue ("But break my heart / For I must hold my tongue" [H, 1.2.333]), might get us close to the "heart" of *Hamlet*. I may be forgiven, therefore, for engaging in an excursus to a counterpart to Pyrrhus's pause that informs a biblical story, "The Binding [*akedah*]," about how a son (Isaac) is almost killed by the quintessential human father, even fore-father (Abraham). Not only is this story often adduced for other purposes when discussing *Hamlet*—a play about fathers, sons, and sacrifices—but the same tale informs the central story of Christianity. That story is the mysterious killing of a Son (Jesus) by a divine Father (the Holy Ghost). The English Roman Catholic Richard Chalonner's eighteenth-century revision of the sixteenth-century Douay Rheims translations of the Bible thus calls the Abrahamic near-act the "holocaust" of Isaac,[58] interpreting that act christologically as the crucifixion of the Father of the Son, or perhaps vice versa, since Father and Son are mysteriously the same.

According to Genesis, then, father Abraham is armed with knife uplifted and set to kill Isaac. Suddenly he stops midstroke. It is as if the heavens themselves had stopped, as when Joshua stills the sun and moon, or like the instant when the Crab constellation that can walk backward turns retrograde. Did armed Abraham stay his arm in midstroke on his own, wholly voluntarily? Or was his arm stayed by some better angel? ("Lay not thy hand upon the lad.")[59]

What happened? Did Abraham himself *stay* his hand, or was his hand *stayed*? Some Christian grammarians[60] say his hand was stayed—his arm was "fixed," or "paralyzed"[61]—by some agency exterior to Abraham. Abraham was presumably more able to hear the "voice walking" than any other human being up to that time.[62] When the angel calls Abraham, Abraham does not hide (as Adam did); he answers "Here I am."[63] Next thing: a ram is caught in a thicket by the horn (shofar).

Hamlet seems to not know what stays him: "I do not know" (H, 2.1.1043). The English churchman John Hacket, in a biography of his patron John Williams (1670), notes about how skeptics are stayed, or paralyzed: "But as our Cambridge term is, he was staid [stayed] with *nescio*'s [statements claiming 'I don't know']."[64]

The reader of the story of the *akedah* (binding), like the spectator of Hamlet—will ye nill ye and will he nill he—both wants the would-be killer to get on with it and to put it off. If comedic death-and-resurrection were realizable, or some new strong-arm man (Fortinbras) might actually incorporate and transcend the contradictions at work in the intermittently stilled actions and stoppered words of such sometime weak-limbed kings, would-be kings, and king-killers—Pyrrhus/Priam, Hamlet/Claudius, Nero/Claudius, Abraham/Isaac, and so on—then all would be well.

And if not? Nietzsche's expression of his disabled physical and psychical state in the 1880s seems relevant here. Nietzsche's "spiritual life" was then broken off by paralyzing illness:[65] "Paralysis of will, where do we not find this cripple sitting nowadays!" The philosopher, attempting to express his condition, speaks of a dancer's loss of little leg (*Beinchen*): more precisely, of a "hamlet."[66] The rhythms of his German dithyrambic "Unter Töchtern der Wüste" (Beneath the daughters of the desert, 1885) match Hamlet's broken iambic pentameter:

einer Tänzerin gleich, die, wie mir scheinen will,	Like a dancer, who, as it would seem to me,
zu lange schon, gefährlich lange immer, immer nur auf Einem Beinchen stand?—	Has stood too long, precariously long Always, always only on one little leg?—
da vergass sie darob, wie mir scheinen will,	For she has forgotten, it would seem to me,
das andre Beinchen?	The other leg?
Vergebens wenigstens	At least in vain
suchte ich das vermisste Zwillings-Kleinod—	I sought the missing Twin-jewel—
nämlich das andre Beinchen—	Namely, the other leg—
sie hat es verloren . . .	She has lost it . . .
Hu! Hu! Hu! Hu! Hu! . . .	Oh my! oh my! oh my! oh my! oh my! . . .
Es ist dahin,	It is gone,
auf ewig dahin,	Gone forever,
das andre Beinchen!	The other leg!
Oh schade um dies liebliche andre Beinchen!	Oh what a shame about that lovely other leg!
Wo—mag es wohl weilen und verlassen trauern,	Where—whence may it be lamenting forsaken,
dieses einsame Beinchen?	This lonely leg?[67]

TRIPLEX

The triplex, sir, is a good tripping measure
—*A MIDSUMMER NIGHT'S DREAM*

For centuries, readers have wondered about the various "threes" in *Hamlet*. Why, according to Horatio, does the Ghost of Old Hamlet walk three times ("Thrice he walk'd / By their oppress'd and fear-surprised eyes" [H])? Why is it on the "third night" (H) that Horatio joins the watchmen at the ramparts. Why it is that Ophelia reports of Hamlet, "thrice his head thus waving up and down" (H). Why Lucianus, nephew to the play King in the dumb show, carries Hecate's poison, "thrice blasted, thrice infected" (H). Why does Osric speak of "three carriages" (H), and Hamlet repeats after him, in case we do not get it, "three liberal-conceited carriages" (H)? In the fencing–gambling game that follows, why the rule that Laertes "shall not exceed you three hits" (H). Everything depends on the third:

> If Hamlet give the first or second hit,
> Or quit in answer of the third exchange,
> Let all the battlements their ordnance fire. (*Hamlet*, 5.2.3910)

During the fencing match itself, Hamlet eggs on Laertes, who is having a moment of hesitation and so, it seems, breaking the measure. (The technical term in Renaissance fencing terminology might be *rompere di misura*.) "Come, for the third, Laertes" (H, 5.2.3910).

An Hegelian thinker might almost welcome as familiar in a forum where a thesis and antithesis are to be subsumed eventually by a synthesis a play where three things are often spoken about triply in this way, as if there were a gradual subsuming or incorporation of Father and Son by Holy Ghost. In this play, however, words themselves are repeated without this overt and logically controlled variation. Words are often also thrice-repeated identical words to indicate, more or less, the same thing. The examples coming from Young Hamlet are legion" "words, words, words" (H), "well, well, well" (H), "except my life, except my life, except my life" (H), and so forth. The influential nineteenth-century critic A. C. Bradley writes, "That Shakespeare meant this trait [of repetition generally] to be characteristic of Hamlet is beyond question."[68]

Bradley, and most all the others too, does not go far enough into the matter. For one thing, he does not distinguish Hamlet's straightforward triples from his simple doublets ("thrift, thrift" [H] and "very like, very like" [H]) or his complex doubles ("one may smile, and smile" [H], and perhaps even "a little less then kind and more than kind" [H]). Near-diacopes ("eye for eye") and ablaut diacope variants ("tit for tat") are right for revenge tragedy.

Relevant here, to understanding Hamlet's prosodic patterns are not only his modes of speaking but also his modes of walking—"amble," "crab," and so forth—and concomitant styles of dancing. Fencing, we shall see, is a type of dance, and Hamlet is in "continual practice" (H) for it. So we move here to another play within the play, namely, the measures and rhythm of the stage combat that provides *Hamlet* with its closing death scene(s).

In *Hamlet*, dancing terminology in general would include not only the various tripping measures of, say, the "jig" (H), but also the several modes of fencing. Dancing includes the choreography of real and fictional battle, including that on the individual level: duels, say, and fencing. Ballet dancing, some historians argue, began in fifteenth-century Italy—the presumed setting for "The Murder of Gonzago," during the performance of which Hamlet asks Horatio to watch for a particular "act a-foot" (H). The balletic art form began as an interpretation of fencing,[69] with its *balestra* (footwork preparation).

The general terminology for fencing resembles that for both rhetoric and choreography. *Conversation*, for example, is "the back-and-forth play of the blades in a fencing bout," and it is composed of *phrases*, or *phrases d'armes*, of the sort at which Fortinbras, we must suppose, would excel. *Feint* (which draws a reaction from the opponent much as did the Mousetrap from Claudius), the crab-like *backstep*. What is more, there is the difficulty throughout Hamlet in determining the line between actual military and "stage combat": the "stage" unto which Hamlet's dead body is to be taken (H), if Horatio has his way, is as much that of a military engagement as the Players' "stage" about which Hamlet had earlier declaimed (H). Small wonder that Shakespeare's Northumberland complains to presumably nobly plotting Hotspur in *Henry IV*: "Before the game is afoote, thou still let'st slip."[70]

There is the partly pathological aspect of Hamlet's diction—he speaks not only trippingly (and doubly) but also in triplets or triple repetitions. Puttenham calls this sort of speaking, *epizeuxis*,[71] literally a yoking together of words or phrases throughout the play. It is both a reminder of a potentially Oedipus-like claudicant limp and a reminder of his stutter or stammer. He encountered that habit in his probably traumatic meeting with the Ghost of Old Hamlet. The Ghost said trippingly to him, "adieu, adieu, adieu" (H), a straightforward epizeuxis, and also "list, list, o list" (H) and "horrible, horrible, most horrible" (H), distinct *diacopes*. Taken to extremes, such speaking would make all words one word, ending finally in that utter silence that is La Mort. Another word for this epizeuxis is, of course, pallilogy. This term in rhetoric, like so many others, would be taken over by nineteenth-century neurologists with a special interest in languages in much the same way, as we shall see below, that they absorbed the terminology of claudication.

The notion that Hamlet, if he is not a neurological specimen—the great Elizabethan clown Richard Tarlton, it is worth remembering, studied actual simpletons and fools as a means to representing—is something of a foolish clown. Some of the sources of Hamlet had also presented him as such.[72] The association of clowning with stage combat is familiar. The clown Tarlton—perhaps referenced in *Hamlet*'s "Yorick" in the Clown Scene set at the cemetery[73]—was a fencing master. Thus there is some warrant here for bringing up the triplex words of the clown Feste in *A Midsummer Night's Dream*, all the more especially so since the clown who played the part of Feste was Robert Armin, the late Tarlton's protégé[74] and author of the doubling *Foole Upon Foole, or Six Sortes of Sottes* (1600).[75] Consideration of Feste's punning on *tripling* and *tripping* in *A Midsummer Night's Dream* seems relevant:

> Primo, secundo, tertio, is a good play; and the old saying is, the third pays for all: the triplex, sir, is a good tripping measure

Triplex, in this gambler's jest[76] (it seems to recall Tarlton's penchant for gambling and losing money) has three likely meanings. The first is "triple time." In musicology, this sort of time is indicated when "each bar [or measure] is divided into three parts." Dance measures in triple meter would include the *courante* ("running steps"), the *gigue* (from the British "jig"), the *minuet* ("pas menus" [short steps]), and the *passepied* ("passing feet"). A second meaning of triplex would be *triplet*. This term refers to "a group of three notes, played in the usual time of two similar ones" referring to "a group of three notes, played in the usual time of two similar ones."[77] Some editors of Shakespeare's work replace *triplex* with *triplet*.[78] The third of *triplex* would be *tercet*, in the sense of "a group of three lines rhyming together." An example informs Shakespeare's "The Phoenix and the Turtle":

Trips of the Tongue in *Hamlet* (1600)

> Truth may seem, but cannot be;
> Beauty brag, but 'tis not she;
> Truth and beauty buried be.

Ariel's five-line rhyming speech about "tripping on his toe" in *The Tempest*, by contrast, would be an extensive quintuplet. To such trips, and clownish pathologies they suggest, we will return in the next chapter.

CHAPTER FOUR

Talking Cures

Dem bones got up walked around
Now hear the word of the Lord
—"DEM DRY BONES" [Ezekiel in the Valley of the dry bones],
African American spiritual with music by James Weldon Johnson

Poets not only do a lot of walking but talk about it in their poems: "I wandered lonely as a cloud" [William Wordsworth], "Now I out walking" [Robert Frost] and "Out walking in the frozen swamp one grey day" [Robert Frost]. There are countless examples, and many of them suggest that both the real and the fictive walk are externalizations of an inward seeking.
—A. R. AMMONS, "A Poem Is a Walk"[1]

In a quasi-literary short story, "On Transience" (1915),[2] Sigmund Freud describes a summer countryside walk he took with a poet—perhaps Rainier Maria Rilke, a poet of walking.[3] The analyst and poet are accompanied by a third person—probably the psychoanalyst Lou Andreas-Salome, who would correspond with Freud about patients whose symptoms involved walking.[4] "Not long ago I went on a summer walk [*Spaziergang*] through a smiling countryside in the company of a taciturn friend and of a young but already famous poet." Elegantly published in the highly literary *Das Land Goethes* (1916)[5] over a reproduction of his signature, Freud's literary "On Transience" imitates the "walking literature" of the British romantic writers, especially the odd walker Wordsworth, as well as referencing the wanderings of Homer's Odysseus. It was as if both poet and analyst were aiming at the same therapy.

The talking cure (*Sprechtherapie*) that psychoanalysis supposes owes a good deal to the broad rhythms of romantic "bumming": walking and talking at the same time. The very term *talking cure* comes from discussions of curing walking-and-talking disabilities by means of talking them through or talking through them. Freud, for example, has it that the origin of the phrase, "talking cure," is a statement by "Anna O.," the pseudonym of Bertha Pappenheim. At the time, Anna O. was being treated for partial paralysis of the limbs and for various intermittent speech disturbances by the neurophysiologist Josef Breuer. In a 1909 lecture, Breuer's coauthor Sigmund Freud tells the story thus: "The patient herself, who, strange to say, could at this time [1880–1992] only speak and understand English christened this novel kind of treatment the 'talking cure.'"[6]

The psychoanalytic talking cure has long been criticized by historians of medicine. (The reporting methods of the investigators are flawed, say some. The investigators' motives are suspect, say others. The patients are deceptive or deceived, claim a third group.) The combined pedagogy and pedagogy of English romantic poetry and German psychoanalysis, we shall see, shed light on the rhetorical and neurological of pedal and vocal ability and disability. *Sprechtherapie* often pretends both to *logopedia* and to *logopaedia* and in much the same way that romantic poetry does.

"WALKING AND TALKING AT THE SAME TIME": WORDSWORTH'S DILATION

DILATION: "Delay, procrastination, postponement."
—*OED*, sv "Dilation" n[1]

I cannot see the wit of walking and talking at the same time.
—WILLIAM HAZLITT, "Going on a Journey"[7]

Pedestrianism
I once told somebody that writing a sestina was rather like riding downhill on a bicycle and having the pedals push your feet. I wanted my feet to be pushed into places they wouldn't normally have taken.
—John Ashbery, interview[8]

William Wordsworth was a self-proclaimed bumbling foot poet. His sister Dorothy records their walks: that on such-and-such a day, they "walked along [as] he was altering his poems"[9] or that, "We walked home almost without speaking—Wm composed a few lines of the Pedlar" (1798).[10] When Wordsworth's "The Pedlar" was published, many people, especially of the upper classes, were nonetheless much offended by the merely "pedestrian" quality of its hero. That explains why the essayist Charles Lamb, trying to defend Wordsworth, wrote in 1814 that anyone who was so offended could simply "substitute silently the word *Palmer*, or *Pilgrim*, or any less offensive designation"[11] if that was required for them to follow along with the poem. Nevertheless, Lamb's words, no matter how well intentioned, tended to dismiss a defining characteristic of Wordsworth's verse: the feet. Lamb tried to sidestep the conjunction between peddling and the foot. *Pilgrim* means merely "a person who makes a long journey" and *palmer* means merely "a pilgrim who carries a palm"; for Wordsworth, though, the essential had to do with foot walking. *Pedestrian*, from Latin *pes* (foot), is important: even its folk etymologies pertain to the activity of "the pedlar," especially when it comes to the issue of rhythms verbal and pedal. Shakespeare writes in *Winter's Tale* (1623): "O Master: if you did but hear the Pedler [Autolycus] at the door, you would never dance again after a tabor and pipe."[12] Autolycus, the poet, peddles rhythm. Or perhaps he was trying to sidestep the conjunction of pedestrianism with being "splay-footed"[13] (a term associated with walking badly) or "barbarian"[14] (a term associated with talking badly) as opposed to being winged like Pegasus, as the actually clubfoot Byron puts it.[15]

In like manner to Hazlitt, some scholars to this day focus on "larger" cultural aspects of rhythm to the exclusion of heeding the pedestrial dance in Wordsworth as footman. Consider, for example, Robin Jarvis's discussion of the rise of pedestrian verse in the romantic period. He supposes that *pedestrian* and all like words were new at the time of the 1780s and 1790s and draws the conclusion, from this supposition, that walking tours, like the cultural and class happenings of the period, were also new.[16] Maybe, like a great many other aspects of walking in the romantic period, they *were* new. A good many other relevant "large" cultural activities may have been new at the time that Wordsworth was writing. Perhaps, on this basis, one could argue that, at this period, talking and walking were parts of the same "mentality"[17] or similar aspects of a novel understanding of "work."[18] Maybe they were now both parts of a general peripatetic[19] that comprehended walking and talking as "instrument[s] of perception"[20] and understood how "walking is thinking."[21] Gilbert writes:

> Ammons and Ashbery are . . . poets of thinking, rather than poets of truth or wisdom. They are more concerned with rendering the experience of reflection, its rhythms and contours, than with delivering completed thoughts that can claim the status of truth. . . . The walk, I would suggest, appeals to poets of thinking precisely because it enables them to anchor thought in the world, to provide the mind with a continuous yet ever-changing point of reference that can keep it from becoming sealed in its own discourse.[22]

Whether or not, it is certain that such terms as pedestrian were a good deal older than Jarvis says. If the argument does not need repositioning on a basis other than history, then the history at least ought to be accurate. *Pedestrial*, after all, belies the history of *ped-* words as Jarvis tells it. *Pedestrial* was, in fact, common already in Shakespeare's day, as in Thomas Palmer's *An Essay of the Means How to Make our Travels into Foreign Countries the More Profitable and Honourable* (1606).[23]

There is the viewpoint that, for some poets who walk, certain processes can "cease to be wholly cognitive" and "become instead a process of wandering as wayward and impulsive as the walk itself."[24] For the large focus on metrics that it seems to provide, this viewpoint ranks with other broad-based historical understandings of walking in the period following the French Revolution: that class and gender differences changed along with habits of walking,[25] for example, and that a walking-tour industry began to thrive. Perhaps such foci are useful in their place. It was, after all, during the 1780s and 1790s that the penchant arose for literary scholars to put together "quotation-collections" about walking,[26] to assemble "companions" for walkers,[27] to provide myriad scholarly "guides" for hikers,[28] and to supply "anecdote-compendia" sometimes with appendices about obsessive walkers.[29] Moreover, in fact, most critics of Wordsworth consider the poet's interest in walking only in broad political and cultural terms, sometimes bordering on scattered journalistic intuitions about "an almost Wordsworthian pedestrianism of style"[30] or the general history of walking as a means for touring. In the present study, it is more useful to begin with smaller observations that more tightly link the two principal sorts of rhythms according to which, some say, Wordsworth actually designed, and to some extent built, his own gardens. For him the natural world was not only the subject of poetry, as for other poets too of the socalled Grand Tour to places like France and Italy and the Picturesque Tour to places to Scotland or Wales; poetry *was* the natural world inasmuch as they shared the rhythm of walking and talking.

Our focus involves the poet's awareness of the narrower linkage between vocal and pedal rhythms. "Dry leaves stir as with the serpent's *walk,* / And, far beneath, Banditti voices *talk,*" wrote Wordsworth in 1793[31] shortly after meeting the athletic John "Walking" Stewart, a "philosopher" of the imperial British age who claimed to have walked from Madras, India, to Europe. (His works include *Travels over the*

Most Interesting Parts of the Globe [1790].) The link that Wordsworth himself explores between talking and walking might help, in circumstances we will describe, to shed definitive light on the larger issues of rhythm in political life.

Bumming
And when at evening on the public way
I sauntered, like a river murmuring
And talking to itself when all things else
Are still, the creature trotted on before;
Such was his custom; but whene'er he met
A passenger approaching, he would turn
To give me timely notice, and straightway,
Grateful for that admonishment, I hushed
My voice, composed my gait, and, with the air
And mien of one whose thoughts are free, advanced
To give and take a greeting that might save
My name from piteous rumours, such as wait
On men suspected to be crazed in brain.
—WORDSWORTH, "The Prelude or, Growth of a Poet's Mind; An Autobiographical Poem"[32]

William Hazlitt, who knew both Wordsworth and Samuel Taylor Coleridge, provides an interesting counterpoint to many descriptions of Wordsworth. "[Samuel] Coleridge has told me," says Hazlitt, "that he himself liked to compose in walking over uneven ground, or breaking through the straggling branches of a copse wood; whereas [William] Wordsworth always wrote (if he could) walking up and down a straight gravel-walk, or in some spot where the continuity of his verse met with no collateral interruption."[33] Dorothy Wordsworth reports that commonly the walking was, as she terms it, "backwards and forwards" on a path, on the orchard platform, in the woods.[34] In fact, Wordsworth composed by *bumming*, even in the closer region of the English Lake District—beyond the "tours"—and his own gardens. John D. Tatter writes in his essay, "Poet as Gardener, Gardener as Poet," published in Stonework, "Wordsworth built with his own hands long terraces and rustic seats out of the local stone. From these he could glimpse the lakes below his property and compose lines of poetry to the rhythm of his strides as he paced back and forth."[35] This method of composition might be called "bumming." I adopt the meaning of *bumming* as conveyed by the *Oxford English Dictionary* and, more particularly, the use of *bumming* by Wordsworth's gardener at his cottage near Ambleside. In his "Reminiscences of Wordsworth Among the Peasantry of Westmorland" (1882),[36] Hardwicke Drummond Rawnsley quotes Wordsworth's gardener's description of Wordsworth's side-to-side ambulatory means of composition at Rydall Mount in the British Lake District, the poet's home near Ambleside:

> [William, when composing,] would set his head a bit forrad, and put his hands behint his back. And then he would start a bumming, and it was bum, bum, bum, stop; then bum, bum, bum, reet down till t'other end, and then he'd set down and git a bit o'paper and write a bit; and then he git up, and bum, bum, bum and goa on bumming for long enough right down and back agean. I suppose, ya kna, the bumming helped him out a bit. However, his lips was always goan'.[37]

Wordsworth's housekeeper confirms that Wordsworth would go "bumming and booing about."[38] The rhythm is animal: *to bum* means "to boom" or "to hum loudly,"[39] like a bumble-bee and Wordsworth's neighbors often recalled the poet as "booing about"[40] like a lowing ox. This "low" or "pedestrian" aspect of Wordsworth's composition bothered some of his contemporaries. Thomas de Quincy, in an essay in *Recollections of the Lakes and the Lake Poets* (1862),[41] thus describes Wordsworth's habit of walking as oblique (like Hamlet's crab), worryingly insectiform, and self-centered:

> But the total effect of Wordsworth's person was always worst in a state of motion; for, according to the remark I have heard from many country people, "he walked like a cade"—a cade [a ked, or sheep tick; MS] being some sort of insect which advances by an oblique motion. This was not always perceptible, and in part depended (I believe) upon the position of his arms; when either of these happened (as was very customary) to be inserted into the unbuttoned waistcoat, his walk had a wry or twisted appearance; and not appearance only—for I have known it, by slow degrees, gradually to edge off his companion from the middle to the side of the highroad.

In his essay, "Going on a Journey" (1821), William Hazlitt says, "I cannot see the wit of walking and talking at the same time."[42] Hazlitt himself wants *to walk without talking*. "No one likes puns, alliterations, antitheses, argument, and analysis better than I do," he says somewhat ingenuously, "but I sometimes had rather be without them," adding later, that we must "give it an understanding, but no tongue."

Hazlitt does, of course, admire Wordsworth's neighbor [Samuel Taylor Coleridge] for being able to walk and talk at the same time "My old friend C—, however, could do both. He could go on in the most delightful explanatory way over hill and dale, a summer's day, and convert a landscape into a didactic poem or a Pindaric ode. "He talked far above singing."

Hazlitt, who cannot do as Coleridge,[43] does not mark how walking and talking might be essentially or rhythmically identical.

Thomas de Quincy's friendship with "Walking" Stewart much affected de Quincy, as de Quincy himself reports in his *Literary Reminiscences*. Walking Stewart's gait was faster, more fluent than Wordsworth's side-to-side bumming. Stewart was as famous for his high-flown pedal swiftness as for his verbal glibness.[44] As for Wordsworth, though, his interest—and this de Quincy did not comprehend—was less in the walking or talking than in rhythm and, significantly, far less in the swift than in the "lame."

Hopping and Ambling

Out walking in the frozen swamp one gray day,
I paused . . .
—ROBERT FROST, "The Wood-Pile"

George Williamson's book on early modern rhythm, *The Senecan Amble: A Study in Prose Form from Bacon to Collier* (1951) defines its focus in terms of the "Lipsian hop," a style and metric that stresses precisely discontinuity, especially that in prose.[45] Approved and displayed by the late sixteenth-century philologist Justus Lipsius, *hopping* refers to "moving by leaping on one or two feet together" (in opposition to regular walking or running), hence also the term involves limping, as in Daniel Defoe's "Away he hops with his Crutch" (1720).[46] The apparent opposite to the Lipsian hop would be the straightforward, easy amble. Samuel Johnson writes thus of ambling in his *Dictionary of the English Language* (1755): "*Canterbury gallop*, the hand gallop of an ambling horse, commonly called a canter; said to be derived from the monks riding to Canterbury on easy ambling horses."[47] The two styles, "hopping" and "ambling," can merge. Thus Williams points out that, although "the Lipsian 'hop' stresses the discontinuous movement, the Senecan 'amble' stresses the antithetic movement"; nonetheless both movements can meet in one, as Shakespeare knew, for 'the skipping king, he ambled up and down'

[1H4.3.2.60]."⁴⁸ Likewise, it is possible to critique both ambling and hopping at the same time. Lord Shaftesbury, in his *Characteristics* (1737), thus mocks both: "The common amble or canterbury is not, I am persuaded, more tiresome to a good rider than this see-saw [hop] of essay writers is to an able reader."⁴⁹ If Walter Scott wrote on horseback, as I have discussed in *Polio and Its Aftermath*, the brilliant Wordsworth wrote lamely.

In France in 1792 Wordsworth met John "Walking" Stewart—presumably a model for the phantom drifter in the poet's *Prelude*.⁵⁰ Soon after meeting this brilliant ambler, Wordsworth was writing the method of writing the world as talk and walk.⁵¹ As we have seen (above) his interest was not in the swift. Rather it was in the impeded. Consider, for example, the "devious feet" about which Wordsworth wrote in "An Evening Walk, Addressed to a Young Lady" (1793):

> ... while I wondered where the huddling rill [a small stream or run" of water]
> Brightens with water-breaks ["piece(s) of broken water"]⁵² the hollow ghyll [rocky ravine]
> As by enchantment, an obscure retreat
> Opened at once, and stayed my devious feet.

In Wordsworth's poetry, as Andrew Bennett has suggested, the narrative often revolves about a "dilatory walk" (as Wordsworth puts it in the *Prelude*).⁵³ It is constructed around an "impediment" or blockage,⁵⁴ as in Wordsworth's *Gordale* (1819), where feet repair. In the *Prelude* itself, we read, "Often of such dilatory walk / Tired, uneasy at the halts I made"⁵⁵—a line that demonstrates enjambment. The rhetorical term *dilation*, or *dilatation*, means "descriptive expansion."⁵⁶

In Wordsworth's *Peter Bell* (1793), there is the narrator's vexation involving *imp*eding lameness: "And I, as well as I was able, / On two poor legs, to my stone-table / [l]*imp*'d on with some vexation." Peter Bell "from a thousand causes / Is crippled sore in his narration"⁵⁷ much as Wordsworth's walking metrics are impeded by dilatory distraction. The connection with walking, or ambulation, is clearest in the influential poet Thomas Warton's discussion, in *The History of English Poetry: From the Close of the Eleventh to the Commencement of the Eighteenth Century* (1774–81), of "needless dilations, and the affectations of circumlocution."⁵⁸ Relevant to this sort of limping is the clubfoot Lord Byron's poem "She Walks in Beauty," written in iambic tetrameter and opening with a famously enjambed line.

Many Wordsworth poems require the pedal cripple: *The Waggoner* (1819),[59] *Simon Lee: The Old Huntsman* (1798) with its "ankles swoln and thick,"[60] the "travelling cripple" in *Andrew Jones* (1800), the cripple in *Home at Grasmere* (published posthumously),[61] and the "cripple from birth" in *The Prelude*.[62] For Wordsworth, moreover, *trip* is both verbal and pedal—as in Shakespeare's *trippingly*. In *The Two April Mornings* (1799), for example, we read, "No fountain from its rocky cave / E'er tripped with foot so free."[63] Lucy Gray "trips along" "o'er rough and smooth" in *Lucy Gray* (1798).[64] The contrast between the impeded pace of an old man and Walter's tripping gait in *The Brothers* (1800) suggests both the stumbling of poetic rhythm contrasted with meter: "His pace was never that of an old man: / I almost see him tripping down the path."[65] Of the four resemblances between walking and talking that A. R. Ammons discovers in his published lecture "A Poem Is a Walk" (1968), the fourth is the most important in this regard: "The fourth resemblance has to do with the motion common to poems and walks. The motion may be lumbering, clipped, wavering, tripping, mechanical, dance-like, awkward, staggering, slow, etc. But the motion occurs only in the body of the walker or in the body of the words."[66] The poetry is in the relation between meter and rhythm.

There would seem no need to revive the psychoanalyses of a dead poet to understand this matter,[67] but the matter does shed light, as we shall see, on the subsequent development of psychoanalysis.

"SLIPS OF THE TONGUE": FREUD'S HINKING

HINK: faltering, hesitation

—*OED* sv "Hink," n¹

At first sight nothing would seem more obvious than the dominant role of language in therapy—the talking cure.

—RAY HOLLAND, *Self and Social Context*[68]

Hysterical Narratives

Nineteenth-century medicine in the West was much concerned with paralysis in general and, more particularly, with what Jean-Martin Charcot—"the founder of modern neurology"[69] with whom Sigmund Freud studied hypnosis and hysteria in 1885—named "intermittent claudication" (1858). This was an often pedal limping that appeared sometimes to be of physiological origin and at other times to be of psychogenic.⁷⁰ The puzzle informed the work of André Halipré and P. Oliver (1896).⁷¹ There was the physio-neurological view of Joseph Babinski⁷² at Charcot's Salpêtrière clinic, which provided new understanding of impaired plantar reflexes.⁷³ There was the physio-electrotherapeutic view of the German Wilhelm Erb concerning the same *intermittende hinken*.⁷⁴ Erb worked also on Erb-Duchenne Palsy with Guillaume Duchenne, Erb-Charcot Palsy with Charcot, Erb-Goldflam Disease (also called *myasthenia gravis*) with Samuel Goldflam, and spastic spinal paralysis, as in his *Spastische Spinalparalyse* (Spastic spinal paralysis, 1875). Charcot's own research also included Charcot's Disease (now known as Amyotrophic Lateral Sclerosis) and polio. Most of the major work in this area took place, in fact, around the time of the first great "infantile paralysis" epidemics in the 1890s. When it came to Cerebral Palsy, so called, there was Halipré's study of pseudo-bulbar paralysis with physiological cerebral origin (1894)⁷⁵ and William Osler's *The Cerebral Palsies of Children: A Critical Study from the Infirmary for Nervous Diseases* (1889).⁷⁶ There was also Sigmund Freud's neuro-scientifically important *Infantile Cerebral Paralysis* (1893) and his "Some Points for a Comparative Study of Organic and Hysterical Motor Paralyses" (1893).⁷⁷ Many authors of the period, including Freud, were concerned whether there might not be a psychogenetic component even to such paralytic diseases as poliomyelitis.⁷⁸

On the international scale, the work on *claudicatio intermittens*, which is still sometimes confused with paralysis, was a definite and eventually defining puzzle. Oftentimes this work included verbal as well as pedal limping as like forms of dyskinesia. Dyskinesia as such is a movement-disorder consisting of involuntary movements. Among these movements are: those that affect walking, as for chorea (from χορεία [dance]), which produces dance-like pedal movements) and tardive dyskinesia, which can produce short "stutter steps"; and those that affect talking, as for tongue dyskinesia as it presents in Wilson's Disease and for the various speech abnormalities that present in other tardive dyskinesia. People interested in intermittent claudication often dealt with both pedal and vocal issues at the same time, as for Herman August Determann in his *"Intermittierendes Hinken*: eines Armes, der Zunge und der Beine" (1905)⁷⁹ and K. Goldstein in his "Intermittierendes Hinken eines Beines, eines Armes, der Sprach- . . . muskulatier: Intermittierendes Hinken oder Myasthenia?" (1908).⁸⁰

Enter now the work of Sigmund Freud, which tends to short circuit much of the above-named physiological research and render to more like, as, the "narratologies" of writers like the well-known writer Arthur Schnitzler in his later novella *Fraulein Else* (1924?).[81] Schnitzler was, of course, a medical doctor, and one of his only entirely independent medical writings was his remarkable "Über funktionelle Aphonie und deren Behandlung durch Hypnose und Suggestion" (1889) in which he presents six case studies of women with various sorts of aphonia (loss of voice), and he finds that he is often successful in restoring the voice through hypnosis.[82] When it comes to potentially psychogenic conditions—an inability to talk, say, or an inability to walk—there is, when it comes to psychoanalysis per se presumably path-breaking *Studies on Hysteria* (1895) by Sigmund Freud and Josef Breuer—a text whose authors came to claim to mark the beginnings of psychoanalysis. Freud and Breuer show there how the "talking cure" treats "walking irregularities" of a particular sort in such a way that the line between "organic" and "hysterical" etiology seems always brought into question. Consider several parallel examples. Consider the narrative "medical case studies" that they bring forward. First, Breuer's analysis of "Anna O." involves the contracture of Anna's right leg and the paralysis of her father. Her cure by talking, say the authors, was "a great step forward" for psychoanalysis.[83] Second, Freud's analysis of "Elisabeth von R." focuses on the point at which Elizabeth's "painful legs began to 'join in the conversation' during our analyses."[84] Third is Freud's analysis of "Dora" in his *Fragments of an Analysis of a Case of Hysteria* (1905). Freud links one of Dora's main symptoms, aphonia, with another one of them: "She had not been able to walk properly and dragged her right foot."[85] Freud interprets "the dragging of one [of her] leg[s]" as having a "secret and possibly sexual meaning of the clinical picture"[86] and interprets this meaning as a sign of the "false step" that Dora had imagined herself to have taken during an attempted seduction. (The psychoanalyst Felix Deutsch, who treated Dora after she had terminated her analysis with Freud, was surprised that the "dragging of her foot, which Freud had observed when the patient was a girl, should have persisted twenty-five years."[87]) Fourth would be Freud's analysis of "Frau Emmy von N." She "spoke in a low voice as though with difficulty and her speech was from time to time subject to spastic interruption amounting to a stammer"; she also had "temporary paralysis" in her legs.[88] All these cases of vocal and/or pedal impedance point in the direction of simply physiological etiology. Nor is it surprising that Freud should find them, given the identities of words for walking and talking, especially in terms of disability. (Roscoe Myrl Ihrig's "The Semantic Development of Words for 'Walk, Run' in the Germanic Languages" [1916] lists words in German that, like those in English, mean "to stumble and stutter at the same time," among them *stammer, hinken,* and *happer*.[89]) Yet, Freud does sometimes seek to separate them. In his "notes" for *Fragments of an Analysis of a Case of Hysteria* (1901), for example, Freud remarks on a patient who "had been for years . . . treated without success for hysteria (pains and defective gait)"; he concludes, in the way of Joseph Babinski, that this particular case "could not be . . . [a case] of hysteria," and so he "immediately instituted a careful physical examination." Because this patient's limp has a merely physiological etiology, he says, he sends her off for the appropriate physiological cure.[90]

Freud's talking cure depends, of course, on "slips of the tongue." There have long been slips of the tongue (*lapsus*) of mere physiological origin; there are also miscues, or "unexpected response[s] to a phonetic cue," perhaps a query from an analyst. Likewise there are so-called Freudian slips wherein, as it were, one is tripped or trapped or says, ironically (or so it goes), what one does not mean, or "intends," or is tricked into saying it. These slips or slip-ups are "unintentional mistake[s] that seem[] to reveal a subconscious intention." There are also, however, meanings that one can intend more or less consciously to slip out. After all, the German *slippen* too means "to pass or go lightly or quietly; to move quickly and softly, without attracting notice; to glide or steal"—trippingly.

One looks for Freudian intentional slips of the tongue and unintentional Freudian slips when reading Freud on the question of verbal and pedal slipping. The most telling expressions of limping (*hinkende*) per se in Freud usually involve the devil, the Bible, and his personal sexual experience. Concerning the devil: Freud—like Karl Marx—much identified with the snake-like "forked-tongued," or "cloven-tongued" devil who has, as Goethe is careful to point out in his *Faust,* the devil's limp: "Was *hinkt* der Kerl auf Einem Fuß?"[91] And, of course, there is the devil's equine or cloven hoof (*Pferdefuß*).[92] Concerning the Bible: The neatest case is the biblical Jacob, namesake of Jakob Freud, who was Sigmund's father by a second or third marriage. The "tricky" forefather Jacob "hinks": "und er hinkte an seiner Hüfte," as Martin Luther's Bible puts it.[93] Thanks to his encounter with the angel, stranger, or (his elder) twin brother, Jacob bears the staff that, some people say, was passed on, from generation to generation, until it reaches the weak-limbed, stuttering Moses. In a letter he sent to Fliess, Freud describes his psychoanalytic career in terms of the biblical Jacob's limping. His name will be lost to science, while the names of others who stuck to the narrow path of science and rhetoric will reap the reward.[94]

> It is different with me [Freud] than with you [Fliess]. No critic (not even the stupid [Leopold] Lowenfeld, the [Max] Burckhard of neuropathology) can see more clearly than I the disparity arising from the problems [in my theories] and the answers to them; and it will be a fitting punishment for me that none of the unexplored regions of psychic life in which I have been the first mortal to set foot will ever bear my name or obey my laws. When it appeared that my breath would fail me in the wrestling march, I asked the angel to desist; and that is what he has done since then. But I did not turn out to be the stronger, although since then I have been limping noticeably.

Concerning his own sexual experience: Freud's "auto psychoanalysis" in this regard shows up often in his correspondence with his confidante and his nose surgeon Wilhelm Fliess. On one occasion, Freud takes on as a patient a relative of Fliess "Miss G. de B" who has a stutter (letter of 4 December 1896). One event, for example, involves his half-nephew and half-niece. In a dream of 23–24 July 1895, writes Freud to Fliess, there appeared to him a limping physician, named "Dr. M.," who "oddly" examines a patient named "Irma." Who are these personages? Freud associates "Dr. M." with two people. First is Josef Breuer, with whom Freud wrote about hysterically disabled walking and talking. Second is Emanuel Freud, Sigmund's half-brother. Emanuel (b. 1833), who was twenty-three years older than Freud (b. 1856), actually limped. One of Emanuel's children, Johann (b. 1855), was Freud's nephew and inseparable companion. (Freud writes, "Until the end of my third year we had been inseparable; we had loved each other and fought each other, and, as I have already hinted, this childhood relation had determined all my later feelings in my dealings with persons of my own age."[95]) Who is "Irma"? She is another of Emanuel's children, Pauline (b. 1856). In his "Screen Memories" (1899), written forty years after the supposed event that is being remembered, Freud "remembers" that he and his half-nephew Johann threw Pauline—Sigmund's half-niece and Johann's full sister—to the ground. Then they "deflowered" her: literally, took her flowers away from her.[96]

Why Freud went to some lengths to try to hide his letters to his epistolary confidante and personal nose surgeon of some fifteen years (1889–1904) soon appears. (Marie Bonaparte saved them.) In a letter to Fliess (1897), he described this childhood incident: "The two of us [Sigmund and John] seem occasionally to have behaved cruelly to my niece [Pauline], who was a year younger [than Sigmund and John were]."[97] In context of kinship and unkindness, it is worth recalling here that, around the year 1875, Sigmund's father Jakob tried to convince Sigmund to marry his kin Pauline.[98] Sigmund refused to do so. Pauline, apparently shattered, died an unmarried woman fully sixty-nine years later. The story, we shall see, probably helps to explain Freud's psychic limp.

Limping Iambics

Hinkende Jamben (*Limping iambics*)
—Title of a 1837 song by Johann Karl Gottfried Loewe[99]

AGE [speaks]: Thy helth sall hynk.
(Thy health shall be in a state of suspense)
—ROBERT HENRYSON, *The Praise of Age and The Ressoning betwix Aige and Yowth*

Freud's attraction to issues of intermittent claudication, or "hinking," included three areas of his life and work. First, there were his actual patients—Anna O., Elisabeth von R., and Dora. Second, there were the literary figures—chief among them being Oedipus. Third, there were his own dreams of a limping uncle and a deflowered niece. The same claudication affected his systems of reference in private and public writing. In correspondence with Fliess, he calls his own theorizing, which partly concerns limping, "my philosophical stammer" (letter 77). In a letter to Fliess in 1895, moreover, he refers to this passage from Friedrich Rückert's German-language 1826 translation of "The Two Gold Coins":

> Whither we cannot fly, we must go limping.
> The Scripture saith that limping is no sin.
>
> [Was man nicht erfliegen kann, muß man erhinken.
> Die Schrift sagt, es ist keine Sünde zu hinken.]

The German verb *hinken* involves verbal as well as ambulatory movement and pertains as much to verbal stammering as to pedal limping.¹⁰⁰ A quarter century later, Freud uses the same lines to close his *Beyond the Pleasure Principle* (1920).¹⁰¹

"The Two Gold Coins"—part of the eleventh-century Arabic-language Al Hariri's *Assemblies*¹⁰²—pertains precisely to the rhetoric of talking and the gait of walking. In this story, Al-Harith, a merchant, narrates the story of how he discovers that the disguised Abu Zayd, a rascal pedestrian wanderer, was pretending to be lame but was not. When the two meet up, Al-Harith asks Abu Zayd to recite verses praising coin money. The limping Abu Zayd does well. Then Al-Harith asks him to recite verses dispraising it. Abu Zayd again responds so fluently and eloquently that the merchant concludes that Abu Zayd cannot be lame. His verbal swiftness is, as it were, a vocal shibboleth showing that his pedal slowness is a sham:

> Thou art recognized by thy eloquence [*dein Witz verriet dich*], so straighten thy walk [*warum gehst du nicht grade?*].

The walker Abu Zayd, whose tongue has betrayed his foot, then explains to Al-Harith why he has *feigned* lameness: "I have feigned to be lame, not from love of lameness, but that I may knock at the gate of relief. For my cord is thrown on my neck, and I go as one who ranges freely. Now if men blame me, I say, 'Excuse me: sure there is no guilt on the lame.'"

> Ich hinke, doch nicht aus Vergnügen am Hinken
> Ich hink', um zu essen, ich hink', um zu trinken.
> Ich hinke, wo Sterne der Hoffnung mir winken,
> Ich hinke, wo Gulden entgegen mir blinken.
> Was man nicht erfliegen kann, muss man erhinken.
> Viel besser ist hinken, als völlig zu siken.
> Die Schrift sagt: *Es ist kein Sünde, zu hinken*.¹⁰³

For Rückert, who did this important translation, *hinken* was a favorite German-language word. In fact, he himself wrote poems with "limping feet" (that is, with "too many" beats) about "limping tongues." There is, for example, his metrically demonstrative poem *Ein Liebchen hatt ich*:

> Ein Liebchen hatt ich, das auf einem Aug'schielte;
> Weil sie mir schön schien, schien ihr Schielen auch Schönheit.
> Eins hatt ich, das beim Sprechen mit der Zung anstieß,
> Mir war's kein Anstoß, stieß sie an und sprach: Liebster! Jetzt
>   hab ich eines, das auf einem *Fuß hinket*
> Ja freilich, sprech ich, hinkt sie, doch sie hinkt zierlich.

[A lover had I, who squinted in one eye;
Because she seemed pretty to me, her squinting also seemed beauty.
One I had, that *stumbled with her tongue* when speaking;
That was no stumble for me, if as she stumbled she said 'beloved'!
Now I have one, who limps on one foot;
Yes freely I admit she limps—but she limps daintily!][104]

The German *anstossen* (stumble, stutter) suggests both stuttering and stumbling. The Berlin-based Hermann Gutzmann Sr., founder of the field of phoniatrics (in 1905) and author of *Spachheilkunde* (Language healing, 1912), argues that stuttering, although a "coordination neurosis," should "not be identified with stumbling [*anstossen*] [in speaking]."[105]

Rückert's title, *Hinkende Jamben*, refers to the poem's choliambic verse, scazon, or lame iambic—with the methodological implication that the meter brings the reader down on the wrong foot by reversing beats.

The Viennese composer Franz Ippisch set Rückert's well-known words to music in 1918,[106] but they were anyways already well known many years before the publication of Freud's *Beyond the Pleasure Principle*. The composer Johann Karl Gottfried Loewe, who enjoyed performing the "stuttering music" of the Queen of the Night in Mozart's *Magic Flute*,[107] had set Rückert's *Hinkende Jamben* (1837).[108] When the baritone Marcus Farnsworth sang Loewe's "Limping Iambics" at London's Wigmore Hall (2009),[109] he "hinked" on stage in such a way as to mime the back-and-forth dialectic, not of regular conversation, but of the halting give-and-take of the talking cure.

CHAPTER FIVE
Walkie Talkies

Soon you'll hear a tune
That's gonna lift you out of your seat
It could be sweeter but then the meter
Was written especi'lly for your feet
—IRVING BERLIN, "Everybody Step"

The advent of "motion pictures" meant that theorists and experimental psychologists—from Christian Alban Ruckmick in *The Role of Kinaesthesis in the Perception of Rhythm* (1913)[1] to Dee Reynold's "Kinesthetic Rhythms" (2008)[2]—became interested in the relationship of the rhythm of walking to the motions of cinematography. With the commercial availability of synchronized voices for motion pictures or "talking pictures"—the "talkies"—interest now focused on the rhythms of talking as well as those of walking. The first feature-length movie with synchronized voice was probably *The Jazz Singer* (1927), and by 1940, the talkie was standard across the world.

There had been earlier experiments: the "early sound films of the silent era,"[3] many dealing with pedal motion and the voice[4] as well as syncopation.[5] One short film, probably directed by Maurice Swaby Wetzel, "Everybody Step in Musicolor" (1922), was a straightforward study of Irving Berlin's sometimes rhythmically offbeat foxtrot "Everybody Step,"[6] from the finale of Act I of his *Music Box Revue 1* (1921).

John Alden Carpenter, composer of *Adventures in a Perambulator* (1915), cited Berlin's song as one of the ten great masterpieces in music history.[7] Already in the seventeenth century, the music publisher and dance theorist John Playford had written in his *A Brief Introduction to the Skill of Music* (1654) about the pedal aspect of musical syncopation: "Notes of Syncopation . . . are when your . . . Foot is taken up, or put down, while the Note is sounding."[8] Filmic works helped to set the pace for pedal and vocal syncopation in music, and animated cartoons were soon to follow, as in the retrospective *Walky Talky Hawky* (1946).

TIN MAN'S "CAN CAN CAN" IN *THE WIZARD OF OZ* (1939)

There is the moment in the movie *The Wizard of Oz* (1939) when Dorothy and her friends meet the being called "The Tin Man." Tin Man is entrapped in, or as, his almost completely motionless, rusted-out, iron-lung-like body: he is a sufferer from something like near-total "locked-in" syndrome. The scene starts with a focus on Tin Man's paralyzed foot and then moves on to his paralyzed mouth.

Dorothy: Oh—
(MS—Dorothy comes forward as she picks up the apples—CAMERA PANS and TRUCKS forward as she starts to pick up two apples—she sees a tin *foot*—reacts—examines it—CAMERA PULLS back and BOOMS up as she stands up by the Tin Man—Scarecrow comes in from left—CAMERA PULLS back as they examine him—he tries to speak—Dorothy picks up the oil can—)
Dorothy: Why, it's a man! A man made out of tin!
Scarecrow: What?
Dorothy: Yes. Oh—look—
Tin Man manages only to move his mouth and lungs, just enough to get out the memorable phrase "Oil can."
Tin Man: Oil can . . . Oil can . . .
Dorothy: Did you say something?
Tin Man: Oil can . . .
Scarecrow: Oil can what?
Dorothy: Oil can? Oh—oh, here it is!

Tin Man's punningly, or cunningly, reduplicated phrase, *oil can,* is worth scanning. The scarecrow takes this to mean "oil is able" and figures that Tin Man's talk is stuck in midsentence, like a stutter blocking. (Consider Tin Man's "stutter" on the otherwise usually exclamatory phrase, "Mm . . . mm . . . mm . . . my . . . m . . . m . . . my, my, my, my goodness." A Jew like Moses, whether lame or not, would have balked likewise stutteringly at this phrase, since he would have been all but unable or unwilling to pronounce the name of his God, or "Goodness" [*Yahweh*].)[9] Scarecrow asks: "Oil can do what?" However, others in *The Wizard of Oz*, including Dorothy herself, figure that "oil can" means "the can of oil." Taken together, the pun on *can* (as "kinetic" verb) and on *can* (as "nonkinetic" noun) suggests to his interlocutors that Tin Man needs to be oiled.¹⁰ And so they oil him:

(MCS—Scarecrow and Dorothy examine the Tin Man—he tries to speak—they oil him about the mouth—)

Dorothy: Where do you want to be oiled first?

Tin Man: My mouth—my mouth!

Scarecrow: He said his mouth.

Dorothy: Here—here—

Scarecrow: The other side . . .

Dorothy: Yes—there.

(CU—The Tin Man tries to speak—squeaks out a few sounds—)

Tin Man: Mm . . . mm . . . mm . . .

(MCS—Dorothy and Scarecrow listen as the Tin Man starts to speak—Dorothy starts to pull the axe arm of the Tin Man down—Scarecrow oils him—)

Tin Man: . . . m . . . m . . . my, my, my, my goodness—I can talk again! Oh—oil my arms, please—oil my elbows.

Dorothy: Oh . . .

(MLS—Dorothy lowers the right arm of the Tin Man so that it hangs naturally—Scarecrow busy with the oil can—the Tin Man begins his story—)

Tin Man: Oh—

Dorothy: . . . Oh, did that hurt?

Tin Man: No—it feels wonderful. I've held that axe up for ages. Oh—

Dorothy: Oh, goodness! How did you ever get like this?

Tin Man: Oh—well, about a year ago—I was chopping that tree—minding my own business—when suddenly it started to rain . . .

(MCS—Scarecrow and Dorothy listen to the Tin Man—he grows weak—they work his arms back and forth—Scarecrow oils his neck for him—Dorothy raps on the Tin Man's chest—they react—Tin Man explains, then steps backward toward tree—)

Tin Man: . . . and right in the middle of a chop, I . . . I rusted solid. And I've been that way ever since.

Dorothy: Well, you're perfect now.¹¹

Tin Man isn't "perfect now"—as everyone soon learns from the hollow sound that comes from his empty (heartless), metallic iron-lung-like, tin-can body. (The song "If I Only Had a Heart" is Tin Man's main vocal performance in the movie *The Wizard of Oz*. The lyrics go, "When a man's an empty kettle / He should be on his mettle.") Tin Man has overcome locked-in syndrome only to note finally about himself that there's nothing—one might properly pronounce this word as "no tin," as Jupiter does in Edgar Allan Poe's story about a gold-bug—that there's nothing in there.

In the end, once rusted-out Tin Man, who could neither walk nor talk, now can can-can, or dance, as well as sing! That is, he is able to talk and walk well. One way or the other, slippery talk—puns—loosens up the rust. It is immediately after his praise of sauntering that Thoreau, whom Emerson says could not write, even really talk, without walking, says, "I . . . cannot stay in my chamber for a single day without acquiring some rust."

In *The Wizard of Oz*, one wants to avoid the arthritis (literally, inflammation of the joints) that farmhand Hickory (played by Jack Haley), the counterpart in Kansas to the Tin Man in Dorothy's adventure in a wonderland (*The Wonderful World of Oz* was Baum's original title), calls rust.

Hickory: Oh! Oh, it feels like my joints are rusted.

Earlier in the century, the American poet Emily Dickinson—an expert adventurer in poetic meter whose mother Emily Norcross would suffer a paralytic stroke[12]—described the sort of verbal and pedal apoplexy from which Baum's Tin Man suffers. In "How many times these low feet staggered—" Dickinson writes:

> How many times these low feet staggered—
> Only the soldered mouth can tell—
> Try—can you stir the awful rivet—
> Try—can you lift the hasps of steel![13]

In "After great pain a formal feeling comes—," with its focus on "freezing persons" and "feet mechanical," Dickinson considers likewise, how "The nerves sit ceremonious like tombs."[14] Dickinson's "[interruptive long] dash" is "key to the [pedal] rhythms and expression of her poetry."[15] (Consider the poems "The feet of people walking home / With gayer sandals go—"[16] and "A bird came down the walk—".)[17] As we shall see, the same dash plays its role in *Talking the Walk & Walking the Talk*.

FOGHORN LEGHORN'S "WALKIE TALKIE" IN *WALKY TALKY HAWKY* (1946)

I define a peripatetic: a peripateck is a two legged living creature, gressible, unfeathered . . .

—*THE COMEDY OF TIMON*[18]

Walkie-talkie, which so obviously conjoins the walking and talking, what does it mean? In the first instance, *walkie-talkie* refers to "a small radio transmitter and receiver that can be carried . . . to provide two-way [talking] communication as one walks." It is not clear whether the carrier-walker must be human or animal. What is clear is that "Walkie-talkie is the Army Signal Corps' way of speaking of unit S.C.R. 195a recently developed radio sending and receiving set so small it is carried on the back and *one talks while one walks*," as put in the *Baltimore Sun* (1939).[19]

The first walkie-talkies were developed in the late 1930s—not long after the so-called talkies (sound/voice films) were developed. Soon thereafter there were small television cameras. These came to be called *walkie-lookies* ("easily portable television camera[s]"; 1946). *Peepie-creepies* ("portable television camera[s] were used for close-up shots on location"; 1952).[20] (The Sony Corporation's "Walkman"— that "small battery-powered operated cassette player and headphones capable of being worn by a person who is on foot"[21]—was introduced in the 1980s.)

Already by the mid-1940s, though, walkie-talkies were already the subject of animated cartoons. These cartoons usually included human beings pretending to be animals that could talk as human beings. One example would be the successful Academy Award Nominee *Walky Talky Hawky* (1946), directed by Robert McKimson, with voice characterizations by Mel Blanc.

The cartoon stars Henery Hawk, a young bird who discovers that he is actually a chicken hawk.[22] (Henery had made an appearance in *The Squawkin' Hawk* [1942].[23] One might compare the *rhyme* of *hawk* with the unspoken *talk* with the assumed rhyme of *squeak* with the unspoken *speak* in the title of Robert Clampett's animated cartoon of the previous year, *We, the Animals—Squeak* [1941].)[24] Henery, who is too young to fly and so must always walk, meets a rooster, Foghorn Leghorn.

(Why this name for the rooster of the piece? *Foghorn* suggests the rooster's loud voice, his verbal tic being the reduplicative, "I say, I say." *Leghorn* suggest both the name of the breed of a domestic fowl known for its strong legs and also the name of "Senator Beauregard Claghorn," a character on *The Fred Allen Show* who would usually end his appearances with the reduplicative sentence, "So Long! So Long, that is!")

Foghorn Leghorn, upon hearing from Henery that he is looking for a chicken to eat, the chicken calls himself a horse. He neighs like a horse, presumably to make his point. (The chicken produces his horse-like sound by holding his nose in the same way that Mel Blanc would have done in life.) Henery then meets a tethered dog (Barnyard Dawg), whom the chicken says is a four-legged chicken (and, later on, a foxy chicken). Eventually the dog and chicken come to blows, but they are stopped by a horse. The chicken hawk eventually is seen dragging off all three animals (chicken, dog, and horse), presumably in order to learn which of them, if any, is actually a chicken.

A second meaning of *walky talky* brings out the possibility that the being may be nonhuman: "a doll that can be made to walk and talk."[25] If the walky talky were an anatine doll that was animated—that is, if there were a "duck-like play-thing" that walked and talked as in the Mel Blanc cartoon "Walky Talky Hawky" (1946)—then its drawing as a robot, instead of as an animation, might look something like a clockwork automaton in the tradition of Tin Man. Here, for example, is an eighteenth-century drawing of an anatine automaton—a mechanical toy that could *walk* like a duck and *quack* like a duck— created by Jacques Vaucanson, whose special interests included what he called "moving anatomy" (see Figure 5.1).[26] Such vaguely "robotic and poetic artworks"[27] recall Ovid's version of the Pygmalion story where Galatea plays the role later occupied by George Bernard Shaw's Eliza—especially where, as in the case of Vaucanson's flute-playing shepherd, the issue is sound.[28]

One antique variant anecdote of the "humanoid duck story" involves the Sinopian Diogenes's criticism of Plato's presumed view that a human being is "a featherless piped [two-foot]."[29] After he heard Plato say this, Diogenes brought to Plato a de-feathered, dead fowl. The same gag informs Cathcart and Klein's *Plato and a Platypus Walk into a Bar*—(2006)[30] and Umberto Eco's *Kant and the Platypus* (1999).[31]

In the animated cartoon movie *The Dixie Fryer* (1960), Foghorn Leghorn is actually rendered featherless. In his biography of his father Robert McKimson Sr., who created all the Foghorn Leghorn cartoons,

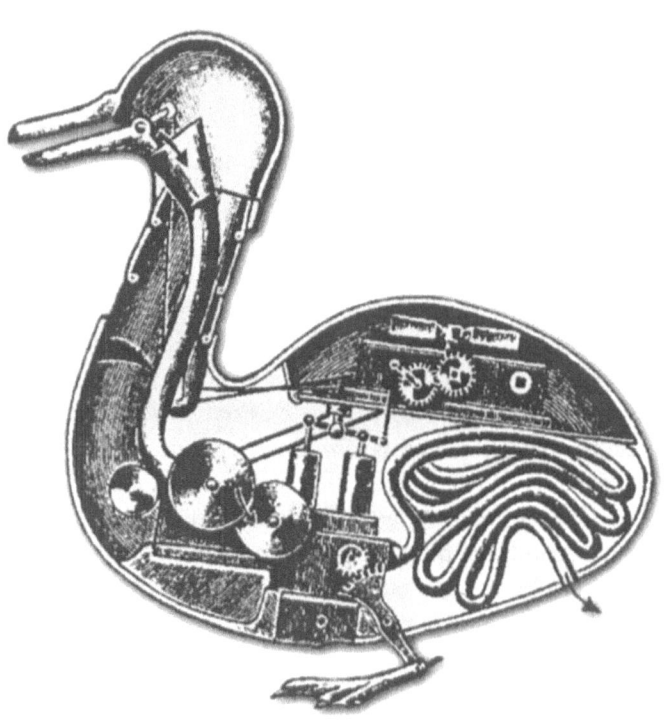

Figure 5.1. A late representation of Jacques Vaucanson's automaton "Digesting Duck" (1739). Vaucanson's original automatons also include "The Tambourine Man" and "The Flute Player" (both lost).

Robert McKimson Jr. points out smartly that Foghorn Leghorn often says, "I Say! I SAY! I tell you what, there, Boy!": the humanoid bird rarely gets his point across in a single swoop.[32]

The third meaning of *walkie-talkie* would be a nonanimal and nonrobotic being that both walks and talks: that is, a Human Being.

LINA LAMONT'S "PIPES AND STEMS"
IN *SINGIN' IN THE RAIN* (1952)

The transitions in early development of photography—from still photography to kinetic photography (the walkies) and from silent cinema to sound (the talkies) required that, from now on, photography actors usually had both to walk and talk. Put otherwise, they would need both stems and pipes: *stems* is slang for "legs," on which human beings walk;[33] *pipes* refers often to the "vocal apparatus,"[34] thanks to which human beings can talk. Both terms play roles in movies' presentation of dancing and singing as well as stillness and muteness.

Consider that speech in the "talkies" of the 1920s cured the dumbness, or verbal paralysis, of "silent cinema"[35] even as "cinema" of the 1890s had cured the stillness, or bodily paralysis, of still photography. There were now technically proficient means of synchronizing sound with moving film, including "lip-synching" and "speaking photoplay." The concomitant question for walkie-talkie production soon became: What shall we do with the old silent-picture "stars" who have no "stage voice"?

Consider these possible answers to this question:

First: One might cure them of their speech "disability" by means of elocution lessons. The film comedy *Once in a Lifetime* (1932)[36] "thematizes" the transition from silent films to talkies by taking up this "talking cure." In this movie, three New York vaudevillians working in 1929 are determined to get rich by teaching silent film stars to speak "properly." They teach acceptable English-language accent and inflection of the sort that nonanglophone immigrants and other nonstandard speakers in America were attempting during the same historical period.

Second: One might turn the screen stars into dummies, through which others speak ventriloquistically or ekphrastically. Dubbing and lip-synching were thus the more-or-less secret "cures" for many film stars whose speaking or singing voices were "wanting." The advent of the talkies thus gave rise to an apparently deceptive ekphrasis, Who, really, is talking? ("When you hear your favorite star sing in the talkies, don't be too sure of it," we read in "The Truth About Voice Doubling," in *Photoplay* for July 1929.)

Third: One might discharge the voice-disabled star. This is what eventually happens to silent screen star "Lina Lamont" (played by Jean Hagen) in *Singin' in the Rain* (1952).[37] In *Singin' in the Rain*, Lina Lamont wants people to believe that she talks as well as she walks. Therefore, she has it put out that "Monumental Pictures [is] Wildly Enthusiastic Over Her Singing Pipes and Dancing Stems." However, Lina can't make the transition to talkies. Her diction and elocution lessons don't help. Her voice ("singing pipes") does not measure up to her body ("dancing stems"). Lina's lower-class New

York and squeaky voice—reminiscent of Judy Holliday's characterization of the not-so-"dumb" blonde Billie Dawn in George Cukor's *Born Yesterday* (1950)—are not easily retrained.

In that sense, Lina in *Singin' in the Rain* is unlike Eliza Doolittle in George Bernard Shaw's *Pygmalion* (1916), in Gabriel Pascal's movie *Pygmalion* (1938), in Alan Jay Lerner and Frederick Lowe's musical *My Fair Lady* (1956), and in George Cukor's movie *My Fair Lady* (1964). Although Lina dances well, as does Eliza, she cannot learn to talk right. Lina has no "Professor Higgins." In fact, Eliza had to learn to walk properly as well as to talk well: to dance as well as to sing. The famous "Ball Scene," which Gabriel Pascal added to Shaw's drama, extends the playwright's original idea for the ball (which was that it should happen "offstage") to the camera's eye. "I Could Have Danced All Night"—one of the best-known routines in *My Fair Lady* (1956)—memorializes Eliza's dancing brilliantly and talking eloquently at the ball.

One of Eliza's famous lines involves walking: "Walk! Not bloody likely!"[38]

Unlike Eliza, Lina the dancer cannot learn to talk well or to sing like a bird. Eventually the producer requires a voice-woman ventriloquist—Kathy Selden (played by Debbie Reynolds). Kathy sings and talks—both dubs and doubles[39]—for Lina. Soon Kathy's audience discovers the "dubbing" deception. (The discovery recalls the unveiling of the marvelous, professorial Wizard in *The Wizard of Oz*, who has both prosthetic body and prosthetic voice.) Kathy then takes over Lina's role on stage, as the lover of the protagonist of the movie, Don Lockwood; Kathy also takes over Lina's old role in reality, as the lover of the actor who plays that protagonist, Gene Kelley.[40]

The diction coaches or elocution teachers in *Singin' in the Rain* are more successful with Don Lockwood than with Lina Lamont. Don does really well on the tongue-twister "Moses Supposes":

> Moses supposes his toes are roses
> But Moses supposes erroneously
> Moses he knowses his toeses aren't roses
> As Moses supposes his toeses to be.

After all, the stutterer Moses needed both a voice-man to speak and a shoulder to lean on: his brother, Aaron.[41]

The hope that stems can replace pipes is one motif of Charles Vidor's movie *The Joker Is Wild* (1957). *The Joker* tells "the real comeback story" of a nightclub performer, Joe E. Lewis (Frank Sinatra),[42] whose vocal cords are cut by a cutthroat member of a speakeasy Chicago mob in 1927.[43] His ability to move is inhibited likewise by cut damaged nerves. At first, Lewis is "unable to walk or talk normally"[44]—as Cohn puts it in *The Story of Joe E. Lewis* (1955), the "biography" on which the movie script is based.

When he is finally rehabilitated, Lewis can stand well enough, but he cannot sing. He then turns to despair. The turning point of the film occurs when he dances behind a cycloramic back-curtain with a beautiful young woman (Jeanne Crain). Only now that he can stand tall can Lewis become a successful stand-up comedian ("the clown supreme") in the tradition of Henny Youngman "(King of the One-liner") and Milton Berle ("The Funniest Man in the World"). In *The Joker Is Wild*, Lewis (Sinatra) never does make a full recovery. He is unable to convert the experience of losing the ability to talk well, or sing, into that of talking well, in the fashion of a sad clown.

Lewis himself—on whose experience the biography and movie were based—appeared as a "mystery guest" on the weekly television show *What's My Line* (12 October 1958) a year after *The Joker Is Wild* opened in the movie theaters. Blindfolded panelists in *What's My Line* attempted to determine the identity of the guest by means of asking him questions. The panelists' series of questions and answers included the following exchange:

Panelist: [blindfolded] Are you a singer?

Joe E. Lewis: [grinning, as if this were *the* question of his life, and sounding almost as if he were singsonging his response] O God! Yes. A little bit.

Panelist: [blindfolded] [addressing the show's host] He's a singer?

Host: And that is a very truthful answer. Just "a little bit."

The stand-up mystery guest's joke about his lost voice was the stand-up comedian's best line.

L. B. JEFFRIES'S "TOTTER" IN *REAR WINDOW* (1954)

TOTTER: walk unsteadily; stutter.
—ROGET'S NEW MILLENNIUM THESAURUS

The relationship between walking and talking informs Alfred Hitchcock's movie *Rear Window* (1954). There the hero, L. B. Jeffries, who cannot walk (he is in a wheelchair), is played by the almost hysterical Jimmy Stewart. As usual, Stewart talks in halting, folksy, stuttering fashion.[45] His "L. B. Jeffries" is a still photographer who has difficulty with motion both physical and verbal.

The intermediating step in cinema, between freeze-frame (stillness or silence) and cinema (movement and speech fluency), would be double-exposure and/or sequential serial exposure in still photographic technique. Double-exposure is essentially the superimposition of two or more still-photograph negatives in such a way as to make a simple positive print.[46] The other intermediating step between freeze frame (or *akinesia*) and cinema (or *kinesis*) that I have mentioned is sequential serial exposure. This was invented much like Freudian theories of hysterical paralysis, by medical-photographer researchers at the time that polio was stilling human beings and photography using cinematography in order to make still pictures move. One principal figure in the development of this sort of cinematography would be Eadweard Muybridge. His serial photographs of crippled, paralyzed children, as well as horses, in motion helped to change both medicine and aesthetics—and in something like the same way.

Released in 1954, *Rear Window* marks a sort of halfway chronological "marker" between our own time and that of the origin of cinema and looks back to the origins of cinema. On the one hand, the protagonist Jeffries is in a plaster cast and wheelchair—his prosthetic legs. He cannot walk. At best he can barely toddle or totter, against the film's jazzy soundtrack. From his rolling chair, he watches the more-or-less discretely plotted events through the windows of tenements in a rear courtyard. *Rear Window* thus alludes not only to the immobility of the spectator in the movie house, who ordinarily cannot join the action, but also to the immobility of the cinema director who ordinarily directs others to act for him. In terms of photography, one might summarize *Rear Window* thus: *Rear Window* is an artwork about the ambiguities of stasis and kinesis in the realms of image photography and bodily paralysis. The wheelchair-bound Jeff is a still (and static) photographer who uses his flash camera, or "flash gun," serially to try to freeze action. Nowhere in *Rear Window* is the problem of movement more intense than in his vertiginous "totter"— defined as "the unsteady or shaky movement or gait of one ready to fall"[47]—in the penultimate scene at his own rear window.

On the other hand, L. B. Jeffries cannot quite say what he means or mean what he says. That "James Stewart won over the masses with a drawl and a slight stutter"[48] helps explain why Hitchcock chose him for the part. At no point is Stewart's "L. B. Jeffries" able to come out and actually *say* what his problem with physical paralysis actually is—whether it derives from sexual hysteria bordering on frigidity (as many have averred) or also, as I have suggested elsewhere, from a sort of repression of the sociopathology of the time involving infantile paralysis, or polio. Infantile was, at the time that *Rear Window* came out, most often considered a disease of "tots"[49]—meaning young children. The movie is thus informed by the "tottering"[50] or vertiginous fall that results not only from apparently incorrect walking but also from hysterical stuttering—itself a sign of presumably incorrect talking.

Jeff is muted (unable or unwilling to talk) and paralyzed (unable or unwilling to walk). He is mute about the things that matter or that he lusts after. Nurse Stella's quasi-psychoanalytic challenge to him, "Is what you want something you can discuss?", has the predictable response: "What?"[51] He is paralyzed, or "listless," in the sense of being withered or encased. *Rear Window* introduces this listlessness as a general condition from the very first time we hear a voice. The voice of a male radio announcer booms asks, "Men, are you over 40 [years of age]? When you wake up in the morning, do you feel tired and rundown? Do you have that listless feeling?"[52] The telephone call that soon follows point to Jeff's unwillingness or inability to have his cast removed.

The relationship between walking (which is tracked by a film camera) and talking (which is tracked with a microphone) is even clearer in *The Conversation* (1974)—directed by the polio survivor Francis Ford Coppola and based partly on *Rear Window*. Rhythmic matching and mismatching between the pedal and vocal is the main theme as a private detective, engaging in something like voyeuristic espionage, tries to follow from a distance a fast-moving and fast-talking couple. The two aspects of so-called *pede-conferencing*[53]—namely, walking and talking—are tracked separately and they need to be.

CHAPTER SIX

Marching and Heiling in *The Great Dictator* (1940)

When they taught me that what mattered most
was not the strict iambic line goose-stepping
over the page but the variations
in that line and the tension produced
on the ear by the surprise of difference,
I understood yet didn't understand
exactly, until just now ...

—LINDA PASTAN, "Prosody 101"

POWERFUL CROWDS

The Swiss poet and theorist Johann Kaspar early noted the "wonderful analogy [for all human beings] between the language, the gait, and the handwriting."[1] His *Physiognomische Fragmente zur Beförderung der Menschenkenntnis und Menschenliebe* (1775–78)—which underlies the principle notions expressed in Balzac's *Theory of Walking* (1833)[2]—claims that the individual gait signals individual character[3] and that a people's way of walking is a clue to its national character. "I know her by her gait," claims Ceres about Juno, "high'st queen of state"[4]—so writes Shakespeare, an ironic pedal physiognomist, for the masque in his *Tempest*.[5] In this section of *Talking the Walk & Walking the Talk*, we wonder less about the walking patterns of an individual (such as William Wordsworth) as about that of a group. The observant neurologist and anatomist Alexander Walker, in his "Character of the French" (1829), allies the supposed general vanity of Frenchmen with the way they walk: "Even the mode of walking in France has more than one relation to vanity—not merely because the rise on the toes, the writhing of the figure, and the paralytic shake of every member, are inspired by that sentiment, but because being, from a curious and accidental circumstance, the very worst mode of walking, it is vainly vaunted as the most graceful."[6] Works by the anthropologists Marcel Mauss followed suit in the twentieth century when he focused on tribal gaits.[7] In all such cases, the motive appears to be partly political.

Small wonder. The political and familial dangers of the attractiveness of rhythm in groups are well known. The Roman poet Ovid famously tells how King Pentheus of Thebes tries to reject the worship of rhythmic Bacchus: "Can the clash of brazen cymbals, pipes of curved horn, and magical tricks be so powerful that men, who were not terrified by drawn swords or blaring trumpets or ranks of sharp spears, are overcome by the shrieks of women, men mad with wine, crowds of obscenities, and empty drumming?"[8] In Euripides's dramatic version of his *Bacchae* (405 BC), Pentheus's mother Agave is the avenging spirit, speaking in dithyrambic ecstasy along with "the vibrant, pulsating entity":[9] the chorus of dancing, chanting Maenads.[10] Whether in perversion or fulfillment of the ritualistic *sparagmos* (rite of sacrifice)—who can say?—Agave pulls Pentheus apart, limb from limb, and then passes around his flesh to be eaten. A few years before the Great War, Joseph Conrad refers in his novel *The Secret Agent* (1907), which deals with anarchism and terrorism, to "the mystery of a human brain pulsating wrongfully to the rhythm of journalistic phrases."[11]

That the politics of walking, as it borders on dancing, may militate brutally against humane justice seems to explain the extraordinary. In *Crowds and Power* (Masse und Macht), which he wrote between 1939 and 1960,[12] Elias Canetti thus brings out a potentially dangerous analogy between human and animal rhythm: "Rhythm is originally the rhythm of the feet." He did so in order to define human "groupiness" in terms of animal rhythm: "The large numbers of the herd which [early human beings] hunted," writes Canetti, "blended into [man's] feelings with their own numbers, which they wished to be large, and they expressed this in a specific state of communal excitement which I shall call the rhythmic or throbbing crowd. The means of achieving this state [excitement] was first of all the rhythm of their feet, repeating and multiplied."[13] In the political practices of Europe, which include mass movements and death camps, the pedal *stamping* of the brutal crowd had a sorry consequence, especially for crippled persons, for example during the Nazi period, who were impeded from joining the *stampede* even as others, with sound bodies, were likewise silenced.

In *Keeping Together in Time: Dance and Drill in Human History* (1995), the historian William McNeil "pursues the possibility that coordinated rhythmic movement has been a powerful force in holding human groups together." He considers kinds of dancing and marching, including Nazi goose-stepping, as a factor in the formation of institutions. However, if these rituals are bonding (as McNeil emphasizes in his treatment of such bodily movements as goose-stepping), they are also separating (which he deemphasizes), and if dance and drill involve the muscular motion of the body, they like to the rhythms of language (which he does not consider). There is the prosodic association, for example, of animal-feet (what we walk on) with verse-feet (what we speak on).[14] Sometimes, we shall see, that association spills over into political rhetoric and the rhetoric of political theory, as if human beings were herd animals, or theory, as in Elias Canetti's influential book, *Crowds and Power* (1960): "Rhythm is originally the rhythm of the feet. . . . Animals too have their familiar gait, their rhythms are often richer and more audible than those of men, hoofed animals flee in herds, like regiments of drummers. The knowledge of the animals by which he was surrounded, which threatened him and which he hunted, was man's oldest knowledge."[15] Canetti is referring partly to the rhythms of Nazi rallies and the movement of crowds. What prosodist, though, would not want to know what sort of rhetoric, informing at once both walking and talking *in the same time*, is actually powerfully charismatic in a given time, place, culture, or language?[16] This is the heart of politics of the twentieth century. And it is no laughing matter.

Or is it? We have seen that, at the level of the individual, the parallel association of walking with talking, taken out of political context, *is* funny, as for Milton Berle in *Let's Make Love* (1960). The present chapter focuses on Charlie Chaplin's dealing with this issue. We look mainly at two factors: the locomotion of German military goose-stepping, which attempts to make the human being walk balanced on a leg as if he were also standing; and the language of nonsense and macaronics, which attempts to make the human being talk in one language while speaking another.

Here we come to the work of Charles Chaplin. He studied Hitler's speech for a long time,[17] in order both to get it right and to properly typify and parody it. (Some people report that Albert Speer—Hitler's architect—said, upon seeing *The Great Dictator*, that it was the most accurate representation of Hitler ever put on screen.) Chaplin claimed that Hitler was one of the greatest actors he had ever seen. "*Den grössten Schauspieler Europas* [Europe's greatest actor]" is, in fact, what Hitler called himself.[18] King George VI seemed also to admire Hitler's charismatic rhetorical abilities.

(King George [1936–52] was a stutterer with a speech therapist: the Australian Lionel George Logue. Even so, Hitler, who suffered from *Stimmbandlähmung* [laming of the vocal cords] had his speaking therapists: Erik Jan Hanussen[19] and Paul Devrient.[20] Logue was attracted to such walking-talking lines as "He the traveller and the talker" [from Longfellow's *Hiawatha*] and focused on issues of cæsura and "correct breathing."[21] As recorded in the movie *The King's Speech* [2010],[22] George VI spoke fluently for the first time when he recited Hamlet's soliloquy "To be or not to be." In Hamlet, as we have seen, the hero's inability to act ["I do not know why yet this thing's to do" (H, 4.4.2819)] matches an inability to speak ["I must hold my tongue" (H, 1.2.333)].)

There have been many studies, rhetorical or prosodic, of Hitler's speech or talk, already from the early 1940s, that focus on mob psychology,[23] most unsuccessful. While even modern theory sometimes attempts to address some of these issues in *The Great Dictator*—and who would not want, along with Deleuze, to understand such powerful charisma apparently partly based in rhythm and the rhetoric of locomotion and language?[24]—yet none does better, for bringing together the dance and oratory, the walk and the talk, than Chaplin, this first time that we hear him.

Chaplin looked like Hitler, people thought, and many knew that he and Hitler were born within a few days of each other in 1889. The rivalry is clear in *The Great Dictator*: not so much Who would dominate the media, but How.

GOOSE STEPS

Goose-step: An elementary drill in which the recruit is taught to balance his body on either leg alternately, and swing the other backwards and forwards.

—*OED* sv "Goose step," n[1]

Oh! the goose step is the walk
And the goose step is the talk
—"In Germany You've Got to Do the Goosestep" (aka "The Goose Step [Is the Thing in Germany])"

Günter Grass, in his memoir *Peeling the Onion* (2007),[25] quotes Theodor Adorno's statement in *Minima Moralia: Reflections from*

Damaged Life (1951): "It is barbaric to write a poem after Auschwitz, and that is why it has become impossible to write poetry today." Already in his Nobel Prize lecture (1999), Grass had commented that the cure to the ills of German culture and politics lay in the Germans' properly attending to the rhythmic dancing march of German soldiers.[26] "No one had the desire or ability to keep silent. It was our duty to take the goose step out of German." One wishes that Grass had talked directly about his *own* goose-stepping earlier than 2007. That is, after all, what the boys do in Will Hay's comedic movie *The Goose Steps Out* (1942), which seems almost to demonstrate the arguments of Heinrich von Kleist's philosophical dialogue, *Über das Marionettentheater* (written 1810), melding robotics with trance.[27] On the English side of the North Sea, in fact, the goose step had long been politically and rhythmically suspect, as in the pseudonymous "Goosestep"'s collection of poems entitled *Splay-feet Splashings in Divers Places* (1891)[28] and, when World War II was finally over, in Herbert Anderson's *The Goosestep over Europe: A Poem of World War II* (1945).[29] Oftentimes such work in prosody combined goose walk with goose talk, as in "In Germany You've Got to Do the Goosestep" (also known as "The Goose Step [Is the Thing in Germany]" [1901]):

> Oh! the goose step is the walk
> And the goose step is the talk,
> That leggy, laggy limber lamber loose step;
> I'd rather march you see,
> In my dear own country,
> For in Germany you've got to do the goose step.[30]

When it came to marches and dances, goose-stepping variably informed the all cinematic ambulation in the English Charles Chaplin's *The Great Dictator* (1940). Documentary footage shows Hitler's troops goose-stepping, and thereafter we see the Jewish barber [played by Chaplin] goose-stepping in the concentration camp yard and barracks,[31] Adenoid Hynkel (played by Chaplin) dancing with the world balloon[32] and with Mrs. Napolini.[33] Why this marching or dance step, both for the Prussian military and for special parodic attention in *The Great Dictator*?

In their pathbreaking *Mechanik der Menschlichen Gehwerkzeuge* (1836),[34] the Prussian brothers, Wilhelm Eduard Weber and Eduard Weber, produced the still classical work on human walking done by observational methods. (Their grandnephew persevered in this work to produce the methods of cinematic gait analysis that we still use today.)[35] The Webers hold that in walking or running the forward motion of the limb is a pendulum-swing owing to gravity, and that walking is a movement of falling forward, arrested by the weight of the body thrown on the limb as it is advanced forward. The "pivot" of this action means that, in walking, the body never moves in the fashion of goose-stepping taken literally. (Other definitions are similar, as put forth in the Prussia army since the time of the eighteenth-century drillmaster Leopold I.)[36] The goose-step, in short, is difficult for human beings, even "mechanistic," and has always been a subject of controversy. Even the Nazis sometimes wanted to abandon the step,[37] partly on that account, and yet it remained, until postwar, when it was abandoned for political or propaganda reasons. Mussolini introduced the goose-step to Italian armed forces in 1938, calling it the *passo Romano*.

The goose-step (German: *Stechschritt*)—"a balance step, practised esp. by various armies in marching on ceremonial parades, in which the legs are alternately advanced without bending the knees."[38] As Marcel Mauss writes, "We laugh at the 'goose-step.' It is the way the German army can obtain maximum extension of the leg, given in particular that all Northerners, high on their legs, like to take as long steps as possible. In the absence of these exercises, we Frenchmen remain more or less knock-kneed."[39] Goose-stepping, partly because it seems to mechanize the human being, becomes an object of laughter in the British Will Hay's movie comedy *The Goose Steps Out* (1942) and remains as such when it surfaces in *Monty Python's Flying Circus* television episode "Ministry of Silly Walks."[40] Goose-stepping is "machine men with machine minds and machine hearts!"—as the Jewish barber describes goose-step talking in *The Great Dictator*; that mechanistic aspect is what can make goose-stepping so funny. Henri Bergson's then still-influential essay "Laughter" (1900) has it that comedy is defined in terms of a human being acting like a machine or automatic-animal, herd, or otherwise, and/or vice versa.

> And laughter will be more pronounced still, if we find on the stage not merely two characters . . . but several, nay, as great a number as possible, the image of one another, who come and go, dance and gesticulate together, simultaneously striking the same attitudes and tossing their arms about in the same manner. This time, we distinctly think of marionettes. Invisible threads seem to us to be joining arms to arms, legs to legs, each muscle in one face to its fellow-muscle in the other: by reason of the absolute uniformity which prevails, the

very litheness of the bodies seems to stiffen as we gaze, and the actors themselves seem transformed into automata . . . [41]

Later in this chapter (in the section "ANATINE QUACKS") we will return to this issue. At this moment, though, it is important to note that, at the same time that goose-stepping elicits laughter, it also, and for the polar-opposite reason, elicits either fear or disgust. Englishmen, for example, find the step, with its eccentric notion of "balance," disgusting or horrible.[42] (You can tell "who a person is," they say, by marking their manner of left-right asymmetry in walking.)[43] George Orwell, in *Why I Write* (1946), says the goose step was common only where people were afraid to laugh at the army.[44] The American movie *Goose Step* (also known as *Hitler Beast of Berlin*, *Beasts of Berlin*, and *Hell's Devils*, 1939)[45] had earlier suggested the same.

Between laughter and fear, goose-stepping enters the world of classical and popular ballet. In the Russian Aram Khachaturian's ballet *Spartacus* (1954), thanks especially to the choreographer Yuri Grigorovich, they are the slave-owning Romans who do the goose-step dance. The Jewish, German-born, French composer Jacques Offenbach's can-can (in *Orphée aux enfer* [Orpheus in the underworld, 1858]), with libretto by Ludovic Halévy, is possibly the first full-length operetta, which includes the can-can (*infernal gallop*)—a complement and opposite to goose-stepping.[46] Offenbach, like composers of marches, was figuring what might be the right words for goose-stepping.

MACARONIC SPEECHES

Barbarus is he that vnderstondyth not yat he readeth in his mother tonge.
—COMPENDIOUS OLDE TREATYSE[47]

The Great Dictator was Chaplin's first full-blown talkie.[48] It was released thirteen years after the first talkies. Chaplin waited a while, as if he wanted to "know his song well," or wanted to know how to sing well, before he started singing. In historical context this makes some sense. On the one hand, there were others—Winston Churchill, a stutterer; Franklin Delano Roosevelt, a polio-survivor; and King George VI, another stutterer—who were nervous about the new media, radio and talkies, and who had to speak for their countries. On the other hand, there was Adolf Hitler, whose apparently unhindered rhetoric spoke powerfully for Nazi Germany. For Chaplin, too, Hitler was a sort of rival.

For starters, then, it was important for Chaplin to diminish the myth of Hitler as a great speaker. In *The Great Dictator*, Chaplin's Adenoid Hynkel (Adolf Hitler) often seems to have adenoid hypertrophy, a condition that sometimes results in a swelling nearly the size of a ping-pong ball that completely blocks airflow through the nasal passages. Hynkel has "talking trouble." He loses his voice when he puts hot English mustard on his strawberries,[49] gagging and blocking up his own mouth with a handkerchief when the heat is too much for him. His speech often devolves into a sickly cough. He becomes tongue-tied when talking to Napoloni (Mussolini) and Mrs. Napoloni.[50]

At one point, Garbitisch (Goebbel) says that Hynkel can't talk: "Just now he's a little horse/hoase." Thanks to interlingual difference, we cannot tell whether Garbitsch might mean, without knowing it, "horse" instead of "hoarse" (even as, due to intralingual difference, we cannot tell whether to hear whores instead of horse).[51]

Chaplin, then, presents the view that Hitler's rhetoric is not "natural" to him—he does not "walk the walk and talk the talk." He is artificial, even mechanical.

It is not only that the real Hitler imitated the fascist Benito Mussolini's mechanical style of talking, official address (*il Duce / Fürher*), and compulsory hand-salute,[52] in much the way that Mussolini imitated Nazi goose-stepping. It is also that Hitler had personal coaches for foot- and hand-choreography and speechifying: Erik Jan Hanussen,[53] for example, and Paul Devrient,[54] whom he visited when he had *Stimmbandlähmung*, which is laming or paralysis of the vocal cords.

In *The Great Dictator*, the Jewish *barber*, with his mastery of shaving the neckline with the dangerous straight-razor, out speaks the barbarian Hitler. Chaplin plays both these parts in *The Great Dictator*. Even so, in *My Hitler*—a cinematographic reinterpretation of *The Great Dictator*—when Hitler develops laryngitis (swelling of the voice box), Hitler calls in the Jewish speech coach, Israel Adolf Grünbaum, in order that Grünbaum, hidden behind the *podium*, become "die Stimme seines Herrn [his master's voice]" as Hitler lip-synchs the words. Grünbaum, playing the role of ventriloquist, is a sort of Professor Henry Higgins (in George Bernard Shaw's dialectal play *Pygmalion*, 1916), and even more is he a kind of Cyrano de Bergerac (in Edmond Rostand's rhetoric play *Cyrano de Bergerac*, 1897), who writes love letters on behalf of his friend Christian.

In *The Great Dictator*, Hynkel's speech is often macaronic rant of the sort that Chaplin had experimented with, just a little, in

Italianate guise, in *Modern Times*. Consider Hynkel's major speech:[55] an *amphigoric* mix of Germerican, Germlish, Gerglish, Germish, Angleutsch, and Engleutsch. The bombast manner and rhythm were already familiar to English audiences from the newsreels of the day showing Hitler.[56]

What interests Chaplin is more the trans-lingual prosody than any substantive meaning.[57] Prosody not only matches cinematic montage. *Montage* is markedly prosodic,[58] says Yury Tynyanov, and Sergei Eisenstein holds that the purpose of film direction was to "balance the rhythmic accents of the visual track [walking, say] with the accents of the audio track [talking, say]."[59] Christian Metz makes a fine point when he writes, in *Film Language: A Semiotics of the Cinema* (1974) that "montage cinema ... came at times very close to being a kind of *mechanical* toy."[60] This mechanical factor helps to explain some of the humor and wit of *The Great Dictator*. It is safe to say, though, that, when it comes to language, scholars have known for centuries that not enough is known about multilingual prosody, which often comes under the rubric of macaronics. Alexander Geddes thus writes, "It is the (1803) characteristic of a Macaronic poem to be written in Latin hexameters, but also as to admit occasionally vernacular words, within their native form, or with a Latin inflection. Other licenses, too, are allowed, in the measure of the lines, contrary to the strict rules of prosody."[61] Charles Anthon (1842) writes similarly about his own System of ... Prosody and Metre, that "at some future day, a separate work will be prepared; and this intended work will also contain the Essay on ... Macaronic Versification."[62] More recently, Gaylord writes, "We could use more study of macaronic verse, where several languages are blended and one prosody confronts, or is overwhelmed, by another."[63] Chaplin's *The Great Dictator* is a filmic essay on macaronic versification with a focus on the movement of walking and hand movement, and on the sound of speechifying. The sound of *Führer* in the hand-salute-accompanied vocal salutation, *Heil, mein Führer* becomes that of "Phooey." It eventually develops, in American cartoon, into the sound of flatulence, as we shall see, even as the salute eventually becomes Dr. Strangelove's possessed arm movements in Stanley Kubrick's movie *Dr. Strangelove* (1964).

Polar opposite to Hynkel's uncontrolled walk and talk would be the amnesiac Jewish barber, who, when he is mistaken for Hynkel, takes the *podium* (one of whose meanings is "foot" that raises one up).⁶⁴ He has to speak, but he can't. This is the dialogue before the speech is made:

Schultz: You must speak.
Jewish barber: I can't.
Schultz: It's our only hope.⁶⁵

The barber is as reluctant to speak as King George in *The King's Speech* and as Chaplin was to speak out in the talkies. Eventually, however, the barber gives a fine kind of talk with a critique of a bad kind of walk (goose-stepping): "Greed has poisoned men's souls, has barricaded the world with hate, has goose-stepped us into misery and bloodshed."⁶⁶ The barber gives a straight-out plea for universal peace and understanding. What Chaplin takes to be the truth comes out of the mouth, not of a barbar[ian] (or stutterer) like Hitler but, which is *almost* the same, out of the mouth of a barber. Saint Paul writes to the Corinthians: "I schal be to him, to whom I schal speke, a barbar."⁶⁷

ANATINE QUACKS

If you expect me to hold forth in a 'scientific' way . . . you are an anserine individual.
—OLIVER WENDELL HOLMES, *Autocrat of Breakfast Table*⁶⁸

The Great Dictator (1940) was followed by dozens of other "funny" movies about the Nazis.⁶⁹ Two that followed in its immediate wake were *Duktators* (1942)⁷⁰ and *Der Führer's Face* (also known as *Donald Duck in Nutzi Land,* 1942).⁷¹ Both of these movies are "Donald Duck"-animated animal cartoons in which the main character, a duck (a bird of the anatine family) is a famously disabled speaker of human languages: his buccal speech avoids using the larynx. For that reason alone, such cartoons conjure up the main turning point in the plot of *The Great Dictator*: the quacking sound of real ducks offscreen, or perhaps, they are merely mechanical, like Vaucanson's duck.⁷² Hynkel, on a tiny rowboat, is surprised by these quacks, falls overboard, and from that time forth, is no longer recognized as Feurher (Phooey).⁷³ The sound of ducks marks the end of Chaplin's reign as Hynkel and the beginning of his reign as barber. After all, a duck, like a goose (a bird of the anserine family), often stands alternately on one leg and then the other.

Silly goose-stepping informs both cartoons. In *Ducktators*, Hitler Duck, Mussolini Goose, and Hirohito Duck *march* while singing a parody of the English nursery, count-out rhyme One, Two, Buckle My Shoe. *Der Fürher's Face* includes a parody, put together by songwriter Wallace Oliver and bandleader Spike Jones, of the official Nazi national anthem and marching song, *Die Fahne Hoch* (The flag on high) played by a goose-stepping "oom-pah" marching band composed of Tojo, Göring, Goebbels, and Mussolini. The Nazi official anthem has this line:

> SA marschiert mit mutig-festem Schritt
> [The storm troopers march with bold, firm step][74]

The comedist Oliver substitutes this one:

> We heil heil right in der fuehrer's face.

What's more, the rhythm of the march's "heil heil" matches the explosive tuba-blasts, fart-like, at each chorus's repetition of *Heil*. (Saint Augustine in his *City of God* [fifth century AD] discusses people who have "such command of their bowels, that they can break wind continuously at will, so as to produce the effect of singing."[75]) The parodic American version of the Nazi anthem became a great hit in the United States, where separate sound recordings put forth the flatulence,[76] now by means of a "bird-a-phone," as Spike Jones called the new instrument, and now by means of a trombone.

The title of the present chapter, "Marching and Heiling," comes from a scene of a third Disney cartoon production: *Education for Death: The Making of a Nazi* (1943).[77] This cartoon is based on Gregor Athalwin Ziemer's 1941 book of the same name.[78] It went on to become a financial success for RKO. Ziemer, who had been headmaster of the American Colony School in Berlin from 1928 to 1939,[79] knew Nazi educational cinema, including *Hans Wessel* (1933), with its story about Communists, who speak poor German; Nazis who march the goose-step; and the storm-trooping, shawm-, or *schalmei*-playing "martyrs for Nazism." In the cartoon version of *Education for Death*, in fact, the "Narrator" seeks thus to define the rhetorical mechanisms of Nazi indoctrination in terms of pedal marching and vocal heiling.

> [The Hitler Youth boys march in formation.]
> Marching and heiling, heiling and marching, Hans grows up. In him is planted no seed of hope, laughter, tolerance or mercy.
> [The boys morph into teenage brown-shirts.]
> For him, only marching and heiling, heiling and marching as the years grind on.

[The brown-shirts become armed German soldiers.]
Manhood finds him still heiling and marching. But the grim years of regimentation have done their work; now he's a good Nazi. He sees nothing but what the party wants him to see, he says nothing but what the party wants him to say, and he does no more than the party wants him to do. And so, he marches on with his millions of comrades, trampling on the rights of others . . . for now his education is complete. His education . . . for death.
[The soldiers change into a row of graves.]

A "voice track of Adolf Hitler in demagogue-rant is heard to punctuate *(stechen)* the goose-stepping *(Stechschritt)*."[80]

MIND THE MUSIC

If the mind can learn to use two rhythms together, why can't it [use] five or worse together? . . . If the mind can understand one key, why can't it learn to understand another key with it?
—CHARLES IVES, *Memos*[81]

"The voice [of Hitler]," said Chaplin, "bangs on your brain."[82] One needs almost to distinguish between pathological and nonpathological walking-and-talking, as if it were possible to complete the project, which Balzac called "Pathology of Social Life,"[83] in anthropological Freudian vein. Yet the French term, *marche*, runs the gamut of meanings, from "walking" to "marching," and, speaking more broadly, marching of one sort or another seems, like walking, almost universally human.

On the one hand, the call of the French national anthem, *La Marseillaise*, that most famous of marches and a French-based foundational myth of Enlightenment humankind, seems all but inevitable.

Marchons, marchons!
[Let's march, let's march!]

Jacques Offenbach's kick-stepping operetta *Orpheus in the Underworld* (1858) and Jean Renoir's movie *La Marseillaise: A Chronicle of Certain Events Relative to the Fall of the Monarchy* (1938) quote this would-be universal march, whose historical counterpart is the historically momentous march of the national guard *(fédérés)* from Marseilles to Paris. So too does the Beatles's song *All You Need Is Love*, first performed on *Our World*, the first live global satellite television link (25 June 1967) with its universally human appeal. The hope is clear: there will no longer be the old divisions—into, say, barbarian and civilized groupings—"neither Gentile nor Jewe... Barbarus or Sithian, bonde or free"[84]—because everyone will be "one" within a promised new political and/or religious dispensation.

On the other hand, the American foundational myth, cast in musical terms, has it that the march is already parodic and the divisions always there no matter what. Consider "The Lexington March," also known as "Yankee Doodle,"[85] still the state anthem of Connecticut, and always considered an American classic. This march marks the American Revolution in something like the way that Wessel's Nazi anthem *Die Fahne Hoch* marks the Nazi movement and the French anthem *La Marseillaise* marks the French Revolution.

Imagine, now, the Lexington March played not with an oboe-like shawm of the sort that Wessel's storm-trooper band preferred, but instead the Yankee-soldiers' piccolo-like fife.

> Yankee Doodle went to town,
> A-riding on a pony;
> Stuck a feather in his cap
> And called it macaroni.

Yankee Doodle is macaronic. *Doodle*, which is probably German, means at least two things at once. The first meaning is "fool" or "noodle,"[86] the sort of person as whom Chaplin casts Hynkel. The second meaning is "to play the militaristic *dudelsack* [bagpipes],"[87] perhaps even in the fashion of Augustinian flatulists. *Macaroni* (what Yankee Doodle calls the feather in his cap), which is probably Italian, likewise means at least two things at once. The first meaning recalls London's "Macaroni Club," much parodied already for its delicate and exotic or mixed tastes.[88] The second meaning suggests the *macaronics* itself: "a mixture of languages" or "nonsense, meaningless talk."[89] Macaronics are the sort of speechifying that Chaplin puts into the mouth of the German doodle Hynkel. Americans are as comfortable projecting charges of being doodles back against their foes as Englishmen recently were comfortable with the gist of Monty Python's "Ministry of Silly Walks." Macaronics fits the lexis of one language with the prosody of another—or macaronics tries to do that. Fitting one language to another is what the American writer Mark Twain does in his translation from English into French and retranslation from French into English of his *The Jumping Frog of Calaveras County*,[90] with interests in intralinguistic dialectal difference (Yankee and West Coast accents) and interlinguistic language difference (French and English). Charles Ives, when he carries Twain's work over into his musical "take off" on Twain's *Jumping Frog* (which Ives called *Rough and Ready*),[91] informs his musical composition with displaced accents.

In much the same way that the quintessentially American composer Charles Ives, son of the marching-band leader George Ives, expresses the difference among marches, arguably the most important influence in his life. Charles Ives was, as he reminds us, the son of a Union bandleader from the Civil War, the second foundational event of the American story. General Grant called George Ives's band the best in the army,[92] and after the war, George went on to become "a public musician."[93] The musical marching interests of his father focused partly on how music filled with poly-vocal, bitonal rhythms and quotations marked how two bands that rhythmically varied crisscrossed each other on the field in such a way that the music, which cannot be totalitarian, never belongs to one march or the other. "On the Fourth of July, he would have separate bands playing different pieces at different locations."[94] Ives's father thus encouraged him to study two marching bands starting at opposite ends of town playing two different songs in different keys while marching toward each other.[95]

Just this sort of thing happens in Ives's *A Symphony: New England Holidays* (1897–1913),[96] toward the end of the part devoted to spring, namely, *Decoration Day* (completed 1912), to commemorate the war dead after the Civil War, now presumably called Memorial Day. The work moves from Henry Clay Work's "Marching Through Georgia" (1865): "Sing it as we used to sing it, 50,000 strong / While we were marching through Georgia." Then it crosses over and into Walter Kittredge's "Tenting on the Old Campground" (1863): "We're tenting tonight on the old camp ground, / Give us a song to cheer / Our weary hearts." Then again it marches crisscross on to David Wallis Reeves's "Second Regiment Connecticut National Guard March" (1888). In his *Essays Before a Sonata* (1920), written partly as a preface to his second pianoforte sonata, Ives famously describes the effect on him of Reeves's march:

> In the early morning of a Memorial Day [in Connecticut], a boy is awakened by martial music—a village band is marching down the street—and as the strains of [David Wallis] Reeves' majestic [Second] Regiment March [1888] come nearer and nearer—he seems of a moment translated—a moment of vivid power comes, a consciousness of material nobility—an exultant something gleaming with the

possibilities of his life—an assurance that nothing is impossible, and that the whole world lies at his feet.[97]

Comparable with George Ives's experiment with band rhythms are his various trials with "an arrangement of singers in which each person sang a different tone of the scale, and that one alone, sounding his tone only when the tune called for that particular note."[98] This notion, says Charles, underlies the songs that Charles later composed with different voices taking different pitches, among them *Aeschylus and Sophocles*.[99]

Ives's song *Walking* (1902),[100] with its walking bass and promise of the future, moves toward funeral and ragtime phases, as the singer sometimes dances, sometimes slows, once pauses, in his musical talking walking.

> A big October morning,
> the village church-bells,
> the road along the ridge,
> the chestnut burr and sumach,
> the hills above the bridge
> with autumn colors glow.
> Now we strike a steady gait,
> walking towards the future,
> letting past and present wait,
> we push on in the sun,
> Now hark! Something bids us pause . . .
> But we keep on a walking,
> 'tis yet not noon-day,
> the road still calls us onward,
> today we do not choose to die
> or to dance, but to live and walk.[101]

The song runs out with the walking rhythm lingering on as a finishing chord. The future toward which the performer, pedal and vocal, moves is not that of uniform march. It walks instead across the line. "Some of the songs in this book, particularly among the latter ones," says Ives, "cannot be sung"[102]—and should not be.

Hitler's "movement signature,"[103] both pedal and vocal, may be what it was, but always aimed at one, as in the totalitarian Nazi slogan, "*Ein Volk, ein Reich, ein Führer.*"[104] Phooey! Balzac says that, if we want to live, we should not pace out all marches as one, but instead strive to vary rhythms and types of marching and walking (*marcher*). When, on 6 February 1788, Massachusetts ratified the Constitution, Bostonians—now citizens of a new country—sang these new words marching out to the old tune:

Now politicians of all kinds,
Who are not yet decided,
May see how Yankees speak their minds,
And yet are not divided.¹⁰⁵

A little later the same year, the politically moderate Quebec City Anglophone newspaper *Quebec Gazette* in loyalist Canada published the following "new song," from the staunchly Federalist Philadelphia newspaper *Pennsylvania Mercury*, reminding everyone that human beings need as well, or better, to mark the rhythm as the mind.

Yankee doodle, keep it up
Yankee doodle, dandy,
Mind the music and the step,
And with the girls by [sic] handy.¹⁰⁶

CHAPTER SEVEN

Knock-Kneed and Tongue-Tied in *The King's Speech* (2010)

Lionel Logue: Any other 'corrections'?
Prince Albert: Knock knees.
—THE KING'S SPEECH[1]

After its first stammering attempts, the orchestra walks, talks, becomes a man!
—HECTOR BERLIOZ, "Exasperations at Rehearsal"[2]

King George VI, known as Prince Albert before his coronation, was a stutterer. One way to tell the story of that stutter is expressed in Tom Hooper's movie *The King's Speech* (2010). That movie begins with the prince delivering a speech, in person, some years before his coronation, at the British Empire Exhibition at Wembley on 31 October 1925.[3] He stutters "badly." The movie climaxes with the king delivering a speech, on the radio, after his coronation, on 3 September 1939. That is the BBC speech that starts the British war against Nazi Germany—an hour that is "perhaps the most fateful in our history." "In this grave hour," he says, "perhaps the most fateful in our history, I send to every household of my peoples, both at home and overseas, this message, spoken with the same depth of feeling for each one of you as if I were able to cross your threshold and speak to you myself.... As if [he] were able," the speech-disabled king now stutters "well." His eloquence on 3 September 1939 resides in a contextually contrapuntal stutter. Winston Churchill explains to the king, just before he makes his speech, how Churchill himself had made an asset of his own "tongue-tied" speech impediment.[4] That is what George VI also does. Perhaps that is what most stutterers should want to do: they want to be entirely rid of their stutter, but they should instead learn to live better with it. *The King's Speech*, then, tells how a stuttering prince—a king-in-training much like Hamlet—learns to speak for the nation by turning his bad speech impediment into a good one. He is helped in that learning by the Australian Lionel George Logue (1926), whose role begins, in fact, with his asking the king to read the soliliquoy in *Hamlet* where the Danish prince considers where to be or not to be.

Lionel Logue's methods involve rhythm and music. He paid attention to the way his stuttering patients walked. Thus Geoffrey Elliott recalls the following about his treatment by Logue:

> As I approached Lionel Logue I remember him saying "hop over here, Geoffrey" and being an obedient child I duly hopped across the room! My father was not allowed to be present during treatment. Dad believed that Logue used hypnosis but I have no evidence whether that is true or untrue. My next recall is of my father's tearful thanks to Logue on my return to the waiting room, when I could speak without the wretched stutter. I shall always be indebted to that great healer.[5]

George VI himself was not only a person who stumbled in talking but also a person who stuttered in walking. That coincidence informs *The King's Speech*.[6] As hopping walker and stuttering talker, the king is not only like Shakespeare's *Hamlet*. He is also like the Roman Emperor Claudius on whom Shakespeare's Hamlet was partly modeled. Robert Graves's best-selling, first-person narrative *I, Claudius* (1934)[7] and his sequel novel *Claudius the God and his wife Messalina* (1934)[8] brought out this association of walking and talking, and in the movie *I, Claudius* (1937) the actor Charles Laughton has it thus: "I l-l-limp with my tongue and st-st-stutter with my leg!"[9] The director Josef von Sternberg never completed his movie *I, Claudius* both because one of the actors was injured[10] and because "the stammering [Roman Emperor] Claudius might be construed as a [politically unacceptable] reflection on the speech impediment of the [then still] new [English King] George VI."[11]

George VI stuttered with his legs not only because he developed Buerger's disease in his adult years but also because, as a child, he had suffered from *genu valgum*—the treatment for which involved his wearing painful metal splints[12] (the standard treatment since 1879).[13] George VI was "knock-kneed"—as Ophelia describes young Hamlet, "his knees knocking each other."[14] The knees "knock together in walking from inward curvature of the legs,"[15] the result often being a rhythmic knocking sound.[16]

The prosodist George Saintsbury, in his *History of Elizabethan Literature* (1887),[17] credits the beginning of English prosody to knock-knees. There was "no theory of any English prosody before [Thomas Wyatt],"[18] he says, and Wyatt's verse is "stumbling and knock-kneed."[19] Saintsbury praised Henry Howard, Earl of Surrey, in *The Earlier Renaissance* (1901), as the first Englishman to write unrhymed iambic pentameter, or blank verse: "Some of [these "knock-kneed"] sonnets are really charming things for all their lisp and stammer."[20]

George VI was not the only British leader of the period who had a speech impediment. There was "tongue-tied" Winston Churchill and, of course, the oddly rhetorical Adolph Hitler. The king and his family watched newsreels of Hitler, commenting on the chancellor's eloquence and on his stormtroopers' goose step.[21] King George did not know *what* Hitler was saying, but he knew that Hitler said it *well*.

There was also the stutterer Aneurin Bevan, who eventually became minister of health in the postwar Clement Attlee government and who helped to pass the National Insurance Act (1946). Like his uncle, Bevan had stuttered since he was a child.[22] He overcame that stutter by following the advice of the therapist Clara Bunn to recite such literary passages as "To be or not to be" as well as prose excerpts from William Morris. Bevan became "the most compelling orator of his generation [1950s]."[23]

These four men—King George, Winston Churchill, Adolph Hitler, and Aneurin Bevan—turned their stutter into eloquence. The turn showed that "there are no [straightforwardly] shambling, knock-kneed verses."[24] The strength of eloquence, as Demosthenes knew, often resides in its charming display of weakness. The trio formed an unlikely alliance even at the level of friendship.

There is also the case of David Seidler, who wrote, "How the 'naughty word' Cured the King's Stutter (and mine)" (2010).[25] Seidler wrote the script for *The King's Speech*, based on Mark Logue's book *The King's Speech: How One Man Saved the British Monarchy* (2010), and his uncle had had Lionel Logue as a speech therapist.[26] Seidler's script shows how a stutterer—the king—can learn to playact at not being a stutterer. It also shows how a nonstutterer—the actor Colin Firth who plays the king—can learn to playact at being a stutterer. Before coming to *The King's Speech*, Firth had played stutterer Tom Birkin, "shell-shocked" by the Great War, in *A Month in the Country* (1987), and stutterer Jamie, who falls in love with a Portuguese-speaking woman with whom he cannot communicate, in *Love Actually* (2003). For *The King's Speech*, however, Seidler himself finally taught Firth how to speak, or how not to speak,[27] like a king who stutters.

The "sound track" for *The King's Speech* moves from silence (as between stutters) toward deafness. When the prince recites Hamlet's soliloquy "To be or not to be," for example, he wears earphones that play back a recording of Mozart's "opera buffa" *The Marriage of Figaro* (1786)[28] that does not allow him to hear himself speak. The opera's libretto is based on the revolutionary play of the same name by Pierre de Beaumarchais (1784), a play about which Georges Danton had said (1789) that it had "killed off the nobility."[29] The commoner Logue breaks the class barrier in *The King's Speech* as much as Horatio does in *Hamlet*.

The British prince is annoyed that he will be unable to hear himself. "How can I hear what I am saying?"[30] That question is the crux of *The King's Speech*. Deafness in *The King's Speech* is no less the "cause" of silence than its therapeutic "cure." It is small wonder, then, that it is the rhythmic and often halting music of the deaf composer Ludwig van Beethoven that accompanies the narratological climax and denouement of *The King's Speech*. During the speech that the king delivers to the empire, for example, it is the second movement of Beethoven's seventh symphony (1812) that overplays for the auditor (in the cinema house) the king's words. Mozart's The *Marriage of Figaro* had likewise overplayed for the prince his recitation of Hamlet's soliloquy (in the therapist's office). The movie score imitates both stuttering and the overcoming of stuttering.

Alexandre Desplat's "original" music score for the movie repeats the same note or extends that note to the point of difficult expectation. That extension, says Desplat, is a musical counterpart to the blockage of the royal voice:[31] "How do you express stuttering in music? Well you can't just repeat the same chord. I found the idea of repeated notes, this thing that can't evolve because it's like it's stuck, the key is stuck. The music is an echo of the king's difficulties."[32] A similar repetition informs the extraordinarily effective, repetitive *ostinato* of the second movement (allegretto) of Beethoven's seventh symphony[33]—where the *ostinato* appears as a quarter note, followed by two eighth notes, and ending with two quarter notes. The French romantic composer Hector Berlioz describes the effect of this rhythm in Beethoven's symphony in his book *A Traver Chants* (1862): "The rhythmic pattern [of the second movement of Beethoven's seventh symphony] consists merely of a dactyl followed by a spondee played relentlessly, either in three parts, or in only one, then in all parts together. Sometimes it serves as an accompaniment, but frequently it focuses attention on itself."[34] "Dactyl and Spondee in Beethoven's Seventh Symphony"—that was the title of a subsection of the textbook *Science of English Verse* (1880), written by the American musician and poet Sidney Lanier.[35] Berlioz had come likewise to issues of rhythm by way of music (Beethoven) and verse (Shakespeare): "Beethoven opened before me a new world of music," he writes in his *Memoirs* (1865), in the same way that "Shakespeare had revealed a new universe of poetry."[36]

In fact, Beethoven's seventh symphony had influenced two relevant works of Berlioz. One is *Tristia* (1852).[37] The third part of *Tristia*, called "Funeral March for the Last Scene of Hamlet," relies on the second movement of Beethoven's seventh symphony even as it presents the last lines of Shakespeare's play about the stumbling, stuttering Prince Hamlet. Prince Fortinbras, almost the new king, speaks about Prince Hamlet, who had been all but king:

> ... and for his passage
> The soldier's music, and the rites of war,
> Speak loudly for him ... (*Hamlet*, 5.2.4064).
>
> [Que sur son passage
> La musique militaire, et les rites de la guerre,
> Parlent hautement pour lui!]

The rhythm of Fortinbras's soldiers shooting would seem to have the ghostly aspect of a ventriloquist therapist speaking, as if one could, for the dead.

A second work of Berlioz that hinges on stuttering and therapeutic musical ventriloquism is *Harold in Italy* (1834),[38] whose first movement recalls the first movement of Beethoven's seventh symphony. In *Harold in Italy*, the solo viola is personal (like a person); its formation of a rhythmic idea precedes its coming forth as melody. Reviews at the time ridiculed *Harold in Italy* for its *stuttering* rhythm: "Ha! ha! ha! ... haro! haro! ... Harold!"[39] *Haro* is often a shout of denunciation,[40] and here it doubly marks a barbarian (Norman) stutter.

The text for the speech that King George delivers to declare war is "scored" with scansion marks that Logue adds in order to lay out graphically the metrical character of the sentences.[41] The effect of the speech as delivered in *The King's Speech* derives partly from the coincidence between prosody and music. In describing Beethoven's work,

Berlioz rightly observes, "The rhythm, a simple rhythm like that of the first movement [*morceau*] but of a different form, is the principal cause of the extraordinary effect produced by the allegretto." One theory of music and stuttering has it that stutterers do not stutter when they sing,[42] but there are those stutterers who might argue that singing, or "warbling" (as King George calls it), is precisely stuttering par excellence.

After King George's excellent delivery of *the* speech there follows a quick denouement accompanied by another work by Beethoven: the second movement (adagio) of the "Emperor" concerto for piano (1811).[43] The piano "takes off" from this work as much as does the personal viola from Berlioz's *Harold in Italy* or the humanoid clarinet from the Mozart concerto (1791)[44] that accompanies the film credits of the movie. "I would not have thought that a clarinet could imitate the human voice so deceptively as you imitate it," wrote Schink about Anton Paul Stadler, for whom Mozart wrote the clarinet concerto.[45]

In *The King's Speech*, the Emperor concerto marks the opening salvo of a war that will destroy both British *Empire* and Third *Reich*.[46] (George VI was the last Emperor of India.) At the same time, the concerto's rhythms recall the opening bars of the first movement of Beethoven's fifth symphony (1808):[47] three short Gs followed by a long *E-flat*. That rhythm became known throughout the world as V, for "victory." In Morse code: • • •—.

There is a political tug of war in *The King's Speech* between ventriloquist and dummy or between therapist and patient. On the one hand is the view that the emperor should be superior to the language. "I am the Roman king [*rex Romanorum*] and above the grammarians" is how the Holy Roman Emperor Sigismund put it (1414 AD).[48] On the other hand is the view that the emperor is no less subject to the language than anyone else. In *What Is Enlightenment?* (1784), the German philosopher Immanuel Kant reminds us of the old notion that "the emperor [*Caesar*] is not above the grammarian,"[49] and the French playwright Molière likewise recalls in his popular *The Learned Ladies* (1672) "grammar, which lords it [régeter] even over kings, / And makes them, with a high hand, obey her laws."[50] *Grammar*'s purview in this context is "the art of speaking and writing a language correctly."[51] Logue makes no more of his behind-the-scenes power and corrective friendship than need be, but the "democratizing" aspect of *The King's Speech* shines through. To the amusement of his children, Logue performs the part of ill-spoken Caliban, the "dispossessed king" in Shakespeare's *The Tempest*.[52] No Prospero he, Caliban is the *barbarian* of the piece: the reduplicative *bar-bar* mimics the rat-a-tat-tat of stuttering. The well-spoken Prospero, master of the nameless isle in Shakespeare's play, was unable to teach Caliban to speak well, but Logue's job is to teach the king of the British Isles to speak well defined in terms of the stutter he cannot cure.

Professor Henry Higgins, the expert phoneticist in George Bernard Shaw's play *Pygmalion* (1916), is able to teach the commoner Eliza Dolittle to talk and walk *like* a royal princess—but only at the cost of Eliza's nearly losing her own voice. The movie version of *Pygmalion* (1938) played in movie theaters the year that George VI was crowned, and few weeks before George delivered his great BBC speech, he went to see a stage performance of *Pygmalion* at Windsor.[53] Shaw's work left its mark on King George, but English Professor Higgins is no more like Australian Dr. Logue than the apparently downwardly mobile King George is like the apparently upwardly mobile Eliza. Higgins teaches a commoner to talk like a king; the commoner Logue teaches a king to discover his own voice as a man. "HIS MASTER'S VOICE" had been the trademark of the old British Gramophone Company since 1899. Logue enables the Master to speak both to a brave new world and also for it.

CHAPTER EIGHT
Sign Languages

Chirologia, or, The Naturall Language of the Hand . . . whereunto is added Chironomia or the Art of Manual Rhetorick . . . with Types, or Chyrograms
—title of John Bulwer's book about "hand rhetoric"[1]

MA BELL'S "LET YOUR FINGERS DO THE WALKING" IN THE YELLOW PAGES (1962)

The inventor of the practical telephone in 1876 was Alexander Graham Bell, whose father was an elocutionist much involved with the education of "deaf mutes" with a focus on lip reading and Visible Speech, and whose mother, who was deaf, taught him a manual finger language.[2] A century after the invention of the telephone, Henry Alexander introduced his well-known "Three-Fingered Walking" logo for the New England Telephone Company's *Yellow Pages* in 1962. (See Figures 8.1 and 8.2.) For hundreds of years already, the digits of the upper limb had been associated both with speaking (as when one uses hand gestures or hand-sign language) and reading (as when one uses a finger-marker). Alexander's logo and its slogan, "Let your fingers do the walking," follows logically from the historical sequence. It represents how, digitally speaking, the foot (*pes*) and its toes ("Moseses toeses") match up with the hand (*manus*) and its fingers. The slogan follows on the notion that with the ancient introduction the reed pen, feather quill, telegraph, and typewriter had allowed the "fingers to do the talking."[3] The rotary telephone dial allowed the fingers to walk to the interlocutor. *The Yellow Pages* was able to talk it and walk it at the same time. Songsters loved the idea: Marty Grosz and Wayne Wright's "Let Your Fingers Do the Walking" (1977),[4] Lindsey LaWanda's "Let Your Fingers Do the Walkin'" (1975),[5] Jebry Lee Briley's "Let Your Fingers Do the Walkin'" (1982),[6] Sort Sol's "Let Your

Figure 8.1. Henry Alexander. "Let Your Fingers Do the Walking." 1962. Public domain. The slogan is a "classic" in the ancient field of literature or rhetoric called "advertisement."

Fingers Do the Walking" (1994),[7] Neil Young's "Let Your Fingers Do the Walkin'" (1984),[8] and so on.

It was a "runner-up" for *Advertising Age*'s Ten Best Slogans of the Twentieth Century. This was the same category where the judges placed "Loose Lips Sink Ships" (1940s), from the War Advertising Council of the United States, and "Does She, or Doesn't She? (1960s), from Clairol.[9] The next best step would become, "Let your feet do the talking."

The study of hand-talking begins with ancient chirology. That was the branch of medicine and rhetoric that focused on "the art or science of gesticulation, or of moving the hands, according to rule in oratory."[10] George Grote puts it thus in his *History of Greece* (1847): "Cheironomy, or the decorous and expressive movement

Sign Languages 125

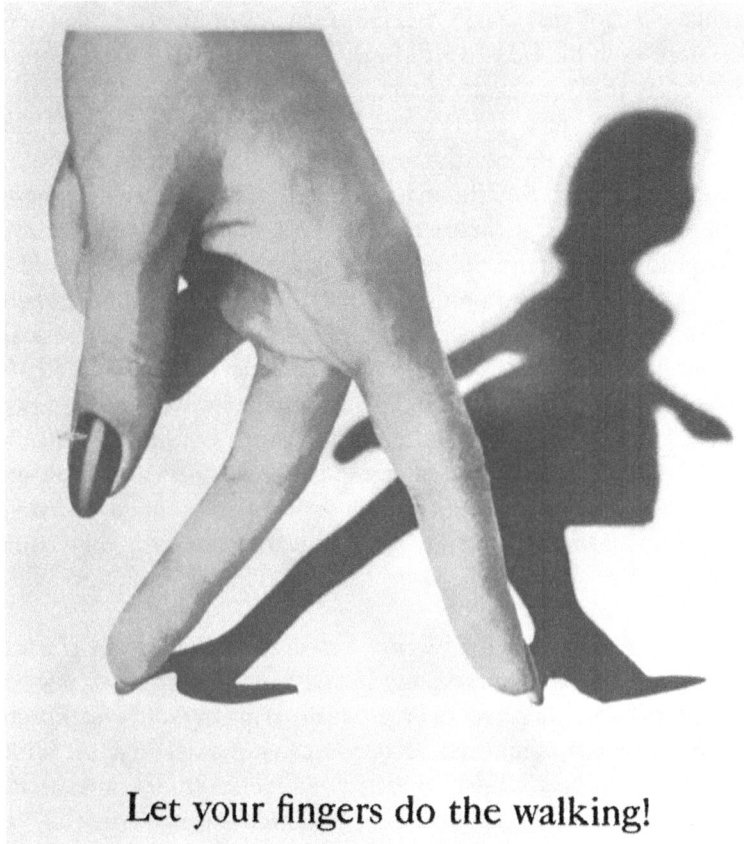

Figure 8.2. Yellow Pages advertisement. LET YOUR FINGERS DO THE WALKING! (shadow motif). Life magazine (16 March 1962), 98. Collection Selechonek.

of the hands."[11] John Bulwer, who tried to introduce this science to the modern world, calls chirology "the natural Language of the Hand"[12] even as Blount, in his *Glossographia* (1656), calls it "a talking or speaking with the hand."[13] (So we read in Rabelais: "Such a fine Gesticulator, and in the Practice of Chirology an Artist so compleat . . . that with his very Fingers he doth speak" [trans. 1693].)[14] Chirology, though, was as concerned on the practical level with sign language—Bulwer presents a fine argument for the education of the deaf in his *Philocopus, or the Deaf and Dumb Man's Friend* (1648)—as it was with issues of rhetoric and neurology. In this sense, chirology was looking forward to such works as the neurological language-psychologist David McNeill's studies of kinetic and visual expression, as in his *Hand and Mind: What Gestures Reveal About Thought* (1992).[15] Bulwer's *Pathomyotomia* (1649) had already aimed . . . "to see in a Chironomer [how] the Muscles of his Hand should be directed so swiftly to the Nerves of his instrument."[16] For our present purpose, the main counterparts to neurologists are Enlightenment musical theorists, above all, Johann Mattheson. A contemporary of Johann Sebastian Bach who maintained an interest in the tritone "devil in music,"[17] Mattheson is sometimes called the "first" professional music critic. Matheson's insightful musical compositions include *Das wol-klingenden Finger-Sprache in zwölf Fugen* (The speech of well-sounding fingers in twelve fugues, 1735 and 1737). (The French translation is *Les doits parlans* [the fingers speak].) In this series of musical compositions, Mattheson took up notions, developed theoretically in his earlier essay-chapter *Von den Klang-Füssen* (On poetic meter, 1739),[18] partly in order to take issue with Bach's *Das Wohltemperierte Klavier* (The well-tempered clavier, 1722).[19]

In a discussion of Bach's *Warum betrübst du dich, mein Hertz?* (Why do you trouble yourself, my heart, 1723)[20] with its bass-aria *Auf Gott steht meine Zuversicht* (I put my trust in God)—a church cantata that Bach composed to accompany the reading of Saint Paul's caution to "*walk* in the Spirit"[21]—Thomas Braatz notes that, according to Johann Mattheson's *Finger-Sprache* (finger-speech), "a composer does not have to use the rhythmic unit of a foot consistently throughout a movement the same way that a poet does in a poem. . . . A composer can quickly turn a musical figure consisting of a specific foot pattern around and transform it to create innumerable melodic feet which are not possible in poetry."[22] For Matheson, after all, "there are 24 different types of feet possible in poetry which might be applied to music, but in music these two dozen feet can be transformed into 620448401733323943936030 musical possibilities."[23] When it comes to the basic rhythmic structure of a foot, poetry cannot match music and fingering-talking beats walking-talking.

DOROTHY MILES'S BODY-SIGN LANGUAGE IN GESTURES (1976)

Six months later a sudden illness, diagnosed as a cerebrospinal meningitis; and a long quiet convalescence during which I had to learn to walk again. Afterwards, the silence that I had accepted as part of the sick-room remained as a fact of my life.
—DOROTHY MILES, *Bright Memory*[24]

The one-time singer Charlie Haden, we have seen, began to walk the bass with his hands after paralytic polio took out his voice. Likewise, the one-time hearer Dorothy Miles—"the source of most of the sign language poetry composed and performed today"[25]—began to talk with her hands after a case of polio (misdiagnosed as cerebrospinal meningitis)[26] took away her hearing. For both Haden and Miles, the sort of thinking that inspired John Bulwer's *Chirologia, or The Natural Language of the Hand* (1644)[27] made possible their partly compensatory, sensibly sensible, musical, and linguistic recoveries—and their uniquely insightful rhythmic art, which one might call a sort of "chirogymnastics."[28]

Two common prejudices concerning "language," of the signal sort in which Miles was a pioneer, deserve unpacking in the context of discussing rhythm and linguistic prosody. The first prejudice is that hand-signing is not a language, a view often attributed to Aristotle, who claimed that fully thoughtful language was impossible without speech.[29] The contrary position had been put forward in Plato's *Cratylus*: there is no essential difference between speaking by mouth and by hand. Socrates says to his interlocutor, "If we had no voice or tongue, and wished to make things clear to one another, should we not try, as dumb people actually do, to make signs (sémanein) with our hands and head and person generally?"[30] Socrates's gist seems to be that the mythical Philomel, having lost her tongue, would still have hands with which to talk, as she does in the story—"the voice of the shuttle"[31]—reported by Ovid in his *Metamorphoses* (8 AD).[32] Socrates seems to suggest likewise that if some counterpart to Philomel were then to lose also her hands, she would find nonetheless a way to talk (as she does Lavinia Shakespeare's *Titus Andronicus*). Yet Socrates adds to this position, with some irony, that such hand-signing might be mere onomatopoeia: "If we wished to mention a galloping horse or any other animal, we should, of course, make our bodily attitudes as much like theirs as possible." Our contemporary understanding of signing with neuro-linguistics goes well beyond ironic onomatopoeia. Edward S. Klima, a neurolinguistic researcher at the Salk Institute, argues for straight-out language in his *What the Hands Reveal About the Brain* (1987).[33] (Miles worked with Ursula Bellugi and Klima at the Salk Institute for Biological Studies, founded by Jonas Salk, the developer of the polio vaccine.[34]) "In the beginning was the foot" is the similar argument made, made at the level of the evolutionary biology and cultural anthropology of the foot, in Marvin Harris's *Our Kind* (1989).[35] The appropriate saying among signers is, "The hands are the head of the mouth."[36]

The second prejudice about signing is that, while spoken language has rhythm, sign language does not, even in its more elaborate formations. The fact about this matter can be as surprising to those who do not know the lingo—as surprising as the facts that stuttering speakers sometimes stutter involuntarily, or break rhythm, even when they write, that stuttering signers do the same,[37] and "the prosody information [in finger Braille] exists in the time structure of finger Braille typing."[38] The fact is that there is a prosody to signing—manually and bodily[39]—as there is to spoken language.[40] For our present purpose, the main consequence is not that the prosody of sign language involves "the rhythm, length, and tension of gestures, along with mouthing and facial expressions," but that the rhythm of signing matches that of walking. Hence the rhythm of the sign for walking (for example, the movement of upturned hands front to back in British Sign Language)[41] and that for talking (the movement of two fingers, placed near the throat, back and forth) match up.

No one was in a better position to understand and express better than Dorothy Miles two interrelated linguistic intersections. The first intersection: how different sign languages (for example, British Sign Language, which she learned first, and American Sign Language, and so on) interact with, or translate into, each other in much the same way as do different spoken languages (for example, English, which she knew, and Welsh, which she did not). The second intersection: how spoken language (sound) interacts with, or is translated into, sign language. Those two intersections, taken together, help to explain how Dorothy Miles's work is pathbreaking.

For the first eight years of her life, Miles lived in a largely Welsh-speaking part of Wales where her father spoke Welsh, her mother spoke English, and although young Dorothy often heard the Welsh language and, as she says, absorbed the rhythms of Welsh, she learned to speak only English. She knew the sound of poems, like Alfred Noyes "galloping" narrative ballad, "The Highwayman" (1906), but, like the Welsh poet Dylan Thomas, with whom she compares herself, she did not speak or read Welsh but knew only its rhythms.[42] After disease took her hearing at the age of eight (1939), she learned British Sign Language and then, in the United States, American Sign Language. Her career in the United States included performances with the National Theater for the Deaf. One signing and largely pantomime performance, meant for both deaf and hearing populations, was *Songs from Milk Wood* (1970), informed by Dylan Thomas's "play for voices" entitled *Under Milk Wood* (1954).[43] Another was the French Molière's seventeenth-century play *Sganarelle*, in which a daughter pretends to be mute and Sganarelle offers to make her father genuinely deaf. Her idea to develop poetry for deaf and hearing readers developed out of this.[44] Within a few years, Miles published the poetry book *Gestures* (1976). She wanted her poetry to be "richer."[45] Eventually, she hoped, it would "combine sign language with spoken English."[46] In a 1975 interview Miles gave a good sense of what this would mean: "I am trying . . . to find ways to use sign language according to the principles of spoken poetry. For example, instead of rhymes like cat and hat, I might use signs like WRONG and WHY, with the same final hand-shape."[47] Miles's poem *Walking Down the Street*,[48] performed with its punning rhythmic beat of digital walk and talk,[49] suggest the success of the experiment.

Much other deaf-talking poetry followed in Miles's footsteps. The "born signer" Paul Scott's *Three Queens*, for example, elaborates on Miles's language.[50] In *Three Queens*, the first Queen Elizabeth, in the sixteenth century, WALKS three times purposefully with her scribes. (It was during the reign of Queen Elizabeth I that sign language as such first came up for serious discussion.) Another of Scott's performances is "The Tortoise and the Hare" (*Testudo et lepus*). Here he signs a patient, walking tortoise, on the one hand, and a disdainful running hare, on the other—with manual articulators showing animal body parts.[51] (See Figure 8.3.) "The hare laughed at the tortoise's feet [ποδῶν] but the tortoise declared, 'I will beat you in a race!'" Famously the hare loses: "The hare, however, lay down to take a nap, confident in the speed of his feet [ποσί]." One guesses that Aesop's hare adopts a plantigrade locomotion while walking—using the podials and metatarsals, like a human being—but employs digitigrade locomotion while running, using the toes, like a dog.[52] (If the

A B

Figure 8.3. Video still. Paul Scott performing, "The Tortoise and the Hare" (19 March 2003). Facial expressions and manual articulators indicate (A) the disdainful hare and (B) the patient tortoise. Radboud University Nijmegen. Open Language Archives Community [OLAC]——Name: BSL_PS_fab2; Title: ECHO BSL Fable 2 (The Tortoise and the Hare) ISLE Metadata Initiative.

story were about groups of animals struggling with each other instead of individuals, then one might guess that he is rather marching in the powerful Roman style, *testudo* [tortoise formation], where shields play the role of the tortoise's shell.)

The signal asymmetry of hopping hare with lumbering tortoise is the aesthetic principle at work.[53] The French composer Camille Saint-Saëns manages to convey the issue when, in the *Carnival of Animals* (1845; first performed 1922), he adopts Offenbach's *gallop infernal* ("can can") for his "opera bouffon," *Orpheus en enfer* (1886), opening with a pulsing triplet and slowing it down to the point where it mimics the tortoise's gait. Ogden Nash provides the poetry for the situation,[54] with its triplex "totley, turtley, torper" and claims to "know the turtoise is a tortle."

One still has to ask: Is the purpose of education—that "leading out of the cave or underworld"—to teach a young person (*pæs*) "to be straight [*orthos*]"? To be straight when using his feet (*pes*)? The surgeon's term *orthopedics* might suggest that the answer is Yes. The anthropologist John Napier asserts that the correct (literally, "orthotic") stride "is [according to many people] the *essence* of human bipedalism and the criterion by which the evolutionary status of a hominid walker must be judged."[55] Certainly the assertion is familiar in the history of evolutionary biology[56] and in the history of literature.[57] Or is the purpose of education to teach "to use words [*logos*] straight"? The language-therapist's term *logopædics* might suggest that the answer is Yes. According to the *Dictionary of Speech Pathology & Therapy* (1963), *logopædia refers only to* "the study and correction of speech and voice defects and disorders as a general field of knowledge."[58]

Worth mentioning in this context is the pervasive English-language conflation of the originally Greek-language term *pæd-* ("education, mostly of the child [*paes*]") with the originally Latin-language *ped* ("foot"). The conflation has at least two explanations. First is the modern orthographic habit of replacing the runic ash (*æ*) with the single letter (*e*). Hence the language therapist's *logopedia* was formed by analogy with the surgeon's *orthopedics,* and the *orthopod* often wanted to make straight (*orthos*) the foot (*podes*) of the child (*paes*). Second is that cultural predilection to blur lines between talking and walking whose subject matter is the general subject of the present book. After all, the confusion of *paed* with *pod* already had a history in the educational practices of pedantry. By way of example, consider such terms as *pedagogue* and the simpler *pedant*. The original Greek and Roman meaning of both terms is "a person who leads [*agógos*] a child walking along a foot-path to or from school." This term, then, would seem to separate or to indicate the conceptual separation of the action of path-walking (to and from school) from the activity of *paedeia* or education itself, which presumably happens only or mainly *at* school. This conceptual separation, along with all the institutional practices that accompany it (the separation of school bussing from schooling itself, the scission between playground and workspace at school, and so forth), fly in the face of beliefs and activities that have "education" taking place in walking conversations. Examples would include the original Academy, Socrates's walk from the Piraeus in Plato's utterly foundational *Republic*, and the philosophers' paths mentioned earlier in *Talking the Walk & Walking the Talk*. (*Path* comes from the early Old English *paed*[59] and/or *paõ*.[60] Some philologists add that English *path* and *foot* are cognate.[61]) In modern times, pedagogy is put down as a mere "pedant." That *orthological* is less tendentious than *logopedia* helps to explain why Charles Kay Ogden and I. A. Richards seriously prefer it both for writing such works as *The Meaning of Meaning* (1923)[62] and for naming the Orthological Institute (1927).[63] On a lighter note, however, one might joke that Oedipus anyways requires both kinds of treatment. One is orthological (or logopaedic), thanks to which he would be able to straighten or interpret the crooked *talk* of the Oracle at Delphi and of Tiresias. The other is orthopedic, thanks to which this lamed man would be able to *walk* straight.

Perhaps, though, the purpose of education is instead to learn to course along, trippingly, with the leporine hare, as in a conga-line version of big-band-leader Duke Ellington's "Bunny Hop Mambo" (1954)[64] with its three-footed "Hop! Hop! Hop!"[65] Or to amble along, with the testudinal tortoise, as in stutterer John Updike's poem "To a Box Turtle" (1989): "Your tentative, stalk-bending walk / resumes."[66]

If so, then Hamlet has one leg up: "Except my life. Except my life. Except my life" (*Hamlet*, 2.2.1316).

CHAPTER NINE
Postamble and Epilogue

[Gabriel Harvey] liked not over-long preambles, or postambles to short discourses.
—JOHN WOLF, "Printer's Advertisement"[1]

REDUPLICATION
I like the way you walk
I like way you talk
I like the way you walk I like the way you talk
Susie Q
—DALE HAWKINS, "Susie Q"[2]

There are, in the English language and especially in jazz lyrics, hundreds of pairs of ablaut reduplicate words like *walk-and-talk*.[3] Just why there are so many we will consider in the present section: a rarely articulated, even often hidden, historical fact and, more importantly, syntactic condition of the English language that affects both the title of the present book and its general subject matters.

The historical fact is this: the English language, characteristically, has many more reduplicatives than other languages. Some of these, that issue from two languages, I would call *twoblets*.[4] These are distinguishable from *doublets*, understood as "one of two words (in the same language) representing the same ultimate word but differentiated in form, as *cloak* and *clock*, *fashion* and *faction*, and so on."[5] Twoblets are words that, although apparently synonymous, come from different languages.

For England, these "twoblets"—*hue and cry, law and order, lord and master,* and *ways and means,* for example[6]—often have special reference to the law.[7] Their historical existence seems to arise from historical circumstances like the Norman "Conquest" (1066). The social consequences of the conquest of England in 1066 resulted, for example, in *beef, pork,* and *veal* (from Norman-French) on the relatively aristocratic table, but *cow, pig,* and *calf* (from Anglo-Saxon) in the stable.[8] (My favorite doublet is the name of Mel Blanc's stutter ring animal: *Porky Pig*.)[9] *Peace and quiet* combines French and Latin; *will and testament* joins Old English and Latin. Oftentimes twoblets appear almost as a single word, as for modern instances of the Anglo-Norman *hu e cri* ("hue and cry"),[10] and sometimes they devolve into "three-lets," as for the *give, devise, and bequeath.* The fact of such twoblets makes palpable "the dualism of [the] elder [French] phraseology"[11] of the English language, says John Earle in *The Philology of the English Tongue.* It also helps to explain why it was "not a very unfrequent [sic] thing in Chaucer for a line to contain a single fact bilingually repeated,"[12] and often makes the English language seem to be a "*walking phrase book* or dictionary"[13] useful in studying other languages. It is no wonder that Earle argued, "This equivalent coupling of words, one [word] English and [the other] one French, is no mere accidental or rhetorical exuberance. It sprang first out of the mutual necessity felt by two races of people and two classes of society to make themselves intelligible to one another."[14]

The widespread existence of twoblets in English is probably due, though, to more than historical circumstances. There had been a widespread existence of this "apparently needless" doubling in English even *before* the Norman invasion in 1066. The duplication recalls those languages where the perfect tense is formed by reduplication of the present, as in the case of the Semitic *rabab*.[15] A relevant example would involve how "the third conjugation [in Ancient Greek] . . . is characterized by the reduplication of the first letter of the verb with a short vowel."[16] Even the rhyme of *talk* with *walk*, insofar as it signals their common membership in the group of English words called the "-alk" words, moves analysis away from history and toward older and sometimes relatively "hidden" grammar and syntax.[17]

The quality of "hiddenness" bears comparison with many reduplicatives with a simply lexical base: the verbal pair *memento* and *memory*, the conjunctions of *mur* and *mur* to form *murmur* and of *bar* and *bar* to form *barbarian*,[18] and such complex terms as *sist* and *exist, nyam-nyam* (becoming *nyam* and *yam*), *gain, go, hullabaloo,* and *piggy back* (picky pack).

Considering such syntactic analysis, one might wonder whether Englishmen have suffered from a sort of redundancy or internalized stutter. Such a stutter would suggest the sort of linguistic pathology that explains the brilliance of Humphrey Chimpden Earwicker's remarkable stutter as the Anglophone Irishman James Joyce presents him in his multilinguistically crabbed *Finnegans Wake* (1939). That would also explain Shakespeare's extraordinary success with the walking pentameter and the talking pun.

The thesis of this book, and the widespread use of terms linguistically similar to the "ablaut"[19] reduplicative *walkie talkie*—there are hundreds of examples,[20] of both differentiated and of nondifferentiated ablaut duplication[21]—suggest a noteworthy conditional situation. If *talk* somehow means "the same" as *walk*—and that has been one thesis of the present book—it is not the way that *law* (in the twoblet *law and order*) means *order* or that *same* (in *same same*) means *same*,[22] albeit that the similarity in ways gives some familiarity and credibility to the mechanisms of meaning.

(Here we may have a "solution" to a celebrated problem in the meaning of *same-same* in global English. "One of the most commonly used expressions [in Anglophone Southeast Asia] is *same same*. Its meaning is nearly identical to the more standard English word [same] said only once. . . . Who knows where this strange habit of repeating *same* two times came from?")[23]

Moreover, if *talk* somehow means "the same" as *walk*, then rhyme between *talk* and *walk* differs from identical sound—both where the rhyming words are the same, as for *same* and *same* (in *same same*) and *tic* and *tic* (in *tic tic*),[24] and where the rhyming words are different or ablaut, as for *tic* and *toc* (in *tic toc*). Such words (*tic tic* and *tic toc*) are often set aside, by presumably serious thinkers and linguists, as "mere baby talk";[25] the ongoing productive formation of such terms in the already creolized *talkee-talkee* English language, some scholars say, ended in the eighteenth century.[26]

Walkie-talkie's duplication involves less word repetition (although, as we shall see, there is some of that) than rhyme. Relevant are such terms as the Christian *hocus pocus*[27] ("*Hoc est corpus meum*" [Here is my body]) and the Hebrew אברא כדברא—Aramaic, *avra kedavra* [I will create as I speak][28]—as if talking and doing were the same. The great philologist Friedrich Max Müller did his dissertation work in the relation between rhyme and ablaut reduplication,[29] and provides the scholarly enthusiasm that modern philology often lacks.

The phrase *Talk the Walk & Walk the Talk* is, like the phrases *tit for tat and tint for tant*, exemplifies not only ablaut reduplication but also epanalepsis. Shakespeare's phrase "Blood will have blood," like the Bible's "Eye for an eye," exemplifies the nonablaut sort. This term, *epanalepsis*, Philips, writing in 1678, defines as "a Rhetorical figure wherein a sentence begins and ends with the same word [or phrase]; as for [']Severe to his servants, to his children severe[']."[30] The title of the present book is epanaleptic: it begins and ends with [nearly] the same word, *Talk*. (Since the title is invertible—that is, *Talking the Walk & Walking the Talk* as *Walking the Talk & Talking the Walk*—*talk* (beginning and ending) could as easily be *walk* (ending and beginning).

This form of uncaesaric[31] invertibility follows the breathless English-language formula of dynastic continuity that provides Shakespeare's regal, ghostly *Hamlet* with its opening passwords: "[The King is Dead] Long Live the King."[32] According to one school, there should be no breathing stop—hence also no breathing, pause, or even comma—between the two parts of the formula. That rule follows both because human breath cannot kill a king (*"The breath of worldly men cannot depose / The deputy elected by the Lord"*)[33] and because the dead king's successor is already the king.[34] The logographic element of the ligature *&* that separates the two parts of this book's title (the phrases *Talking the Walk* and *Walking the Talk*) is a union of two letters (*e* and *t*) that already expresses the invertibility of the title whose center that it occupies.

Inversion as such is the meaning of *epanados* in English.[35] Insofar as one part of the title of this book, *Walk the Talk*, reduplicates the other, *Talk the Walk*, the title taken as a whole is not only epanaleptic, as we have just considered, but also ablaut-reduplicative. Epanalepsis means, literally, "a taking back" (*lambanein*, a root of *epanalepsis*) as if by way of echo.[36] Epanalepsis with absolute reduplication—*eye for eye*, say, or *tat for tat*[37]—suggests an impossible condition in the political economy.

That is one other reason why so many differentiated reduplicates are lumped together as a language fit only for children, or for little ones, because the duplicates seem to belittle speech itself, which adults need, for various reasons, so seriously to consider.[38] In infancy too there is humor.

TALKING THE WALK & WALKING THE TALK

Although he has no gilded medals upon his bosom, Howard Herring of the North American Watch Company, walks the walk, and talks the talk, of a hero today.

—*MANSFIELD NEWS* (Ohio, 1921)[39]

Each of the two sentences, *Talk the walk* and *Walk the walk*, that name this book, takes one of the several "-alk" words in the English language[40] and uses it, first as a verb, and then as a noun. The two sentences are often collocated (placed side by side) or contrasted with (stood with or against) each other.[41] How come? Is it mainly because they happen to rhyme with each other? Alternatively, is it *also* because there is a reasonable or an actual relationship—neurological, or metrical, or logical—between talking and walking?

Let us approach this question by asking what each sentence means—separately from the other, in their simpler formulation, as *Talk the talk* and *Walk the walk*.

Consider first *Talk the talk*. This sentence can have two polar opposite meanings. (1) The first meaning suggests duplicity, as if the first term, *talk*, were not the same as the second, *talk*. To *talk the talk* means "to speak convincingly or effectively, or in a manner consistent with the image one projects or the values one advocates, usually with the implication that such speech is *mere* rhetoric or posturing without substance."[42] That is to say, one talks, but one does not really mean what one says. (The question, Must one mean what one says?, is left in abeyance.) (2) The second meaning suggests genuineness. In this case, "talk the talk" means "to speak, esp. creatively or effectively, in a manner associated with or considered distinctive of African-Americans, such as joning, jiving, etc." J. A. Walker thus writes in his *Harangue* (1969), "You don't even know how to talk that talk. You're so goddam un-Negro you make me sick."[43]

How can one know when a given person is talking the talk in the first sense (dishonesty) or in the second sense (honesty)? Sometimes one can tell by the dialect.[44] More often, one can tell by whether the way that a person talks matches up or down to the way that he walks. Thus the *OED* says, "Walk the walk means 'behave in a manner consistent with the image one projects or the values one advocates . . . ' " The editors of the *OED* go on. They add that, in the case of "walk the walk," the purpose is " . . . to back up rhetoric with action." "Money talks, bullshit walks," says Fran Drescher ("Bobbi") in Rob Reiner's faux-documentary rock-movie *This Is Spinal Tap* (1984).

"Talk the talk" in its first meaning (1) can have a negative connotation—"usually with the implication that such speech is mere rhetoric or posturing without substance." "Walk the walk" implies positive genuineness. So "Walking the walk" is a test for genuine talk (2). There is a relevant example in *POW* [Prisoner of war] magazine (2002), "After taking a real beating from McMahon during the Street Fight, 'The Dirtiest Player in the Game' proved that he could still walk the walk as he eventually defeated McMahon with his trusty figure-four leglock."[45] There is also the statement in *Rolling Stone* magazine (1991) that "Rob Tyner, more than anyone, walked the walk and talked the talk."[46] What does this mean?[47] Mosher points out that "the African-American notion of genuineness is brought to bear on singing and dancing, talking and walking.[48]

Talking, which is merely ideal, is oftentimes preliminary to walking, which is pleasantly real. So, we read in the *New York Times* (1972): "I've talked that talk, and now I'm ready to walk that walk."[49] In such cases, walking is what really "counts." Like "good works" in the Protestant Christian tradition, walking even counts for getting us to heaven. "It is not talking but walking that will bring us to heaven," wrote Matthew Henry in his early eighteenth-century *Concise Commentary on the Bible*. If talk is theory, then walk is practice. Walking, again, is what seems to count.[50] Van Morrison sings, "Walk that walk, / Talk that talk";[51] McCoy Tyner sings, "Walk Spirit, Talk Spirit."[52] In their movie title song for the movie *You Gotta Walk It Like You Talk It* (1970), which stars Richard Pryor and Robert Downey Jr., songwriters Donald Fagen and Walter Becker propose much the same thesis. (The soundtrack has the song, "Ain't no man can tell you / what's right or wrong for you / 'cause you got to know what you need to know / to know what you got to do.")[53]

Sometimes, in American popular music, walking is all that's left to do. In the later part of his career, the songwriter Bob Dylan wrote, "Ain't Walkin', Just Talkin'" (2006):

> Ain't talkin', just walkin'
> Carrying a dead man's shield
> Heart burnin', still yearnin'
> Walkin' with a toothache in my heel.[54]

Bob Dylan's pained narrator, whose disability is at once oral and pedal, is, in part, the old, crippled hero of Sophocles's tragedy *Oedipus at Colonus*: punning Oedipus, whose ankles or heels were driven through according to the command of his parent, so that he can hardly walk at all. He "walk[s] through the cities of the plague" and, as Dylan reports it, the protagonist commands, "Hand me my walkin' cane."[55] His talking is marred by doomed slippages of meaning and sound.

THE FINISH LINE

That strain again! it had a dying fall
—SHAKESPEARE, *Twelfth Night*

In the movie *Let's Make Love* (1960), Marilyn Monroe plays the most beautiful woman in the world just as Milton Berle plays the funniest man in the world and Yves Montand plays the richest. She both walks and talks the part. She moves breathlessly and talks sashayingly all the while.

Rafael Campo, a poet and medical doctor at Harvard University, says, "While I do certainly hear the rhythms of the body's heartbeat or breathing in iambic poetry, or of walking in syllabic verse, I have to be cautious about what might be understood too reductively in this regard."[56] Balzac asserts, in his *Pathology of Social Life* (1839) that "the voice, the respiration, and the . . . walk, are identical."[57] If you're gonna *talk the talk*, then you gotta *walk the walk*. It's not so much, "If it talks like a duck and walks like a duck then it's a duck," as the saying goes. ("If it waddles like a duck and quacks like a duck, then it is a duck . . . in my book.")[58] It's more that, as the saying goes, if it talks like a duck, it also walks like a duck—because talking and walking, deep down, are the same. An anatine quack becomes a cycnean flight.[59] (See Figure 9.1.)

I am not being—I am trying not to be—[merely] metaphorical or circumlocutory about walking and talking or about stumbling and stuttering. On the one hand, many recently trendy philosophers do claim, rather metaphorically, that real philosophy is a stuttering or a walking. These thinkers would include Friedrich Nietzsche, Susan Sontag, Gilles Deleuze, Charles Péguy, and Paul de Man—to name a few. Their essentially "literary" views are, in the present context, often distractions from the puzzle at hand as well as fascinating

Figure 9.1. Still photograph. Walt Disney's animated short, *The Ugly Duckling* (dir. Jack Cutting, 1939). Number 75 in Disney's *Silly Symphony Series* of 75 shorts. Based on Hans Christian Andersen's "Den grimme ælling" (The ugly duckling, 1843).

indications of it. When Walter Benjamin focuses on the *flâneur*, in his review of Franz Hessel's work about walking (*spazieren*) (1929) and in his "Paris Arcades Project,"[60] he both contributes to the study of urban modernity and distracts attention away from the focus on talking as walking. In his chapter "Walking in the City" in *The Practice of Everyday Life* (1984), Michel de Certeau describes walking as "a space of enunciation,"[61] remarking that the "long poem of walking"[62] carries a personalized politics mobilizing resistant meanings beneath the city's smooth surface.[63]

Marcel Mauss, in his "Techniques of the Body" (1935),[64] focuses on how the gait of Frenchman changed after the widespread introduction of American cinema to Parisian audiences, and likewise shifts attention away from the likeness of walking and talking. The myriad anthropologists of walking who follow in his wake critique the Western elevation of the upright style of walking. They argue that there is no natural or universal style of walking[65] and emphasize how gaits differ from culture to culture but do not ally that with how speaking differs likewise not only from culture to culture but also from language to language to language.

In much the same way, the sociologist Erving Goffman, focusing in his *Relations in Public* (1971) on the visual aspects of a pedestrian trying to avoid obstacles, neglects the rhythm of walking.[66]

There are those who claim that philosophy is a way of life that amounts to such "exercises" as physical "bodily walking" and spiritual "inward orientation": *Innenwendung*. That is how Pierre Hadot, following Paul Rabbow, sometimes likes to put it. The theme has common roots in the nineteenth century. The polio sufferer and novelist Sir Walter Scott, who often wrote on horseback, thus refers to his "paralytic custom of stuttering with my pen." The stutterer Henry James likewise allies his English-style of writing with his stammering in the English language and his relative fluency in French. What obtains for limping and stuttering carries over into dancing and singing.

Finally the relationship between walking and talking may be less critical for students of metaphysical philosophy than for science-minded students of prosody, linguistics, handwriting, and especially neurology, who have often taken their terms from classical rhetoric as items for further investigation, as for *palilalia*. "Just as when we are children," writes one of the medical authors who attribute their work to Aristotle, "we always have less control over hand and feet and at a still younger age cannot walk at all, so the young cannot control their tongue."[67] Neurologists, in fact, already often investigate "dual tasking deficits" in diseases like ALS and Alzheimer's,[68] as well as in strokes and regular aging.[69] Journals like *Annals of Neurology* are replete with such articles and letters as "'Stops Walking When Talking' Does Not Predict Falls in Parkinson's Disease."[70] Others write on the "Effect of a Combined Walking and Conversation Intervention on Functional Mobility"[71] and "Walking While Talking: Effect of Task Prioritization in the Elderly."[72] Various biology-based studies similarly discuss how to disassociate walking from talking.[73] Michael Barilan reminds us, "Alas, whereas one can walk 'brainless' (relying on the spinal cord only), one must have a functioning higher-brain in order to talk."[74] Stutterers, I know, are often told by therapists and neurologists that their thoughts outrun their tongues, so that they should "slow down." "My poor Bianca," says Matilda to her servant in Walpole's *Hamlet*-inspired Gothic novel *The Castle of Otranto*

(1765), "How fast your thoughts amble!"[75] Thomas Dekker writes in *The Guls Horne-Book* (1609), "It will add much to your fame to let your tongue walke faster than your teeth."[76]

Post-nineteenth-century neurology often comes down to working out issues of walking and talking that were first introduced as questions in rhetoric. Scientists are still seeking to unpack the original insights of the prosodists and rhetoricians. *Logopedia*, etymologically speaking, means "language-foot,"[77] in much the same way that *logopædia* might mean "education in speaking."

That's no ending, however.

A WALKING SOLUTION

Ineptum est hoc Sophisma 1. Quia solvitur ambulando; quod fecit Diogenes.

—HENRY ALDRICH, *Rudiments of the Art of Logic*[78]

The rule for speakers, that one should "THINK ON YOUR FEET"—"react to events or arguments quickly and effectively"[79]—suggests that one ought not to use a written or memorized text. One should be or appear to be extemporaneous in much the way that a stand-up comedian is or appears to be. The audience adores the extemporaneous song and dance man who talks with his feet, southern dance style,[80] or makes jokes, like Milton Berle, the funniest man in the world.

Scientists may not like the rule. The geologist Charles Lyell thus complains to Charles Darwin (1838) that "[England] is a country where . . . a most exaggerated importance is attached to the faculty of thinking on your legs."[81] Serious political thinkers too have their qualms. Thomas Jefferson, some say, "had but small power of thinking on his feet."[82] Jefferson was a great walker, but unlike many of the Rousseauist ambulators we have considered in *Talking the Walk & Walking the Talk*, Jefferson sought to separate walking entirely from talking and thinking. He writes to Peter Carr (1785), "You should not permit yourself even to think while you walk."[83] But like it or not, song and dance are powerfully attractive.

Artworks, we have seen, increase ability to think on our feet. When it comes to architecture, furthermore, there is the environmentally scaled steel sculpture that Richard Serra constructed in the 1990s.[84] While Serra's smaller and earlier works, mostly paintings, already had "walking" titles—like *Labyrinth* (1960) and *[Hyena] Stomp* (1962). His later work, though, already has for its dictum "thinking on your feet"—curiously translated into German as *Sehen ist Denken* (seeing is thinking).[85] The large Serra sculptures concern the space around the construction and require one to move about, thinking on one's feet.[86] "Painting before [Michelangelo's architectural fresco] *Last Judgment* [1536-41]," Stella writes in *Working Space* (1986), "was painting one could look at, or at least into; after the *Last Judgment* painting became something one could walk through."[87] It is as pedestrian that one reaches, if at all, the aesthetic end.

Solvitur ambulando (it is solved by walking), which the Oxford English Dictionary says is now an English-language phrase, suggests here how one might deal with logical conclusions or solutions that cannot be spoken of. One solves talking problems by walking, or by appealing to practical experience for the solution of a problem or for proof of a statement. At least for those who can walk, walking can presumably even trump talking.

The proof *solvitur ambulando* is a subject in the Oxford philosopher, architect, and composer Henry Aldrich's influential works on logic (quoted as the epigraph to this Postamble). Aldrich wrote such musical church standbys as "Hold Not Thy Tongue" (after Palestrina) and "Give Ear O Lord."[88] In philosophy, Aldrich's major work, based loosely on the medieval textbook by Peter of Spain,[89] was the *Artis logicae rudimenta*. This work was employed insistently by thousands of philosophy students at Oxford University and elsewhere for two hundred and fifty years, from the time of its earliest publications in the later seventeenth century until the mid-twentieth century.[90] Among these Oxford scholars who read Aldrich was the stutterer and philosopher Lewis Carroll.[91]

In the Rudimenta, *solvitur ambulando* is introduced as the response of Diogenes the Sinope (called Cynic) to the famous paradox of Zeno of Elea, "Achilles," purporting to show that motion, of the sort that stops Pyrrhus in Hamlet, is essentially impossible.[92] In a race between tortoise and Achilles, it does not matter who is faster because neither one can *ever* get to the finish line.

In his *Physics* (350 BC) Aristotle says that this paradox "amounts to this, that in a race the quickest runner can never overtake the slowest, since the pursuer must first reach the point whence the pursued started, so that the slower must always hold a lead."[93] One has always to traverse the first half of the previous distance covered and thus never gets to the end. According to Simplicius, who calls the story "Achilles and the Tortoise," Diogenes of Sinope, called the Cynic, when he overhead Zeno putting forth this vertiginously disturbing argument, stood up, and walked out of the room, thus proving, for practical purposes, that one can get somewhere.[94] *Solvitur ambulando*; "it is solved by walking."

In his lectures at Oxford University in the mid-nineteenth century, Henry Longueville Mansel—professor of moral and metaphysical philosophy—stressed this heels-over-head "walking solution." This solution wavers, as if in some Wonderland, between two poles: the evidence of "the senses" which shows that one *can* walk somewhere (Diogenes of Sinope); and the evidence of "reason" that shows that one *cannot* get anywhere (Zeno of Elea).[95]

Paradoxes of infinity like Zeno's require the sort of abstract response that "Achilles" has received during 2,500 years since his teacher, Parmenides, first proposed it.[96] Yet the paradox "still perplexes" the mathematician,[97] and what's more, it still provides grist for popular human concerns,[98] partly because the way in which the paradox is presented in, pace the mathematician, an ongoing part of its substance, or, put otherwise, partly because mathematics as such is not its only concern. What if the *way* that one presents the paradox, in terms of the "human faculty" of human and testudinal talking and walking, suggested a concern with an ongoing rhythm of never quite getting there, like to the mathematical puzzle and without which the mathematical puzzle will remain just that, puzzling?

Most all thinkers, including Hegel and Russell,[99] have set aside the rhetoric of the paradox as irrelevant to its significance. Consider, however, the cleverly wise reaction to the "Achilles" from Lewis Carroll, who was famously a student at Oxford in the mid-nineteenth century. The story of an Achilles who can't get anywhere walking was especially attractive to Carroll, a stutterer, who often could not get anywhere by talking and who, on that account, identified with animals that could talk, but only in a manner of speaking. In Zeno's "Achilles," the human hero Achilles's Homeric epithet was "swifted-footed" (*podarkés*),[100] which seems fair enough, but Achilles's weak-point, his Achilles heel, is likewise both Oedipal and pedal. What sets him up also brings him down,[101] as in the Player's Speech in Hamlet, where his voice is stilled and his hand is stayed. Carroll's philosophical work, "What the Tortoise Said to Achilles," published in the philosophical journal *Mind* (1895), thus reports the following conversation between Achilles and the tortoise about the right finish line.

> Achilles had overtaken the Tortoise, and had seated himself comfortably on its back. [¶] "So you've got to the end of our race-course?" said the Tortoise. "Even though it does consist of an infinite series of distances? I thought some wiseacre or other had proved that the thing couldn't be done?" [¶] "It can be done," said Achilles. "It has been done! Solvitur ambulando. [It is solved by walking.] You see the distances were constantly diminishing; and so—"[102]

The English-language phrase *solvitur ambulando* suggests that there will be no "absolute" empirical proof. F. W. Maitland (1906) writes about Leslie Stephen that he would have to proceed empirically: "*Solvitur ambulando*—the motto of the philosophic tramp or wandering walker—had also to be the motto of the editor."[103]

That is where we are now: tramps, we must tread lightly enough also to saunter. The em-dash stroke that we have used to mark a pause in motion or speech (like that indicated for the action of Achilles, or Pyrrhus, in the Player's Speech in *Hamlet*) is just like the long em-dash (——) with which Carroll's *Sylvie and Bruno* (1890) begins. A foot is missing there by way of a metrical pun.

Lewis Carroll's "talking proof," which talks of a *tortoise* walking, puns the word *tortoise* as *taught us*. Carroll thus demonstrates the stuttering "rhotacism," or difficulty in pronouncing the sound of the letter *rho*, or *r*, that afflicted the young Athenian Demosthenes. (Demosthenes taught himself how to become a fluent talker by *walking* along the seacoast and, at the same time, *talking* above the rut, or racket that the water and stones make together as the waves and the rocks grind against one another.[104])Teacher Carroll's Achilles, now riding the animal, learns from the "*taught us*" that he can never get to where he's going, or rather, to where he's not going. Lewis Carroll writes in *Mind*, "Achilles was still seated on the back of the much-enduring Tortoise, and was writing in his note-book, which appeared to be nearly full. The Tortoise was saying, Have you got that last step written down? Unless I've lost count, that makes a thousand and one. There are several millions more to come."

Is walking talking? In his accusation that the Guatemalan government of the 1950s was communist, Richard Patterson (US ambassador to Guatemala) applied what he calls a "duck test" of Wonderland. Here's how it goes:

> Suppose you see a bird walking around in a farm yard. This bird has no label that says "duck." But the bird certainly looks like a duck. Also, he goes to the pond and you notice that he swims like a duck. Then he opens his beak and quacks [, or talks,] like a duck. Well, by this time you have probably reached the conclusion that the bird is a duck, whether he's wearing a label or not.[105]

When it comes to the further understanding of walking and talking, no matter what some quack says, walking the talk amounts, almost any way, to talking the walk.

"Who dare say he's mad, whose words *march* in so good aray?"[106] It is daring to accuse someone of madness when his words march well because there is, behind it all, something like a powerful army. The rhythm of words, no matter their semantic content, comes to trump their meaning, if any. Elias Canetti, in his book on the rise of Nazism, *Crowds and Power*, allies the rhythm of animal herds, which so affected early humankind, with that of the political stampede—*démarche*—in humankind's later political manifestations.[107]

The quick jump, from the realm of prosodic rhythm to that of political danger, serves to recall how much we have yet to accomplish, in the intellectual and scientific realms, since the time that Balzac proposed: How it matters that walking and talking, taken together, are formative parts of the "philosophical, psychological, and political systems which preoccupy the world."[108]

If what distinguishes man from other creatures is how "the human gait is a continuously arrested falling," as Straus puts it,[109] then the walker, like the talker, needs to remember, as does the dying Young Hamlet, that "this feel sergeant, death, / Is strict in his arrest" (H, 5.2.3990). The "dying fall"—what George Saintsbury, remembering the rhythms at the beginning of *Twelfth Night*, calls the "falling cadence" in the prosody of language (talking)[110]—is the vertiginous experience in the rhythm of ambulation (walking) that the Prussian Immanuel Kant most dreaded. The concomitant role of gravity in human walking was discussed by the Weber brothers; they argued that "during ambulation the leg that is not contacting the ground mirrors the motion of a pendulum."[111] In *The Roots of Mankind* (1970), John Napier figures concomitantly, "Human walking is a risky business. Without split-second timing man would fall flat on his face; in fact with each step he takes, he teeters on the edge of catastrophe."[112] There are few better descriptions of stuttering.

The fall, in talking as in walking, both makes for human being and ends that being. In the vertigo of walking and talking, so much remains to be done at the finish line that we require already a fresh start. I recall at last Maurice Merleau-Ponty's inaugural lecture, "In Praise of Philosophy" (1953), delivered at the Collège de France in Paris. (At the time, I was a seven-year-old child in Montreal, unable to walk and talk well.) Known for his insistence on somatic silences, Merleau-Ponty described philosophy as limping: "*Il est inutile de contester que la philosophie boite* [it is useless to contest that philosophy limps]."[113] He thus linked thinking with a little ham and praised philosophy as a claudicant: "The limping [*claudication*] of philosophy is its virtue."[114]

NOTES

1. STARTING OUT: PROLOGUE AND PREAMBLE

1. MV 1.3.35–39.
2. *The Works of Ralph Waldo Emerson in Five Volumes* (Bohn's Library), vol. 2, ed. George Sampson (London: George Bell & Sons, 1906), 286. "Le regard, la voix, la respiration, la démarche sont identiques" (Honoré de Balzac, *Théorie de la démarche* [Paris: L'Échoppe, 1992], 123). Balzac's *Théorie* is an essay that first appeared in the journal *L'Europe littéraire* (1833); it was later incorporated as a "chapter" in his *Pathologie de la vie sociale* (Pathology of social life, 1839), which is part of the *Études analytiques* in his *Comédie humaine* (in Balzac, *Oeuvres complètes*, vol. 19 [Paris: Les Bibliophiles de l'Original, 1968]).
3. The English word *pedal*, from the Latin *ped*, *pes* (foot), means "of or relating to a foot or feet" (OED, sv "Pedal," adj.). Cf. *orthopaedics*, which presumably aims at getting the feet right.
4. References not included in the notes below may be found in the indices and notes in my books *Polio and Its Aftermath: The Paralysis of Culture* (2005) and *Stutter* (2006), both published by Harvard University Press.
5. Friedrich Wilhelm Nietzsche, *Twilight of the Idols* (1895), "Maxims and Arrows," no. 34, in *The Portable Nietzsche*, trans. Walter Kaufmann (New York: Viking Press, 1954). Nietzsche here confronts Flaubert's thought that "one cannot think and write except when seated."
6. Gospel According to Saint John 1:1. Marvin Harris, *Our Kind: Who We Are, Where We Came From, Where We Are Going* (New York: Harper & Row, 1989).
7. In his essay "Walking" (published posthumously 1862), Thoreau offers several etymologies of *saunter*. One current suggestion is that the word is "a. AF. *sauntrer* (= *s'auntrer*), to venture oneself, is unlikely (apart from difficulties of meaning) on the ground that the AF. word, of which only one instance has been found . . . is app[arently] an adoption of ME. *auntre* to adventure *n*., and possibly a mere nonce-word."
8. On Hegel's stutter, see Terry Pinkard, *Hegel: A Biography* (New York: Cambridge University Press, 2000), esp. 5.

9. Rebecca Solnit, *Wanderlust: A History of Walking* (New York: Viking, 2000).

10. Gretel Ehrlich, *Islands, the Universe, Home* (New York: Viking, 1991), 28: "Walking is almost an ambulation of mind." See also Gretel Ehrlich, "River History," in *Montana Spaces: Essays and Photographs in Celebration of Montana*, ed. William Kittredge and John Smart (New York: Nick Lyons Books, 1988), 70: "Walking is also an ambulation of mind."

11. Against the view that man is a featherless biped, see below.

12. Joseph A. Amato, *On Foot: A History of Walking* (New York: New York University Press, 2004), see "In the beginning was the foot," 19–26.

13. Gospel According to Saint Mark 8:24: "ως δενδρα ορω ϖεριϖατουντας."

14. In the Cartesian *Discourse* (1637), part 4. *Discours de la method*. See *The Philosophical Writings of Descartes*, vol. 1, ed. and trans. J. Cottingham, R. Stoothoff, D. Murdoch, and A. Kenny (Cambridge: Cambridge University Press, 1984–91).

15. In the Cartesian *Principles* (1644), part 1, paragraph 7.

16. *OED*, sv "Amble," v. 1. On equine movement, see below.

17. *OED*, sv "Amble," v. 2. On wheelchair-like movement, see below.

18. *OED*, sv "Amble," v. 3. On humanoid cartoon-character movement, see below.

19. See George MacDonald Ross, "Hobbes and Descartes on the Relation between Language and Consciousness," *SYNTHESE* 75.2 (1988): 217–29; and Lisa T. Sarasohn, "Motion and Morality: Pierre Gassendi, Thomas Hobbes, and the Mechanical World-View," *Journal of the History of Ideas* 46.3 (1985): 363.

20. For Walpole, see below.

21. Trans. C. J. M. Hubback, 50–51.

22. See Fliess, *Der Ablauf Des Lebens: Grundlegung zur Exacten Biologie* (Leipzig: F. Deuticke, 1906); Fliess, *Vom Leben und Vom Tod: Biologishe Vortage* (Jena: Diederichs, 1916); Fliess, *Das Jahr im Lebendigen* (Jena: Diederichs, 1924); and Fliess, *Zur Periodenlehre* (Jena: Diederichs, 1925), as well as his associate Hans Schlieper's *Der Rhythmus im Leberedigen* (Jena: Diederichs, 1909). On Freud, Fliess, and both slips of the tongue and trips of the leg, see below.

23. Le nombre d'or. Rites et rythmes pythagoriciens dans le development de la civilisation occidentale, pref. Paul Valéry (1931).

24. Paris: Boivin & Cie.

25. S.l.: s.n., 1905.

26. Bonn: Bouvier, 2000.

27. Trans. Stuart Elden and Gerald Moore, introd. Stuart Elden (London: Continuum, 2004).

28. Munich: Liliom.

29. Paris: Gallimard.

30. Paris: Prairies ordinaries.

31. Robert Plumer Ward, *Tremaine, or, The Man of Refinement* (London: n.p., 1825), 2:106.

32. "Introduction to Metrics," in *The Theory of Verse* [1925], trans. C. F. Brown (Hague: Mouton, 1966), 12. On formalism and rhythm, see Boris Eichenbaum, "The Theory of the 'Formal Method,'" in *Russian Formalist Criticism: Four Essays*, ed. and trans. Lee T. Lemon and Marion J. Reis (Lincoln: University of Nebraska Press, 1965).

33. In *Problems in General Linguistics* (1966/1974).

34. Benveniste, *Problems in General Linguistics*, trans. Mary Elizabeth Meek (Coral Gables, FL: UMP, 1971), 285–86.

35. *OED*, sv "Rheology." See also Marc Shell, *Islandology* (Stanford: Stanford University Press, forthcoming).

36. Meschonnic, *Critique du rythme*, 216.

37. Paris: Verdier.

38. With Gérard Dessons. Paris: Dunod.

39. Paris: Verdier.

40. With Jean-Gilles Badaire. Paris: Jacques Brémond.

41. Meschonnic, *De monde en monde* (Cahiers d'Arfuyen, no. 178), (Paris: 2009).

42. Meschonnic, *Puisque je suis ce buisson* (2001), 45.

43. Gn 34:5.

44. Solomon Barrett, The Principles of Grammar: Being a compendious treatise on the languages, English, Latin, Greek, German, Spanish, and French; founded on the immutable principle of the relation which one word sustains to another, revised edition (1860), "Prosody," 1st page.

45. Peter Riley, *Noon Province et autres poèmes*, bilingual edition, trans. Lorand Gaspar, Sarah Clair, and Claire Malroux (Saint-Pierre-la-Vielle: Atlier La Feugraie, 1996), 56. Riley writes, "The English text of *Noon Province* here does not correspond exactly to the other English editions and was in some places modified to accommodate the demands of being translated into French."

46. http://www.baltimoregaylife.com/Features/122807.htm.

47. Dorothy Richardson Jones, *"King of Critics": George Saintsbury (1845–1933), Critic, Journalist, Historian, Professor* (Ann Arbor: University of Michigan Press, 1992), 244. See Saintsbury, *History of Prosody*, 2d ed., 2:106, 3:381.

48. Joost Daalder, "A Literary Reaction to 'A Phonetician's View of Verse Structure,'" *Language and Style: An International Journal* (preprint). Archived at Flinders University: dspace.flinders.edu.au.

49. One example here would be the first section of Amato's book, *On Foot*, a section that is called "Walking Is Talking" (1–19), but which never really makes any such argument.

50. The Velvet Underground's "Walk and Talk It" (c. 1969) is an outtake from 1970. In *Peel Slowly and See*, 5-disk box-set, disk 5, number 12.

51. Thus Thomas Wright writes, "The Saxons did not measure their verse by feet" (*Essays on Subjects Connected with the Literature, Popular Superstitions, and History of England in the Middle Ages* [London: J. R. Smith, 1846], I.i.14).

52. See Alfred Corn's Braille book, *The Poem's Heartbeat: A Manual of Prosody* (Brownsville, OR: Story Line Press, 2001), and on finger Braille typing, see below.

53. See Tim Ingold, "Culture on the Ground: The World Perceived Through the Feet," *Journal of Material Culture* 9.3 (2004): 315–40.

54. Barbara Weiden Boyd, *Vergil's "Aeneid": Selections from Books 1, 2, 4, 6, 10 and 12*, 2d ed. (Mundelein, IL: Bolchazy-Carducci Publishers, 2008), 314.

55. M. L. Gasparov, *A History of European Versification*, trans. G. S. Smith and Marina Tarlinskaja (Oxford: Clarendon Press, 1996).

56. *OED*, sv "Length," 4c.

57. *OED*, sv "Length," 8a.

58. The poet Gary Snyder writes in his collection of essays entitled *The Practice of the Wild* (San Francisco: North Point Press, 1990): "Walking is the great adventure, the first meditation, a practice of heartiness and soul primary to humankind. Walking is the exact balance between spirit and humility" (19). In his introduction to Snyder's "High Sierra journals," Tom Killian writes: " . . . walking sets the rhythm of our days . . . " (Snyder and Killian, *The High Sierra of California* [Berkeley, CA: Heyday Books, 2002], 26).

59. Mark Twain, *Sketches New & Old* [1871] (Hartford, CT, and Chicago: The American Publishing Company, 1875), 248.

60. In his *Traité de la poësie françoise* (Toulouse: Boude, 1697).

61. For a complementary view, see Nicolas Etienne Framery, *Avis aux poëtes lyriques, ou De la nécessité du rhythme et de la césure* (Paris: L'Imprimerie de la République, Brumaire, an IV [i.e., 1796]).

62. See Ada Laura Fonda Snell, *Pause: A Study of its Nature and its Rhythmical Function in Verse, Especially Blank Verse* (Ann Arbor, MI: Ann Arbor Press, 1918).

63. Conrad, *The Secret Agent* (London: Methuen, 1907), chap. 1.

64. *L'Art poétique* (1674), Canto 1, ll.105–6.

65. Clarence King, *Mountaineering in the Sierra Nevada* (London: Sampson Low, Marston, Low, and Searle, 1872), 208.

66. On the comparative aspect from language to language, see Andreas Dufter, "Remarks on Rhythmic Typologies and Comparative Metrics," *Cologne Workshop on Prosody*, 2–3 July 2010.

67. *OED*, sv "Caesura," n 1a.

68. George Puttenham, *The Arte of English Poesie* (1589), ii.iv.62.

69. Consider, however, the recognition early on: "There are laws of cæsuric effect in blank verse" (Eugene Lee Hamilton, "Apollo and Marsyas, and Other Poems," *Athenæum* no. 2981 [1884]: 765).

70. Including Hölderlin's *Anmerkungen* on *Antigone* and on *Oedipus*.

71. Michael Spitzer, *Music as Philosophy: Adorno and Beethoven's Late Style* (Bloomington: Indiana University Press, 2006), esp. "Caesura of the Classical Style," 226, 245.

72. Dirk Cysarz, Dietrich von Bonin, Helmut Lackner, Peter Heusser, Maximilian Moser, and Henrik Bettermann, "Oscillations of Heart Rate and Respiration Synchronize During Poetry Recitation," *American Journal of Physiology* (5 April 2004).

73. Joachim Latacz, *Troja und Homer* (Berlin: Koehler und Amelang, 2001).

74. Barbara Denjean and Dietrich von Bonin, *Therapeutische Sprachgestaltung* (Stuttgart: Urachhaus, 2000).
75. *OED*, sv "Eurythmy," 2 [Pathology].
76. See Edmund Munk, *Metres Greeks and Romans*, trans. Charles Beck and Cornelius Conway Felton (Boston: n.p., 1844), 1.
77. Rudolf Steiner and Ita Wegman, *Grundlegendes für eine Erweiterung der Heilkunst nach geisteswissenschaftlichen Erkenntnissen* (Dornach, Switzerland: Philosophisch-anthroposophischer Verlag am Goetheanum, 1925), 86; and Arthur Pearce Shepherd, *Scientist of the Invisible: An Introduction to the Life and Work of Rudolf Steiner* (Edinburgh: Floris, 1983).
78. Emile Jaques-Dalcroze, *Rhythm, Music, and Education*, trans. Harold Frederick Rubinstein (London: Chatto & Windus, 1921), 196.
79. Mauro, "My Iron Lung et Cetera," quoted in Shell, *Polio and Its Aftermath*, 35.
80. O'Brien, "The Man in the Iron Lung," in *The Man in the Iron Lung* (Berkeley, CA: Lemonade Factory, 1997), 1; quoted in Shell, *Polio and Its Aftermath*, 108. See also Jessica Yu's documentary movie *Breathing Lessons: The Life and Work of Mark O'Brien* (1996).
81. AC 5.281-3 refers to Plutarch even as it glosses over what it might mean to write poetry for recitation by mermaids.
82. *OED*, sv "Walk," v^1.
83. Coleridge, *Friendship's Offering* (1834).
84. Coleridge, *Poetical Works*, ed. J. C. C. Mays (Princeton, NJ: Princeton University Press, 2001), vol. 1, pt. 2, no. 395.
85. So goes the story according to the comparative musicologist Jean-Laurent Le Cerf de La Viéville, *Comparison de la musique italienne et de la musique française*, 2 pts. (Brussels: n.p., 1704-5), pt. 2, "Life of Lully."
86. In drama, there is the gate-keeping Porter's often-repeated "Knock, knock, knock!" in *Macbeth*. The words are rhythmically percussive and semantically meaningful even as they imitate the actual "knocking within"; it is not only because the porter in *Macbeth* wants a "tip" that Shakespeare, greatest master of the English-language's easy pentameter, has the Gatekeeper say, "I pray you, remember the porter" (MB 2.2).
87. Private collection.
88. Ny Carlsberg Glyptotek (Denmark).
89. Paul Gauguin, Letter to Emile Schuffenecker (written from Point-Aven, Brittany, February 1888), in Victor Merles, ed., *Correspondence de Paul Gauguin* (Paris: 1984), letter 141, p. 172.
90. Letter from Vincent van Gogh to Theo van Gogh, sent from Saint-Rémy, 10 or 11 February 1890; in *The Letters of Vincent van Gogh to his Brother: 1872-1886*, memoir by Johanna van Gogh-Bonger (London: Constable & Co., 1927). Among thinkers who have written about Vincent van Gogh's interest in shoes are: Martin Heidegger, in *The Origin of the Work of Art* (1935); Meyer Schapiro, in *The Still Life as a Personal Object* (1968); and Jacques Derrida, in "Restitutions of the Truth in Pointing [*Pointure*]" (1978). In 2009, the Wallraf-Richartz Museum (Cologne, Germany) held an exhibition entitled "Vincent Van Gogh: Shoes."

91. Diodorus of Sicily (1st century BC), *Library of History* 4.64.4.

92. See Lévi-Strauss, "The Structural Study of Myth" (*The Journals of American Folklore* 68.270 = *Myth: A Symposium* [October–December 1955]: 428–44); see, in particular, the discussion of the various "impediments" of three members of the same family: Labdacos (Laius's father) is lame, left-sided Laius (Oedipus's father) is left-sided, and Oedipus is swollen-footed. See also Lévi-Strauss's observation that in myths generally, men "born from the earth" (like Cadmus) are, at first, lame (ibid., 433).

93. Some have it that the phrase "foot in mouth" comes from a pun on "hoof and mouth disease" and the colloquial saying "put one's foot in one's mouth." See J. E. Lighter, *Random House Historical Dictionary of American Slang (A-G)*.

94. Glasgow: Maclehose, Jackson and Co., 1923, 92.

95. Susan Stewart, *Poetry and the Fate of the Senses* (Chicago: University of Chicago Press, 2002), 212–13.

96. For more on this rhyme, see Martha Warren Beckwith, "Signs and Superstitions Collected from American College Girls," *The Journal of American Folklore* 36.139 (Jan.–Mar. 1923): 1–15.

97. Terry Spencer Hesser, *Kissing Doorknobs*, afterword A. J. Allen (New York: Delacorte Press, 1998).

98. For the meaning of this term, see p. 20n.

99. Stewart, *Beauty and the Fate of the Senses*, 213.

100. William Hazlitt, "My First Acquaintance with Poets," in *Selected Writings*, Oxford's World Classics, ed. John Cook (Oxford: Oxford University Press, 1998), 255.

101. Schlegel, *Werke* VI, "Etwas über William Shakespere," ed. Eduard Böcking (Leipzig: Weidmann'sche Buchhandlung, 1846–47), 7:55; cited by Francis Barton Gummere, *The Beginnings of Poetry* (New York: The Macmillian Company, 1901), 41.

102. http://poeticinvention.blogspot.com/2007/02/talking-with-barry-schwabsky.html.

103. Patrick Dorn, *Teaching Shakespeare in School: Some Pointers on How to Teach Shakespeare to Drama Students*. An excerpt from newsletter; http://playsandmusicalsnewsletter.pioneerdrama.com/public/blog/105415.

104. Gill Stoker, "Oxford University Shakespeare Summer School: A Tutor's View"; http://www.britishtheatreguide.info/otherresources/shakespeare/oushakespeare.htm.

105. Marcel Mauss, "Techniques of the Body (1935)," in *Techniques, Technology and Civilisation*, ed. Nathan Schlanger (New York: Durkheim, 2006).

106. OED, sv "Pedal," n^1, 3.

107. OED, OED, sv "Pedal," n^1, 6. So Herman Melville writes in *Mardi, and A Voyage Thither* (London: Richard Bentley, 1849), II.xliv.204: "To cool his heated pedals, he established . . . stopping-places."

108. "Walking" was Dupree's only major R&B hit: a recording he made for King Records with Teddy McRae (vox, foot tapping), Joe Williams (b) and

George DeHeart (d); recorded in Cincinnati on 29 May 1955 and released as King 4812 (as "Jack Dupree and Mr. Bear"); on *R&B Hits of 1955.*

109. Was recorded in Chicago on 20 April 1931. In *You're Driving Me Crazy.*

110. "I's up this mornin' / ah, blues walkin' like a man / I's up this mornin' / ah, blues walkin' like a man / Worried blues give me your right hand." Recorded in San Antonio on 27 November 1936; in *Complete Recordings.* Robert Johnson, *Preachin' Blues.* Consider here Eric Clapton's version of Johnson's "Walkin' Blues" in *Unplugged* (1992).

111. In the recorded version of "Walk Around," which I have heard, the lead singer, R. H. Harris, dodges ahead of his partners, then falls behind, soars beyond them, then comes back to bolster them. In *Swing Time Gospel, Vol. 1: "The A Cappella Groups,"* CD, Night Train, 2004 (releases from the 1940s and 1950s).

112. Recorded February 1950 and released as Chess 1426. This piece was first recorded by Son House in 1930.

113. Recorded 10 October 1956 and released in January 1957 as Old Town 1034, c/w "Please Kiss This Letter"; in *Walking Along with the Solitaires* (doo-wop group).

114. Recorded in Los Angeles on 22 July 1957 in *Benny Carter: Jazz Giant.*

115. Released as Imperial 5676 in *Fats Domino Jukebox: 20 Greatest Hits.*

116. Recorded in Hollywood in September 1964, released as Philles 123 in *The Best of The Ronettes.*

117. Little Milton's "Walking the Back Streets and Crying," from 1972. Released as Stax 0124 in *Stax Profiles: Little Milton.*

118. Consider Patsy Cline's *Walking After Midnight*, Van McCoy's *Night Walk*, and Sleepy John Estes's *Runnin' Around.*

119. *De motu animalium* (Rome: A. Bernabo, 1680).

120. *De motu animalium*, published posthumously. See too his *De motionibus naturalibus a gravitate pendentibus* (Bologna: n.p., 1670)

121. *Der Gang des Menschen: Versuche am unbelasteten und belasteten Menschen* (Leipzig: S. Hirzel, 1895) Eng. trans. (1985) P. J. G. Maquet and R. Furlong.

122. A major source here, including for the title: Joseph Tate, "Numme Feete: Meter in Early Modern England," *Early Modern Literary Studies* 7.1/ special issue 8 (May 2001): 3.1–31; see http://purl.oclc.org/emls/07-1/tate-feet.htm.

123. Ovid, *Amores*, 40: The speaker mourns an unusual theft: "Arma graui numero uiolentaque bella parabam / edere, materia conueniente modis. / par erat inferior uersus: risisse Cupido / dicitur atque unum surripuisse pedem" [I was preparing to bear arms in solemn numbers, with subject-matter appropriate to the measure. The subsequent line was well-matched: Cupid is said to have laughed and stolen one foot.] ¶ Hexameters (verses with six feet) are the epic meter (as in Homer and Vergil). By stealing a foot in the second line, Cupid has turned it into elegiac meter, used for

love poetry (as in Ovid's *Amores*). Ovid's speaker proceeds to reprimand Cupid for ignoring poetry's province as the reserve of the Muses. Cupid responds to the accusation with an arrow that quickly inflames the speaker's heart, who sullenly resigns: "sex mihi surgat opus numeris, in quinque residat; / ferrea cum uestris bella ualete modis" [Let my work march in six numbers, and fall in five; farewell iron wars with your measures] (Ovid 42). ¶ [13] Marlowe's translation of these lines does not support my own, but neither is it terribly faithful to the original: "Let my verse be six, my last five feet; Farewell stern war, for blunter poets meet" (ll.31–32). ¶ The verb *surgat* (from *surgo*, *surgere*) denotes "to rise, to stand up," but also has the connotation "to march" in war-like contexts, as in the mock military epic tone of this poem. Given Ovid's proposed preparation to write heroic war poetry, this allows a translation to read "Let my work march in six numbers" instead of the less concrete "rise in six numbers" preferred by most translators.—¶—Other aspects of the topos—for example, the common notion, introduced by Ovid, that we are to think of one or another metric as associated with a genre—say hexameter with heroic epic—of a dropped foot as having been "stolen"—we leave aside for purposes of the present paper, albeit that they too play an ancillary role in discussing the matters, that go beyond metrics and extend to marching, that we are concerned with.)

124. In *Ancient Critical Essays in upon English Poets and Poësy*, ed. Joseph Haslewood (London: Robert Triphook, 1815), 2:201.

125. Ed. R. C. Alston (Menston, England: The Scolar Press Limited, 1972), a6.

126. Thomas Nashe, *Strange Newes* (1592), in *The Works of Thomas Nashe*, ed. Ronald B. McKerrow (London: Sidgwick and Jackson, 1910), 1:247–335. Here, p. 299.

127. Puttenham, *The Arte of English Poesie* [1589] (Menston, England: The Scolar Press Limited, 1968), 55–56.

128. Puttenham, *English Poesie*, 57.

129. Ibid., II.xiii.[xiv].(Arb = Edward Arber), 135.

130. James D. Hart, "Jazz Jargon," *American Speech* 7.4 (1932): 242.

131. *OED*, sv "Walkies."

132. Edmund Spenser, "To Master G.H." *Works* (1580), (Globe) App. ii. 709/1.

133. John Florio, *Queen Anna's New World of Words* (1611), Versaccij (1611).

134. Manuscript Bodleian Library (c. 1625), 30.13a.

135. David Dalrymple [Lord Hailes], *Ancient Scottish Poems* (Edinburgh: Printed by A. Murray and J. Cochran for John Balfour, 1770) 243 (Jam.). The alternate lines are composed of shreds of the breviary, mixed with what we call Dog-Latin . . . "

136. *Letters of Ford Madox Ford*, ed. Richard M. Ludwig (Princeton, NJ: Princeton University Press, 1965), 16 March 1938 (1965), 290: "He will at least write comprehensible dog-English."

137. New York Times Book Review (22 Jan. 1961), 6/4.

138. Puttenham, *English Poesie*, II. iv. (Arb.) 89.
139. Ward, *Tremaine, or, The Man of Refinement* (London: n.p., 1825), 2:106.
140. Peter Watt, "Introduction," *Peer Gynt*, trans. (Harmondsworth, England: Penguin, 1966), 17.
141. Stopford Augustus Brooke, *Tennyson, His Art and Relation to Modern Life* (London: Isbister and Company, 1894), 92.
142. See "Byron, George Gordon Noel, 6th Baron Byron," *Microsoft Encarta Online Encyclopedia 2007;* http://au.encarta.msn.com. The Italian stanza often has eleven syllables and had an iambic variant (*endecasillabo*); the English, iambic form differs somewhat.
143. "In terms of dance music, the merengue is the Dominican Republic's national style. A fast, galloping 2/4 rhythm, it is very different from the mellower Haitian meringue and from other 'merengues' on the Latin American continent" (Philip Sweeney, *Virgin Directory World Music* [New York: Henry Holt, 1992], 205).
144. Compare Franz Liszt's *Grand galop chromatique* (1838),; and Herman Koenig's "Post Horn Galop."
145. AYL 3.2.111–12.
146. Nashe, *Strange Newes*, 275.
147. H41 3.1.120–21.
148. H41 3.1.126.
149. AYL 3.1.127–31.
150. Edmund Spenser and Gabriel Harvey, *Correspondence 1579–80*, in *Elizabethan Critical Essays*, ed. and introd. G. Gregory Smith (London: Oxford University Press, 1967), 1:96.
151. Edmund Spenser and Gabriel Harvey, *Correspondence*, 99.
152. Dorothy Leigh Sayers, *Gaudy Night* (1935), xviii. 382.
153. Compare human beings, which are *plantigrade*, dogs, which are *digitigrade*, and hares, which are *plantigrade* when they walk and *digitigrade* when they run. See below.
154. For moving pictures of animal locomotion in this context, see http://bowlingsite.mcf.com/Movement/locoindex.html.
155. Sung on a BBC Broadcast on 11 June 1963 on the show called "Pop Goes The Beatles." CD: *The Beatles, The British Broadcasting Corporation, Live at the BBC*. "Young Blood" was written by Jerry Leiber, Mike Stoller, and Doc Pomus; performed by The Coasters around 1958.
156. OED, sv "Catalexis."
157. Puttenham, *English Poesie* (Arb.), 142.
158. Pliny the Elder declares in his *Natural History*, "The face of Hipponax was notoriously ugly." See also Douglas E. Gerber, *A Companion to the Greek Lyric Poets* (Leiden: Brill, 1997), 345.
159. Fragment 59.
160. Herondas, in Willis Barnstone, trans., and William E. McCulloh, intro., *Ancient Greek Lyrics* (Bloomington: Indiana University Press, 2010), 103.
161. Babrius, in his *Fables*, used this meter.

162. Karl Otfried Müller, *History of the Literature of Ancient Greece to the Period of Isocrates,* trans. George Cornwall Lewes (London: Robert Baldwin, 1847), 142.
163. Müller, *History,* 142.
164. *OED,* sv "Brachy."
165. Obadiah Walker, *Of Education, Especially of Young Gentlemen* (1673) (Oxford: Printed at the Theatre, 1677), xi.124.
166. Thomas Parnell, *The Poetical Works* (London: W. Pickering, 1833).
167. Edmund Spenser writes in his *Faerie Queene* (1590) of the limping Hag, "And euer as she went, her tongue did *walke* / In foule reproch, and termes of vile despight, / Prouoking him by her outrageous *talke,* / To heape more vengeance on that wretched wight" (book 2, canto 4, stanza 4).
168. *OED,* sv "Acephalous," 5.
169. *OED,* sv "Diastole," 1, 2.
170. Matthew Prior, "Alma, or the Progress of the Mind" [1718], III.144.
171. Samuel Johnson, *Somerville* (1779–81).
172. John Dryden, "Preface," *Fables Ancient and Modern* (1700), Globe edition, 499.
173. Roger Ascham, "Of Imitation": *The Scholemaster* (Book II) (1570), vol. 1, Smith 1–45.
174. Ascham, *Scholemaster,* ii. f. 61ᵛ.
175. *OED,* sv "Numb."
176. Ascham.
177. *The Selected Poetry of Robinson Jeffers* (New York: Random House, 1938), 328. The poem was suggested to Jeffers from his reading a novel from the pen of the (lame) novelist Walter Scott (Jeffers, "Foreword").
178. John Dryden, "Preface" to *Fables, Ancient and Modern* (Globe) (1700), 499.
179. AYL 3.2.
180. COR 4.7.
181. AYL 3.2.
182. Cf. The dramatic character "John Gower's" attempts in Shakespeare's play *Pericles of Tyre* to "carry wingèd Time / Post on the lame feet of my rhyme" (PER 4.47–48).
183. "The Measure is English Heroic Verse without Rime, as that of Homer in Greek, and Virgil in Latin; Rhime being no necessary Adjunct or true Ornament of Poem or good Verse, in longer Works especially, but the Invention of a barbarous Age, to set off wretched matter and lame Meeter" (Milton, preface to *Paradise Lost*).
184. PER 4.47–48.
185. Sig. A3ᵛ. Quoted 55 in Joseph Tate, "*Shakespeare Prose and Verse: Unreadable Forms,*" PhD diss. (University of Washington, 2005), 55.
186. 32.
187. Roger Ascham, "Of Imitation": *The Scholemaster (Book II)* [1570], vol. 1; Smith, 1–45; here p. 33.
188. Decimus Junius Juvenal, *Satire,* 10.356: "Orandum est ut sit mens sana in corpore sano." Kant's *Philosopher's Medicine,* trans. Mary Gregor,

is included in Immanuel Kant, *Anthropology, History, and Education*, ed. Gunther Zöller and Robert Louden (Cambridge: Cambridge University Press, 2007), 63–77.

189. Kant, *Philosophers' Medicine*, 184.

190. Olivier Guard and François Boller, "Immanuel Kant: Evolution from a Personality 'Disorder' to a Dementia," in *Neurological Disorders in Famous Artists*, ed. J. Bogousslavsky and F. Boller (Basel: Karger, 2005), 76–84.

191. Harald Weinrich, *Lethe: The Art and Critique of Forgetting* (Ithaca, NY: Cornell University Press, 2004), 67.

192. David Warrilow, who plays the part of Kant in *The Last Days*, had experience in walking and breathing accordingly. First, he had earlier presented a particular "slow-motion" walk for the role of Old Dantes in Peter Sellars's *The Count of Monte Crisco* at the Kennedy Center. One critic wrote, "Warrilow created a walk for Old Dantes in which his head is bowed slightly forwards and his knees are bent enough so that he steps onto a flat foot rather than a normal heel-to-toe stride. He glides across the floor, head and upper body remaining still." Laurie Lassiter, "David Warrilow: Creating Symbol and Cypher," *The Drama Review* [TDR] 29.4 (Winter 1985): 3–12.

193. For many other biographical ideas, see also Rolf George, "Review: The Lives of Kant," *Immanuel Kant. Der Mann und das Werk*, Karl Vorländer, Felix Malter, Konrad Kopper, Wolfgang Ritzel; *The Life of Immanuel Kant*, J. W. H. Stuckenberg; *Immanuel Kant*, Arsenij Gulyga, Sigrun Bielfeldt; *Kant's Life and Thought*, Ernst Cassirer, James Haden, Stephen Körner; Kant, *Eine Biographie*, Wolfgang Ritzel, *Philosophy and Phenomenological Research* 47.3 (March 1987): 485–500.

194. 161.

195. Quoted in Andrew Cutrofello, *Discipline and Critique: Kant, Poststructuralism, and the Problem of Resistance* (Albany: State University of New York Press, 1994), 53.

196. Another translation: "For one cannot subtract dancing in every form from a noble education—to be able to dance with one's feet, with concepts, with words: need I still add that one must be able to do it with the pen too—that one must learn to write?" (from Kimerer L. LaMothe, *Nietzsche's Dancers: Isadora Duncan, Martha Graham, and the Revaluation of Christian Values* [New York: Palgrave Macmillan, 2006], 93, K6, 110; Nietzsche, *Twilight of the Idols*, 512–13); see also Lamothe, *Between Dancing and Writing: The Practice of Religious Studies* (New York: Fordham University Press, 2004).

197. Joseph Warton, *Sappho's Advice* (c. 1740), 30.

198. T. S. C. Hans, *Walking is Dancing, Talking is Singing = Sen ge susun, kaji ge duran: The Development of Munda Poetry, Music, and Dance: Contribution of the Christian Church* (Ranchi, Jharkhand, India: Project Vikas, 1990).

199. Frank Kermode, "Poet and Dancer Before Diaghelev," in *What Is Dance?* ed. Roger Copeland and Marshall Cohen (New York: Oxford University Press, 1983), 156. See Paul Valéry, "Philosophy of the Dance: The

Plane of Walking, the Prose of Human Movement" (in Copeland and Cohen, eds., *What Is Dance?*, 61).

200. Paul Valéry, "Philosophy of the Dance," in Copeland and Cohen, eds., *What Is Dance?*, 50.

201. Hansgörj Bittner, "The Metrical Structure of Free Verse," PhD diss. (University of East Anglia, May 1997). See also Elizabeth den Otter, *Rhythm, a Dance in Time* (Amsterdam: Royal Tropical Institute, 2001).

202. Jonathan Richardson, *Morning Thoughts: or, Poetical Meditations, Moral, Divine and Miscellaneous* [1745], together with several other poems on various subjects; with notes by his son, lately deceased (London: J. Dodsley, 1776), 1:346.

203. John Dryden, *Rival Ladies* (1664), 3.1.32.

204. *OED*, sv "Poetry," 6a.

205. *OED*, sv "Poetry," 6b.

206. Balzac, *Théorie*, 123.

207. Balzac, *Théorie*, 92. See below: "Let Your Fingers Do the Walking."

208. The song/dance was written by Hal David together with Burt Bacharach. Included in *Very Dionne* (Scepter LP 587).

209. It was in 1822, a decade before Balzac published his *Théorie de la marche*, that Jean-François Champollion published work deciphering the Rosetta Stone. On the Romantic period and walking, see below.

210. *OED*, sv "Cursive, of writing: Written with a running hand, so that the characters are rapidly formed without raising the pen, and in consequence have their angles rounded, and separate strokes joined, and at length become slanted."

211. P. Ansell, G. Kitchener, and S. Potter, *The Dance of the Pen: Developing a Cursive Handwriting Style for Children* (1994); cited in Charmian Kenner and Gunther Kress, "The Multisemiotic Resources of Early Childhood Literacy," *Journal of Early Childhood Literacy* 3.2 (2003): 179–202.

212. See Alfred Fairbanks, *Renaissance Handwriting: An Anthology of Italic Scripts* (New York: The World Publishing Company, 1960) and *A Book of Scripts* (Harmondsmith, England: Penguin, 1949); Fairbanks is discussed in *New York Times, Obituaries* (5 January 2008).

213. Lin Yutang, *My Country and My People* (New York: Reynal & Hitchcock, [1935]), 285.

214. Yang Hao-cheng, "The Art of Chinese Calligraphy: A Brief Introduction," 8; forthcoming. Consulted in manuscript by the author in Nanjing, 23 December 2007.

215. Chiang Yee, *Chinese Calligraphy: An Introduction to its Aesthetic Technique* (published by Chiang Yee), 126, 129. See also the exhibition catalogue *Calligraphy and Paintings by Change Yee* (Hong Kong: Chiang Yee, 1972).

216. Chiang Yee, *Chinese Calligraphy*, 126, 129; Collection Selechonek.

217. Michael P. Garofalo, "Great Star of the Literary God—Zhong Kui, K'uei Hsing, Kui Xing—Chief Star, Big Dipper Constellation, Point to the Major Luminary," http://www.egreenway.com/taichichuan/swordmyth1.

htm. See also Cheng Man-Ch'ing, *Master of Five Excellences*, trans. Mark Hennessey (Berkeley, CA: Frog Books, 1995).

218. This English-language formulation of the Classical idea, already in the ancient Greek Euripides, is from Edward Bulwer-Lytton's play *Richelieu* (London: Saunders and Otley, 1839), 2.2. In the English Renaissance, George Whetstone was writing, "The dashe of a Pen, is more greeuous then the counterbuse of a Launce," which formulation has the advantage, in the present contact, of comparing the *motion* of pens that that of lances instead of pens with lances (*An Heptameron of Ciuill Discourse* [London: Richard Jones et al., 1582], Iii.sig.I.i. [*margin*]).

219. H 2.2.

220. Included in Yang Haocheng, "Chinese Calligraphy," illus. 7.

221. See Chiang Yee, *Chinese Calligraphy, an Introduction to Its Aesthetic and Technique*, foreword Sir Herbert Read, 2d ed. (Cambridge, MA: Harvard University Press).

222. Jean Shen, *The Dance of the Brush: A Nontraditional Approach to Learning Chinese Brush Painting*. Marc Shell's copy. See also http://www.paulnoll.com/China/Culture/language-Cursive-script.html.

223. Soen Nakagawa, *Endless Vow: The Zen Path of Soen Nakagawa*, presented by Eido T. Shimano, trans Kazuaki Tanahashi and Roko Sherry Chayat (Boston: Shambala, 1996), 98–99. See also http://zenart.shambhala.com/Product.jmdx?action=displayDetail&id=39&searchString=39.

224. Trans John D. Langlois Jr., in "Introduction," 18–19, in Langlois, ed., *China under Mongol Rule* (Princeton, NJ: Princeton University Press, 1981).

225. Yasin H. Safadi, *Islamic Calligraphy* (New York: Thames and Hudson, 1978).

226. *OED*, sv "Crawl," n¹c.

227. Milton, *Paradise Lost*, 5:200–201.

228. The edition we used was David Charles Bell and Alexander Melville Bell, *Standard Elocutionist: Principles and Exercises*, rev. and enlarged edition (London: Hodder and Stoughton, 1889), 388.

229. Alexander Melville Bell there enjoins stutterers to practice sentences that have such "double sounds" as "solemn march" (H) whereby Horatio describes how the mysterious ghost of Old Hamlet "thrice . . . walk'd" (H).

230. Matthew 14:25.

231. See Andy Martin's surfing book *Walking on Water* (London: J. Murray, 1991).

232. *Literary Digest* (11 October 1930), 48/3.

233. *OED*, "Tread," v., 7.

234. *Esquire* (September 1993), 126/2.

235. Hans Christian Andersen, *The Little Mermaid* [den lille havfrue] (1836); trans. H. B. Paull (1872).

236. *Satirical Poems of the Time of the Reformation*, ed. James Cranstoun, 4 vols. (Edinburgh: The Scottish Text Society by William Blackwood and Sons, 1891), vol. 3, lines 53–55.

237. Edward Munk, *The Metres of the Greeks and Romans*, trans. Charles C. Beck and C. C. Felton (Boston: J. Munroe, 1844), i.

238. The first instance cited in OED is Frank Pierce Foster, ed., *Illustrated Medical Dictionary, Being a Dictionary of the Technical Terms Used by Writers on Medicine and the Collateral Sciences*, in the Latin, English, French and German languages, 4 vols. (New York: D. Appleton and Company, 1888–94), 1:392/1.

239. Compare the Polish *puszczanie kaczek* (letting the ducks out).

240. For "ducks and drakes," see Hadrianus Junius, *The Nomenclator, or Remembrancer of Adrianus Iunius physician*, trans. John Higgins ([London]: Ralph Newberie, and Henrie Denham, 1585): "A kind of sport or play with an oister shell or stone throwne into the water, and making circles yer it sinke, etc. It is called a ducke and a drake, and a halfe-penie cake."

241. Percy B. Green, *A History of Nursery Rhymes* (London: Greening, 1899) reports this version: "A duck and a drake, / And a halfpenny cake, / With a penny to pay the old baker. / A hop and a scotch / Is another notch, / Slitherum, slatherum, take her."

242. For a more recent view, see I. J. Hewitt, N. J. Balmforth, and J. N. McElwaine, "Continual Skipping on Water," *Journal of Fluid Mechanics* 669 (2011): 328–53.

243. Presso S. Occhi.

244. For a more recent view, see Jay Ingram, "Skipping Stones," in his *The Velocity of Honey: And More Science of Everyday Life* (New York: Thunder's Mouth Press, 2003), 170–79.

245. Bombs can move over the surface of the water while bouncing or ricocheting. See Barnes Wallis, "Spherical Bomb—Surface Torpedo" (April 1942), where he described a method of attack in which a weapon would be bounced across water until it struck appropriately under the water.

246. See Ralph Lorenz, *Spinning Flight: Dynamics of Frisbees, Boomerangs, Samaras and Skipping Stones* (New York: Springer, 2006).

247. TN 1.1.

248. State University of Iowa, MA.

249. Harry Levin, "Core Canon Curriculum," *College English* 43.4 (April 1981): 352–62.

2. WALKING VOICES

1. Milton, *Comus*, 91–2.

2. Milton, *Comus*, 961–62. Cf. the pedal metrics of Milton, *L'Allegro* (1645), 33: "trip it, as you go, / On the light fantastic toe."

3. Milton, *Paradise Lost*, 10.1539. Milton would often walk three or four hours a day in his garden.

4. At the Pitti Palace, Florence, Italy.

5. Eric Levy, "When God Walks: A Syntactic and Lexical Analysis of Genesis 3:8"; http://www.ericlevy.com/Writings/Writings_Gen3-8.htm.

6. Milton, *Paradise Lost*, Book 9, lines 97–98.

7. Milton, *Paradise Lost*, Book 9, lines 103–4.

8. See Shakespeare's reference to "Hedg-hogs, which . . . mount / Their pricks at my foot-fall" (TMP).

9. French, eleventh century. Rashi, on Gn 3:8.
10. Catalan, thirteenth century. Gn 3:8.
11. Jewish Palestinian, 3d century CE.
12. Milton, *Paradise Lost*, Book 9, 116.
13. Provence, twelfth-thirteenth centuries. Kimchi, Gn 3:8. Cf. the interpretation of "The voice thereof shall go like a serpent" (Jer. 46:22).
14. Spain/Egypt; twelfth century. Maimonides, *The Guide for the Perplexed*, I, 24. It is the "voice" that is stated to be walking (*mit'halekh*), not God *per se*.
15. Abraham ibn Ezra also puts forward this gloss: "As he [Adam] was walking . . . "
16. France, fourteenth century.
17. Persia, tenth century.
18. See Eric Levy, "A Syntactical and Lexical Analysis of Genesis 3:8" (2004); ericlevy@ericlevy.com; accessed 24 September 2012.
19. Ex 19:19.
20. Abraham Ibn Ezra thus discusses several cases of walking voices in his commentary.
21. *OED*, 7. "To talk volubly; to rail, storm at. Also, to talk excessively or tiresomely about (a subject); to discuss ad nauseam." Charles Cowden Clarke, *Shakespeare—characters* (1863): "Her first scene with Fenton is inimitable, where she goes on about a wart on his face" (162).
22. *OED*, 17. "Of verses: To glide along rhythmically." Cf. *OED*: "Of a song: To admit of being sung; also, to follow the measure of, to adapt itself to (a tune)."
23. Puttenham, *Arte Eng. Poesie* (1589), i.vii.9: "When they could make their verses goe all in ryme."
24. *OED*: "Of a document, language, etc.: To have a specified tenor, to run, as in Shakespeare's *Macbeth*'s 'You shall be King. And Thane of Cawdor too: went it not so?'"
25. Shakespeare, *Winter's Tale*: "This is a passing merry one, and goes to the tune of two maids wooing a man."
26. Richard Baxter, A *Paraphrase of the New Testament* (1685), Matt. i.10: "In a very ancient Hebrew Copy of the Gospel, this verse goeth (and Eliakim begat Abner [and so on])."
27. *Woman's Will: A Comedy in Five Acts* (London: A. J. Valpy [printer], 1815), ii.1: "Why do you go about with me thus—why not speak to be understood?"
28. 28 October 1980.
29. See Mary Corey and Victoria Westermark, *Fer Shur! How to Be a Valley Girl—Totally* (New York: Random House, 1982).
30. http://www.urbandictionary.com.
31. See Janice Kay Whitelaw, ed., *Jacob Ruff's "Adam und Heva"* [*1550*], critical edition with introduction and notes, l. 1444.
32. See Richard Rastell, "The Construction of a Speaking Tube for Late Medieval Drama," *European Medieval Drama* 4.4 (2001): 231–44.
33. See stage direction, "durch ein starkes Sprachrohr," in *Siegfried*, act 2, scene 1. More generally on the history of hearing aids and megaphones,

see Rainer Hüls, *Die Hand am Ohr: Eine kleine Geschichte der Hörhilfen* (Hamburg: Innocentia-Verlag, 2009).

34. The brand-name still exists as *HMV*.

35. "Und sie hörten die Stimme Gottes des HERRN, der im Garten ging" (Gn 3:8; trans. Martin Luther).

36. First published 1976. Martin Luther translated the Hebrew term *shofar* as the German word *Posaune*.

37. Dt 34.5.

38. Yitzchak Hutner, *Pachad Yitzchak*, Rosh Ha-Shana 25, points out that the blowing the shofar is the only mitzvah done through breathing and remarks on the breath that God breathed into the nostrils of Adam.

39. New International Version (translation).

40. King James Version.

41. Vulgate.

42. Luther.

43. On this similarity, see Shell, *Stutter*, esp. "Moses' Tongue."

44. The Latin Vulgate Bible calls the marching around Jericho an ambulation.

45. Handel, *Joshua*, act II, scene 1, Solo and Chorus/Israelites: "Glory to God! The strong cemented walls, / The tott'ring tow'rs, the pond'rous ruin falls. / And the shivering music that accompanies the tempest: / The nations tremble at the dreadful sound, / Heav'n thunders, tempests roar, and groans the ground."

46. HWV 64.

47. Handel, *Joshua*, act II, scene 1, Recitative/Joshua.

48. Handel, *Joshua*, act II, scene 7, Solo/Joshua and Chorus/Israelites.

49. In the chorus "O feeble boast" ("The lingering sun his fiery wheels delay'd, the moon obedient trembled at the sound")?

50. *West Side Story* was originally planned as a conflict between Irish Roman Catholics and Jewish groups on the (Lower) East Side. On the shofar-whistle motif, see Jack Gottlieb, *Funny, It Doesn't Sound Jewish: How Yiddish Songs and Synagogue Melodies Influenced Tin Pan Alley, Broadway, and Hollywood* (Albany: State University of New York Press, 2004).

51. Ruth Smith, "Early Music's Dramatic Significance in Handel's *Saul*," *Oxford Journals* 35.2 (2007): 173–90.

52. David Hunter, "George Frideric Handel and the Jews: Fact, Fiction and the Tolerances of Scholarship," in *For the Love of Music: Festschrift in Honor of Theodore Front on his 90th Birthday*, ed. Darwin F. Scott (Lucca, Italy: Lim Antiqua, 2002), 22–27.

53. Ps 150:3.

54. Anthony Baines, "Trombone," *Grove's Dictionary of Music and Musicians*, 5th ed., ed. Eric Bloom, 9 vols. (London: MacMillan, 1954), 8: 557; quoted (approvingly) by David M. Guion, *Trombone: Its History and Music, 1697–1811* (New York: Gordon and Breach, 1988), 206.

55. HWV 53.

56. Handel, *Saul*, the "symphony" at the beginning of act II, scene 9: "Saul at the Festival of the New Moon." See also Smith, "Early Music."

57. Ps 89:15. What modern-day Jews call Rosh Hashannah is called, in the Bible, Yom Teruah.

58. For an example of an ear-trumpet made from a ram's horn, see that in the collection of the Becker Medical Library at Washington University School of Medicine (St. Louis).

59. Dt 6:4.

60. Mk 12:29.

61. Dt 11:19.

62. Rahel Musleah, "A Concerto for Ancient Hebrew Ram's Horn," *Forward* (20 November 2009).

63. Alexander Ringer, *The Composer as Jew* (Oxford: Clarendon Press, 1990), 203.

64. Opus 46.

65. In a letter to the composer Anton Webern (4 August 1933), Schoenberg writes, "I have long since resolved to be a Jew . . . I have also returned officially to the Jewish religious community. . . . It is my intention to take an active part in endeavors of this kind. I regard that as more important than my art, and am determined . . . to do nothing in future [sic] but work for the Jewish national cause" (qtd. in Willi Reich, *Schoenberg: A Critical Biography*, trans. Leo Black [London: Longman, 1971], 49).

66. Schoenberg did versions of the following: Matthias Georg Monn's *Symphonia a quattro* (A-Dur), *Concerto per Violoncello o Cembalo* (g-Moll) (Klavierauszug und Kadenzen), and *Concerto per Clavicembalo* (D-Dur), Johann Christoph Mann's *Divertimento a tre* (D-Dur), and Franz Seraf Ignaz Anton Tuma's *Sinfonia a quattro für Streichorchester* (e-Moll). He also did three partitas a tre by Tuma: *A-Dur für zwei Violinen, Violoncello und Generalbaß*; *c-Moll für zwei Violinen, Violoncello und Generalbaß* [im 5. Satz zusätzlich: Violino obligato]; and *G-Dur für zwei Violinen, Violoncello und Generalbaß*.

67. Schoenberg, Opus 9.

68. Adorno, "Arnold Schoenberg, 1874–1951," trans. Samuel M. Weber and Shierry Weber, in Adorno, *Prisms* (Cambridge MA: MIT Press, 1983), 194–95.

69. Handel's *Concerto Grosso* Op. 6, No. 7. HWV 325.

70. The phrase is discussed in Johann Joseph Fux, *Gradus ad Parnassum* (1725). Rheinhold Hammerstein, *Diabolus in musica: Ikonographie zur Musik im Mittelalter* (Bern: Francke, 1974), discusses the ways in which musical theorists forbad the use of the triton.

71. Cf. Greek *herpein*. Phineas Fletcher, *Purple Island, or, The Isle of Man: An Allegorical Poem* (1633), ix.xiii.125: "But when he could not go, yet forward would he creep."

72. See below, Part IV.

73. Gn 3:15.

74. See below, Part V.

75. Ido Abravaya, "On Bach's Rhythm and Tempo," revised PhD diss. (University of Tel Aviv, 1999) (Kassel: Bärenreiter, 2006).

76. In Leonard Stein, ed. *Style and Idea* (Berkeley: n.p., 1975), 216–44.

77. Some music historians hold out for Jacopo Peri's *Dafne* (1597), now lost, and others for his *Euridice* (1600), in which Orpheus actually succeeds in retrieving Eurydice from the underworld.
78. *OED*, sv "Walking," adj., "Walking bass."
79. See Merulo's *Sonata concertate* for two violins with basso continuo (1637).
80. See Frescobaldi's *Arie musicali* (published 1630).
81. *OED*, sv "Walking," adj., "Walking beat." Marshall Winslow Stearns writes in his *Story of Jazz* (Oxford: Oxford University Press, 1956), 205: "The string-bass began to 'walk', or play melodic figures instead of pounding away at one or two notes."
82. "Up here in the north all the jazzmen are playing too fast or too slow—nobody walks" (*Mademoiselle* magazine [December 1952], 118).
83. For some practical information about the walking-bass, see Ed Friedland, *Building Walking Bass Lines* (Hal Leonard Corporation; CD edition, 1995).
84. Comparable with *walking base* is the *basso ostinato* ("a continuously repeated melodic or rhythmical figure or phrase") as well as *passus duriusulus* and *basso continuo*.
85. On the walking base in Monteverdi's *Laetatus Sum*, see Jeffrey Kurtzman, *The Monteverdi Vespers of 1610: Music, Context, Performance* (Oxford and New York: Oxford University Press, 1999), 223–26, 243.
86. Trans. Maria Steiner, CD booklet for *Il combattimento di Tancredi e Clorinda, Madrigals* (Hungaroton, 1988; HCD 12952).
87. Corelli, Opus 4, no. 1.
88. So says Craig Wright, *Listening to Western Music* [CD] (Belmont, CA: Thomson/Schirmer, 2008), chap. 12.
89. HWV-60. "A chorus of Handel followed, 'Let none despair'; it is upon a fine walking bass, and the voices burst in upon it with an expression of confidence truly admirable" ("The Musician at York," *London Magazine* [new series] 13 [October 1825], 269).
90. Handel, *Hercules*, act 1, scene 3. HWV-60.
91. See his Historical Dictionary of all Religions from the Creation of the World to the Present Times (1742)
92. HWV-56.
93. BWV-645.
94. BWV-645.
95. BWV-140.
96. These are the opening lines:

> Wachet auf, ruft uns die Stimme : *Wake, arise, the voices call us*
> Der Wächter sehr hoch auf der Zinne : *Of watchmen from the lofty tower* . . .
> Zion hört die Wächter singen, : *Zion hears the watchmen singing,*
> Das Herz tut ihr vor Freuden springen : *Her heart within for joy is dancing* . . .
> Gloria sei dir gesungen : *Gloria to thee be sung now*
> Mit Menschen- und mit Engelzungen : *With mortal and angelic voices* . . .

97. BWV-659 (organ). Russell Stinson, *J.S. Bach's Great Eighteen Organ Chorales* (New York: Oxford University Press, 2001), discussing BWV 659, overstates his case when he writes that it includes "the only instance of a true 'walking-bass' pedal in any of Bach's organ chorales." See BWV-61 (cantata) and BWV-62 (chorale cantata).

98. BWV-232. Cf. BWV-1082: *Credo in unum Deum in F Major* (1747–48).

99. BMV-243. Reference: http://www.sfbach.org/notes-march-2012. Camperi's program notes for a March 2012 performance of Bach's Magnificat at the San Francisco Bach Choir; see also Camperi, *Philippe Verdelot: Madrigali a sei voci: edizione critica* (Pisa: ETS, 2003).

100. Quoted in Rudi Blesh and Harriet Grossman Janis, *They All Played Ragtime* (London: Jazz Club [Sedgewick and Jackson], 1960), 192; and Len Lyons, *The 101 Best Jazz Albums* (New York: William Morrow and Company, 1980).

101. In *Stand Up* [LP] 1969.

102. BWV-996.

103. Arpeggiato (dir. Christina Pluhar), [CD] *Teatro d'Amore: Monteverdi—Zefiro Torna, Etc.* Virgin Classics #36140.

104. Ben Finane, "Liner Notes" for *Teatro d'Amore*. See also Finane, *Handel's Messiah and His English Oratorios* (New York: Continuum, 2009).

105. See "Walking the Strings," in *Eddie Pennington Walks the Strings* [CD] (Smithsonian Folkways, 2004). Joe "Flip" Wilson ("Liner Notes") writes about Pennington that "he's completely at home, letting his fingers do the talking."

106. See Tony Osborne, *The Double Bass Sings* [solo instrument (string bass) with piano accompaniment] [sheet music] (Dochroyle Farm, Barrhill, Girvan, Ayrshire, Scotland: Piper Publications, n.d.), whose cover art personifies the string bass. Collection Selechonek.

107. John Lindberg and Burrill Crohn, *Bass Walk* (Lindy Film).

108. These cuts include "Would You Like to Take a Walk," "Walkin' My Baby Back Home," "I'll Walk Alone," and Vinnegar's original "Walk On." See also Vinnegar's *Jazz's Great "Walker"* (1964; Vee Jay) and *Walkin' the Basses* (1992; Contemporary Records).

109. It was notably covered by his protégé Robert Johnson (1936) and by dozens of others since then.

110. Included in *This is Ray Brown* [LP] (Verve, 1959).

111. See too *Walk On* [CD 2 disc] (Telarc Records, 2003).

112. See "Jazz Legend Charlie Haden on His Life, His Music and His Politics," interview in *Democracy Now* (1 September 2006); http://www.democracynow.org/2006/9/1/jazz_legend_charlie_haden_on_his. "The disease weakened the nerves in his face and throat"; http://www.allmusic.com/artist/p83212/biography.

113. Andrea Lewis, "Charlie Haden's Progressions," *The Progressive* (April 2008).

114. National Public Radio staff, "Charlie Haden: A Moment of Clarity"; http://www.npr.org/2012/01/15/145172275/charlie-haden-a-moment-of-clarity.

115. Of the Orbison songs discussed below, Orbison collaborated with Joe Melson for the writing and/or composing of the following: "Only the Lonely" (1960), "Running Scared" (1961), and "Crying" (1961).

116. Consider Orbison's earlier work, "Claudette" (1958), which appeared on the B-side of the (Phil and Don) Everly Brother's hit single "Dream": "Whenever I want you, all I have to is dream." Dreams continue throughout the period of the 1960s, as in Orbison's fine rendition of Don Gibson's "Sweet Dreams," his cover of Johnny Mercer's "Dream (When You're Feeling Blue" (1944), and his representation of Cindy Walker's "Dream Baby (How Long Must I Dream?)."

117. There is, for example, Joshua Gunn's talk, "The Big O: A Psychoanalytic Account of Roy Orbison's Voice," Roy Orbison Tribute Symposium sponsored by the Center For Film, Media and Popular Culture, Arizona State University, Temple, Arizona (25 January 2008).

118. Quoted by Ellis Amburn, *Dark Star: The Roy Orbison Story* (New York: Carol Publishing Group, 1990), 212. The Irish Bono's offstage name is Paul David Hewson.

119. See Alan Clayson, *Only the Lonely: Roy Orbison's Life and Legacy* (New York: St. Martin's Press, 1989), 109–13.

120. "America's Got Talent," Season Two: 21 August 2007.

121. The part of Ben is played by Dean Stockwell.

122. Lehman, *Orbison*, 93.

123. Ibid., 190.

124. Written by Wally Gold and Aaron Shroeder.

125. Bob Dylan, obituary for Orbison, 1988. Quoted in Peter Lehman, *Roy Orbison: Invention of an Alternative Rock Masculinity* (Detroit, MI: Wayne State University Press, 2007), 21.

126. David Gates, "The Voice that Sang in the Dark: Roy Orbison, Rock and Roll's Mr. Lonely: 1936–1988," *Newsweek* (19 December 1988): 73.

127. Act 4. *Isis* was first published in 1719. Its libretto is written by Phillippe Quinault.

128. The same theme informs Antonio Vivaldi's "Winter Concerto" in *The Four Seasons* (1723).

129. See Robert Shay, "Dryden and Purcell's *King Arthur*: Legend and Politics on the Restoration Stage," in Richard W. Barber, ed., *King Arthur in Music = Arthurian Studies* 52 (Cambridge: n.p., 2002).

130. Purcell and Dryden, *King Arthur*, act III, scene 2.

131. The aria provides the soundtrack for Ariane Mnouchkine's movie *Molière* (1978), in particular, for the scene about the French dramatist Molière's death.

132. Act 3.

133. Eliot, *The Wasteland*, opening passage.

134. Ibid.

135. Nikolaus Hamoncourt's version of the opera at the Salzburger Festspiele (2004). Starring also Isabel Rey, Barbara Bonney, and Michael Schade.

136. Widmer stutters (chatters) out the words along with the shivering strings. Oliver Widmer's performance of Purcell's *Cold Genius* in Nikolaus

Hamoncourt's version of the opera at the Salzburger Festspiele (2004). Starring also Isabel Rey, Barbara Bonney, and Michael Schade.

137. Also known as Klaus Sperber.

138. See Andrew Horn's movie *The Nomi Song* (2004). Nomi also did an excellent version of "Dido's Lament" (also known as "When I am laid in earth"), a piece formed on a ground bass with chaconne-like descending chromatic line in Henry Purcell's *Dido and Aeneas* (1688).

139. See Michael Nyman Band, "Memorial," in *The Cook, the Thief, His Wife & Her Lover* (CD album release). See, too, the versions of "Memorial" in *After Extra* (CD album release, 1996).

140. At the Théâtre du Châtelet in Paris.

141. Susan Kerschbaumer, review, *Opera News* (9 December 1995).

142. At the Savonlinna Opera Festival in Finland (1994).

143. Also known as Gordon Matthew Thomas Sumner.

144. In Durham Cathedral 14 July.

3. TRIPS OF THE TONGUE IN *HAMLET* (1600)

1. Erwin W. Straus, "The Upright Posture," *Psychiatric Quarterly* 26.1–4 (October 1952): 529–61.

2. Mills, 83.

3. Kean "crawled upon his belly towards the King like a wounded snake" wrote the first night reviewer for the *Herald*.

4. Now at the Tate Gallery.

5. See Alan Young's book, *Shakespeare and the Visual Arts, 1709–1900*; see also artist Keeley Halswelle's painting (1878) of Hamlet's play within the play.

6. Lewis Carroll, *The Private Journals of Charles Lutwidge Dodgson [Lewis Carroll]*, ed. Edward Wakeling, intro. Roger Lancelyn Green (Luton, England: Lewis Carroll Society, 1993–2007), 1: 73.

7. *Society Magazine* (May 1884); qtd. on p. 585 in Marvin Rosenberg, *The Masks of Hamlet* (Cranberry, NJ: Associated University Presses, 1992), 484. See also James Thomas, "Wilson Barrett's *Hamlet*," *Theatre Journal* 31.4 (December 1979).

8. "*Hamlet* at the Haymarket," Saturday Review, 30 January 1892, 126–27.

9. See Harry Rusche's "Shakespeare Illustrated" webpage for more illustrations and sources for the above. For further discussions of the crawl, the fan, and the play scene in general, see Hughes, 58–61; Sprague, 157–59.

10. Alan Young, *Hamlet and the Visual Arts, 1709–1900* (Cranberry, NJ: Associated University Press, 2002), 187. See also Robert Gottlieb, *Sarah: The Life of Sarah Bernhardt* (New Haven, CT: Yale University Press, 2010), 142.

11. The movie, directed by Svend Gade and Heinz Schall, is based partly on Edward Payson Vining's book *The Mystery of Hamlet* (Philadelphia, PA: J. B. Lippincott, 1881) in which Hamlet is a woman disguised as a man.

12. Frank Marshall, *A Study of Hamlet* (N.p.: Longmans, Green, & Co., 1875), 43–44.

13. Gn 3:1; KJV.
14. Gn 3:13; KVJ.
15. Gn 3:14.
16. Gn 3:8.
17. The philosophie, commonly called, the Morals, written by the learned philosopher, Plutarch of Chæronea (1603), 1:1072.
18. Richard Grant White, *Every-day English. A Sequel to "Words and Their Uses"* (Boston and New York: Houghton Mifflin Company, 1908), 303.
19. Vergil, *Aeneid*, trans. Henry Rushton Fairclough (Chicago: B. H. Sanborn, 1934), 2.526ff. "But lo! escaping from the sword of Pyrrhus, through darts, through foes, Polites, one of Priam's sons, flees down the long colonnades and, wounded, traverses the empty courts. Pyrrhus presses hotly upon him eager to strike, and at any moment will catch him and overwhelm him with the spear. When at last he came before the eyes and faces of his parents, he fell, and poured out his life in a stream of blood. Hereupon Priam, though now in death's closest grasp, yet held not back nor spared his voice and wrath: 'For your crime, for deeds so heinous,' he cries, 'if in heaven there is any righteousness to mark such sins, may the gods pay you fitting thanks and render you due rewards, who has made me look on my own son's murder, and defiled with death a father's face! Not so did Achilles deal with his foe Priam, that Achilles whose sonship you falsely claim, but he had respect for a suppliant's rights and trust; he gave back to the tomb Hector's bloodless corpse and sent me back to my realm.' So spoke the old man and hurled his weak and harmless spear, which straight recoiled from the clanging brass and hung idly from the top of the shield's boss. To him Pyrrhus: 'Then you shall bear this news and go as messenger to my sire, Peleus' son; be sure to tell him of my sorry deeds and his degenerate Neoptolemus! Now die!' So saying, to the very altar stones he drew him, trembling and slipping in his son's streaming blood, and wound his left hand in his hair, while with the right he raised high the flashing sword and buried it to the hilt in his side. Such was the close of Priam's fortunes; such the doom that by fate befell him—to see Troy in flames and Pergamus laid low, he who was once lord of so many tribes and lands, the monarch of Asia. He lies, a huge trunk upon the shore, a head severed from the neck, a corpse without a name!"
20. Puttenham, *Arte of English Poesie*, 102.
21. *To walk* means "To move or travel at a regular and fairly slow pace by lifting and setting down each foot in turn, so that one of the feet is always on the ground" (*OED*, sv "Walk," IV.9).
22. OED.
23. In ancient Greek prosody, especially that of Aristophanes of Byzantium, the comma originates from discussion of colometry, or measurement of verses.
24. H 2.2.325–26.
25. The same opposition between mobility and immobility informs Hamlet's worries that "the lady shall say her mind freely, or the blank verse shall halt for't" (H 3.2.30–32). Like Hamlet in his reference to halting blank

verse, in *Much Ado About Nothing*, Claudio mocks Benedict's "halting sonnet" (5.4.86). Similarly, the speaker of Sidney's *Astrophil and Stella*, having sought for "words to paint the blackest face of woe," bemoans that "words came halting forth, wanting Inventions stay" (*Poems* 165), and Francisco in John Webster's *The White Devil* proclaims: "I am in love, / In love with Corombonà, and my suit / Thus halts to her in verse" (4.1.120–22).

26. There have been many previous attempts at answering this question. Alexander Pope, for example, says "mobled" should have been printed as "enobled" (in Pope, ed., *The Works of Mr. William Shakespear*, 6 vols. (London: Jacob Tonson, 1723), Hamlet (in vol. 6). Marginalia in the 1743 British Library's "Third Folio" of Shakespeare say, "mobled [means] removed, or undressed" (British Library F3 with MS marginal and interleaved notes, dated 1743. BL C.39.i.20 [1463–64, 1524, 1535, 1542, 1547, 1637, 1721, 1733, 1935].) William Warburton (1747) says, "Mobled or mabled, signifies veiled." (Warburton, ed., *The Works of Shakespear* (London: Printed for J. and P. Knapton, 1747), *Hamlet* (in vol. 8.) John Upton (1748) says, "The mobled queen: this designedly affected expression seems to be formed from Virg[il]. Aen[eid]. II, 40. *Magnâ comitante caterva* [followed by a crowd; in reference to *Laocoön*]. I once thought it should be *mabled*, I. carelessly dressed. The word is used in the northern parts of England; and by the seventeenth-century author [George] Sandys in his *Travels*, p. 148. 'The elder mabble their heads in linnen,' &c." (John Upton, 2d ed. of *Critical Observations on Shakespeare* (1748), 320–21). George Stevens (1773) admires how Alexander Pope makes the entire speech ludicrous: "The folio reads—the innobled queen; and in all probability it is the true reading. This pompous but unmeaning epithet might be introduced merely to make her Phrygian majesty [Hecuba] appear more ridiculous." Samuel Wesley (1790), claiming to follow Upton, argues for the meaning "mob-led": "Upton reads says the mob-led Queen. [George] Tollet points out that mob was first used with this meaning during the reign of Charles II" (Samuel Johnson and George Stevens, eds., *The Plays of William Shakespeare, Hamlet*, 10 vols. [London: Printed for C. Bathurst, 1773], vol. 10). Samuel Coleridge (1819) writes, "A mob-cap is still a word in common use for a morning cap, which conceals the whole head of hair and passes under the chin—It is nearly the same as the night-cap—i.e. an imitation of it so as to answer the purpose ('I am not drest for company') and yet reconciling it with neatness and perfect purity. [etymologically connected with mop?]" (Samuel Coleridge, ms. notes [1819]; in Samuel Ayscough, ed. 1807 [BL shelf mark C.61.h.7]). The person known as "GH" (1864) writes, "In the more primitive parts of Yorkshire, where old words still survive, there is one in common use, which, I think, exactly hits poor Hecuba's condition. It is madlet or maddled; which means, not 'absolutely mad,' but 'bewildered almost to madness.'" "Thus it is said, a man maddled, is maddling, or is maddled, when he talks or acts in a vague, feeble, and irrational manner. I respectfully submit the suggested 'emendation' to the critical readers of Shakespeare" (G.H. [1864], 66; "G.H." is probably Browne). Other emendations refer to the Celtic story of the fairy Queen Mab (W. P. Reeves, *Modern Language Notes* 17.6 [1902]: 341–45). Mab is the subject of Mercutio's speech in RJ.

27. Andrew Becket, *Shakespeare's Himself Again*: or, The Language of the Poet Assessed: Being a Full but Dispassionate Examen of the Readings of the Several Editors, the Whole Comprised in a series of Notes, and Further Illustrative of the More Difficult Passages in his Plays, to the various editions to which the present volumes form a complete and necessary supplement, 2 vols. (London: A. J. Valpy, 1815). See, too, Becket, *Shakespeare's Himself Again*, 38: "The commentators are all on a wrong scent. I am persuaded that Shakespeare has here coined a word from mobilis Lat. without knowing the particular meaning of the Latin term. By mobiled queen,—he means the moved, agitated, queen, as the context will clearly show."

28. William Caxton, *The Boke yf Eneydos* [1490] (=EETS 1890), 19.71.

29. TMP 2.1.

30. Caxton, *Eneydos*, 27.103.

31. Jean-François Lyotard approaches differently the Player's pause or lapse. For him it is more a *lapsus linguæ*, slip of the tongue, than a *lapsus calami*, slip of the [quill/reed] pen. See Jean-François Lyotard, *Discours, figure* (Paris: Klincksiek, 1971), esp. 386; and Ann Tomiche, in her essay "Lyotard and/on Literature," *Yale French Studies*, no. 99, Jean-Francois Lyotard, *Time and Judgment* (2001): 149–63.

32. (London: Victor Gollancz, 1955), 110.

33. For the meaning of the verb *to ham* as "to hamstring," see in R. F. Williams's *Birch's Court & Times James I* (1618), (1849) (modernized text), II.114: "The bailiffs assaulted him in his coach, hammed his horses, and threatened no less unto himself."

34. *OED*, sv "-grade."

35. Back-and-forth walking is what Thomas Chaloner associated with the crab. See James Anthony Froude's *History of England* [1564] (1879), VIII:45/1: "[I am] now further from wealth . . . than I was eighteen years agone. Methinks I became a retrograde crab." See also Joshua Sylvester's translation into English of Guillaume de Salluste du Bartas's *Essay of the Second Week* (1598): "Southward Sol doth retrograde, / Goes (Crab-like) backward." For the constellation, see Patricia Parker, "Spelling Backwards," in *Rhetoric Women and Politics in Early Modern*, ed. Jennifer Richards and Alison Thorne England (London: Routledge, 2007), 31, 33.

36. See Marc Shell, *Polio and Its Aftermath: The Culture of Paralysis* (Cambridge, MA: Harvard University Press, 2006).

37. Cf. *OED*, sv. "Infant."

38. Cf. Middle English *hamme*, Old English *hamm*, and the toponym *Ham*, which names the part of the London Tideway at the bend of the Thames River upstream from Shakespeare's Globe Theater.

39. Trans. Krishna Winston (London: Harcourt, 2002).

40. Relevant are such works in experimental theatre as Claire Heggen and Yves Marc, *Attention à la marche*, which the French acting company Théâtre Du Mouvement "performed" in May 1986.

41. *OED*: pork, int. (and n^2). Francis Grose, *Classical Dictionary of the Vulgar Tongue* [1796] (1963), 267: "*Pork, to cry pork*; to give intelligence to

the undertaker of a funeral: metaphor borrowed from the raven, whose note sounds like the word pork."

42. Hamlet, dressed in black, seems to identify with a croaking raven that black bird that was a device of the Danish and other Vikings. The Old English word for a raven was *hræfn*; in Old Norse it was *hrafn*; the word was frequently used in combinations as a kenning for bloodshed and battle.

43. J. Sylvester, trans. Guillaume de Salluste du Bartas, *Essay of the Second Week* (1598) (new ed.), ii.iv.89: "From the Mountains nigh / The Rav'ns begin with their pork-porking cry."

44. See ii.i.44. Griffin acted in Shakespeare's plays. His roles included Justice Silence in *2 Henry IV*; see [William Shakespeare?], *Double Falsehood*, 3d ser., ed. Brean Hammond (London: Methuen, 2010), 173.

45. John Milton, *Colasterion* (1645), 12: "I mean not to dispute Philosophy with this Pork, who never read any."

46. See John Lyly, *Euphues and his England* (new ed.) (1580). f. 13ᵛ: "Wring not a horse on the withers"; and Thomas Nashe, *Have With You to Saffron Walden* (1596), sig. P4: "That wrung him on the withers worse than all the rest."

47. *OED*, sv. "Claudication."

48. Joannes Boemus, trans. William Waterman, *Fardle of Facions* (London: John Kingstone and Henry Sutton, 1555), i.vi. 91: "Claudicacion or limping."

49. Eucharius Roesslin, trans. Thomas Raynald, *Byrth of Mankynde* (London: n.p., 1545), i.x: "The brayne, of whom all the sinewes take their originall."

50. KJ: "You bloody Neroes, ripping up the womb / Of your dear mother . . . "

51. *Promptorium Parvulorum et Clericorum* (compiled in 1440): 224/1 Haltare, claudicator.

52. David and Ben Crystal, *Shakespeare's Words: A Glossary and Language Companion* (London: Penguin, 2002), 211.

53. John Frith, *Another Book against Rastell* [1533] (1829) 228.

54. Abraham Fleming, *Panoply of Epistles* (1576) 388.

55. *Hamlet* 2.2.339.

56. The Passionate Pilgrim (1599), 308.

57. There are those who say that this refers to the metrics only. For various references, see esp. Michael Carl Schoenfeldt, *A Companion to Shakespeare's Sonnets*, 364.

58. *Bible* (Richard Chalonner). Gn 2:10–14: "And he put forth his hand, and took the sword, to sacrifice his son. And behold an Angel of the Lord from heaven called to him, saying: Abraham, Abraham. And he answered: Here I am. And he said to him: Lay not thy hand upon the boy, neither do thou any thing to him: now I know that thou fearest God, and hast not spared thy only begotten son for my sake. Abraham lifted up his eyes, and saw behind his back a ram amongst the briers sticking fast by the horns, which he took and offered for a *holocaust* instead of his son. And he called the name of that place, The Lord seeth. Whereupon even to this day it is said: In the mountain the Lord will see."

59. Gn 22:12.

60. William Stevens Balch, *Lectures on Language, as Particularly Connected with English Grammar* (Providence, RI: B. Cranston and Co., 1883): "The allied powers of Europe combined their forces to defeat Napoleon. In this instance the whole expression is in the past tense; nevertheless, the action expressed in the infinitive mood, was future to the circumstance on which it depended; that is, the defeat was future to the combination of the forces. Abraham raised the knife to slay his son. Not that he did slay him, as that sentence must be explained on the common systems, which teach us that to slay is in the present tense; but he raised the fatal knife for that purpose, the fulfilment of which was future; but the angel staid his hand, and averted the blow."

61. Guy de Chauillac, *Guydon's Questionary of Cyrurgens* Qiv, trans. Robert Copland (London: 1541): "Than beholde . . . yf his [the lazar's] loke be steyed and horryble [orig. *aspectus fixus & horribilis*]."

62. "The blowing of the Shofar turns out to have been originally the imitation of the voice of the dying God" (Review of Theodor Reik's *Ritual: Psychoanalytic Studies* [1928], pref. Sigmund Freud, trans. Douglas Bryan [London: Hogarth Press and Institute of Psychoanalysis *Times Literary Supplement*] [24 September 1931], 722/2).

63. Gn 22:11.

64. John Hacket, Scrinia reserata: A Memorial Offered to the Great Deservings of John Williams, D.D. (London: 1693), II.94.

65. Jaspers, *Nietzsche: An Introduction to the Understanding of His Philosophical Activity*, trans. Charles F. Wallraff and Frederick J. Schmitz, 106.

66. Regarding the word bone, says *OED*, "the Old Norse, Old High German, Middle High German, and Dutch [languages], have, beside the general sense 'bone', the specific sense 'shank (of the leg)', which is the ordinary sense in modern German" (*OED* sv "Bone," etymology).

Shank itself means *ham* in German, being cognate with "Old Saxon *scinka*, gl. Latin 'basis', 'tibia' (Middle Low German *schinke* thigh, ham), Old High German *scinko* (masculine), *scinka* (feminine), leg-bone, thigh (Middle High German *schinke* (masculine), thigh, ham, modern German *schinken* (masculine), ham); . . . Low German (Koolman) *schunke* thigh, ham" (*OED* sv. "Shank," etymology).

67. Nietzsche, "Unter Töchtern der Wüste," one of his "Dionysus Dithyrambs," also in *Thus Spake Zarathustra: A Book for All and None* (1892), pt. 4, sec. 76.

68. Andrew Cecil Bradley, *Shakespearean Tragedy: Lectures on Hamlet, Othello, King Lear, Macbeth*, 2d ed. (London: Macmillan, 1905), 105.

69. See Sydney Anglo, "The Barriers: From Combat to Dance (Almost)," *Dance Research: The Journal of the Society for Dance Research* 25.2 (winter 2007): 91–106; and Kate van Orden, *Music, Discipline, and Arms in Early Modern France* (Chicago: University of Chicago Press, 2005).

70. Shakespeare, *1 Henry 4*.

71. "Ye have another sort of repetition, when . . . ye iterate one word without any intermission, as thus: 'It was Maryne, Maryne that wrought

mine woe. . . . The Greeks call him, Epizeuxis, the Latines Subiunctio'" (Puttenham, *Arte Englishe Poesie* [1589], iii.xix.167).

72. There is, for example, Saxo Grammaticus, for whom *ambleth* involves not only ambling but also foolishness.

73. Peter Thomson, "Hamlet and the Actor in Shakespeare's Theatre," in *Shakespeare's Theatre* (London: Methuen, 1992), 115–16.

74. See the relevant anecdotal details in *Tarlton's Jests* (London: Andrew Cook, 1638).

75. London: William Ferbrand.

76. For the "gambler's saying"—"The third time pays for all"—, see Robert William Dent, *Shakespeare's Proverbial Language: An Index* (Berkeley and Los Angeles: University of California Press, 1981), T319.

77. John Hiles, *Musical Dictionary*.

78. Among them is Samuel Johnson.

4. TALKING CURES

1. *Epoch* 18 (fall 1968): 114–19. Delivered to the International Poetry Forum in Pittsburgh (April 1967).

2. This work is much discussed in Matthew von Unwerth, *Freud's Requiem: Mourning, Memory and the Invisible History of a Summer Walk* (New York: Riverhead Books, 2005).

3. See, for example, Rilke's "Gott spricht zu jedem nur, eh er ihn macht, / dann geht er schweigend mit ihm aus der Nacht" (1899), and his "Spaziergang" (1924).

4. She would later write to Freud about patients who had symptoms involving walking, as in her letter to Freud written from Gottingen in 22 February 1919. See *Sigmund Freud and Lou Andreas-Salomé: Letters* (New York: Harcourt Brace Jovanovich, 1972).

5. *Das Land Goethes 1914–1916. Ein vaterländisches Gedenkbuch*, ed. Berliner Goethebund [Isidor Landau und Eugen Zabel] (Stuttgart: Deutsche Verlags-Anstalt, 1916).

6. Sigmund Freud, *Five Lectures on Psychoanalysis, Lecture 1*; in *The Standard Edition of the Complete Psychological Works of Sigmund Freud* [hereafter SE], ed. James Strachey et al. (London: Hogarth Press, 1953–), 11:8.

7. William Hazlitt, "On Going a Journey," *The New Monthly Magazine* (1821); also in his *Table-Talk*.

8. "Craft Interview with John Ashbery," *New York Quarterly* (winter 1972); quoted from William Packard, *The Craft of Poetry: Interviews from the New York Quarterly* (Garden City, NY: Doubleday & Company, Inc., 1974), 124.

9. Dorothy Wordsworth, 12 July 1800, *The Grasmere Journals*, ed. Pamela Woof (Oxford: Clarendon Press, 1991), 17.

10. Dorothy Wordsworth, 22 December 1801, *Grasmere Journals*, 50.

11. Charles Lamb, *Quarterly Review* 12 (1814): 111; quoted in Alfred C. Ames, "Contemporary Defence of Wordsworth 'Pedlar'," *Modern Language Notes* 63.8 (December 1948): 543–44. My emphasis.

12. WT 4.4.182
13. Myles Davies, *Athenae Britannicae; or, A Critical History of the Oxford and Cambri[d]ge Writers and Writings* (London: [printed for the author], 1716): II.139: "The rest moulded upon Lucretius's Splay-footed numbers, with some pedestrian spoilings [*printed* spoulings] out of Horace's Epistles."
14. William Roscoe, *Life and Pontificate of Leo the Tenth* (Liverpool: Cadell, 1805), I. Pref. p. xxii: "The diary [of Hans Burckhardt] is written in a pedestrian and semi-barbarian style."
15. Lord Byron, *Don Juan* (1824), dedication, in *Works* (1833), XV.104: "Who wandering with pedestrian Muses, / Contend not with you on the winged steed."
16. Consider Robin Jarvis, *Romantic Writing and Pedestrian Travel* (London: Macmillan Press, 1997).
17. Ibid.
18. However, see Jarvis's chapter "Walking and Talking: Late Romantic Voices."
19. Anne Wallace's *Walking, Literature, and English Culture: The Origins and Uses of Peripatetic in the Nineteenth Century* (Oxford: Clarendon Press, 1993).
20. Anne D. Wallace, "Farming on Foot: Tracking Georgic in Clare and Wordsworth," *Texas Studies in Literature and Language* [TSLL] 34.4 (1992): 527.
21. Gilbert, "The Walk as Thinking: A. R. Ammons and John Ashbery," from *Walks in the World*, reprinted in abridged form in *Critical Essays on A. R. Ammons*, ed. Robert Kirschten (N.p.: G.K. Hall & Co., 1997), 246–70.
22. Roger Gilbert, "A. R. Ammons and John Ashbery: The Walk as Thinking," in *Walks in the World* (Princeton, NJ: Princeton University Press, 1991).
23. London: Mathew Lownes, 1606.
24. Gilbert (1991), 11.
25. Jarvis, *Romantic Writing and Pedestrian Travel*.
26. Roger Gilbert and Anne Wallace, eds., *The Quotable Walker* (N.p.: Breakaway Books, 2000).
27. Roger Gilbert, Jeffrey Robinson, and Anne Wallace, *The Walker's Literary Companion* (2000).
28. See Gilbert's Afterword, in Jeffrey Cane Robinson, *The Walk: Notes on a Romantic Image* (Champaign, IL: Dalkey Archive Press, 2006).
29. Wordsworth, *An Evening Walk*, ed. James Averill (Ithaca, NY: Cornell University Press, 1984).
30. "[Algernon Charles Swinburne's verse play] The Sisters [London: Chatto and Windus, 1892]," review essay, in *Saturday Review* (21 May 1892): 602/1. Swinburne was a master of metrics.
31. Wordsworth, "Descriptive Sketches in Verse. Taken During a Pedestrian Tour in the Italian, Grison, Swiss, and Savoyard Alps" (1793).
32. Wordsworth. Published posthumously. Bk. 4
33. William Hazlitt, "My First Acquaintance with Poets" [1823], in *English Critical Essays: Nineteenth Century* (London: Oxford, 1916), 84.

34. Dorothy Wordsworth, *Grasmere Journals*, 219n.
35. *Stonework* issue 4. *Stonework* is published by Houghton College (New York State); John Tatter teaches at Birmingham-Southern College (Alabama); http://faculty.bsc.edu/jtatter/stonework.html; accessed 20 September 2012. See also Carol Buchanan, *Wordsworth's Gardens* (Lubbock: Texas Tech University Press, 2001).
36. London Corresponding Society. "Reminiscences" is included in William Angus Knight, ed., *Wordsworthiana: A Selection of Papers Read to the Wordsworth Society* (London and New York: Macmillan & Co., 1889).
37. Hardwicke Drummond Rawnsley, *Reminiscences of Wordsworth Among the Peasantry of Westmorland* (London: London Corresponding Society, 1882). The chapter "Reminiscences" is included in Knight, ed., *Wordsworthiana*.
38. Rawnsley, *Reminiscences*.
39. *OED*, sv "Bum," v^2.
40. *Quarterly Review* 92 (December 1852): 121.
41. Thomas de Quincy, *Recollections of the Lakes and the Lake Poets*, ed. David Wright (1970; reprint, Harmondsworth, England: Penguin, 1985), 136. Quoted in Bennett, "'Devious Feet': Wordsworth and the Scandal of Narrative," *ELH* 59.1 (Spring 1992): 145.
42. William Hazlitt, "On Going a Journey," *The New Monthly Magazine* (1821); also in his *Table-Talk*.
43. "If I could so clothe my ideas in sounding and flowing words, I might perhaps wish to have some one with me to admire the swelling theme; or I could be more content, were it possible for me still to hear his echoing voice in the woods of All-Foxden [the location of the homes of Coleridge and of Wordsworth's in Somersetshire]."
44. Anon [William Thomas Brande], *The Life and Adventure of the Celebrated Walking Stewart* (London: E. Wheatley, 1822), refers to Stewart's "swiftness of feet" (5).
45. Williamson, *The Senecan Amble: A Study in Prose Form from Bacon to Collier* (Chicago: University of Chicago Press, 1951), 142.
46. *OED*, sv "Hop," vi, esp. 3. Daniel Defoe, *Memoirs of a Cavalier* (London: A. Bell, J. Osborn, W. Taylor, and T. Warner, 1720), 1:250.
47. Johnson, *Dictionary of the English Language*, 4th ed. (1773).
48. Williamson, *Senecan Amble*, 148; discussed also in David Lawrence Cole, "James Howell and the Speech of Commonwealth: Seventeenth-Century Prose Style in Transition," PhD diss. (Texas Tech University, 1974).
49. Anthony Ashley-Cooper, 3rd Earl of Shaftesbury, *Characteristics of Men, Manners, Opinions, Times*, ed. J. M. Robertson (London: n.p., 1900), 2:170; Misc. 1, chap. iii., quoted by Williamson, 353.
50. Prelude, book 5. So argues Kelly Groovier, "Dream Walker: A Wordsworth Mystery Solved," *Romanticism* 13.2 (2007): 156–63.
51. Grovier, "'Shades of the Prison House': 'Walking' Stewart and the Making of Wordsworth's 'two consciousnesses'," *Studies in Romanticism* (Fall 2005): 341–66.
52. *OED*, sv, "Water-break."
53. Bennett, "'Devious Feet.'"

54. "Impediments that make his task more sweet" (Wordsworth, *Prelude* 4:261).
55. Wordsworth, *Prelude* 4:108–9.
56. *OED*, sv. "Dilatation," n3, and "Dilation."
57. Wordsworth, *Peter Bell*, 1084–85.
58. Wharton, *English Poetry* (London), 3:377.
59. Wordsworth, *The Waggoner*, 379–80.
60. Wordsworth, *Simon Lee*, 35.
61. Wordsworth, *The Recluse*, Part First, Book First: *Home at Grasmere*, 504–9. First published in *The Complete Poetical Works of William Wordsworth*, Globe Edition, intro. John Morley (London and New York: Macmillan and Co., 1888).
62. Wordsworth, *Prelude*, 7.93–108.
63. Wordsworth, *Two April Mornings*, 49–50.
64. Wordsworth, *Lucy Gray*, 61.
65. Wordsworth, *Brothers*, 220–21.
66. Ammons.
67. See Richard D. McGhee's *Guilty Pleasures: William Wordsworth's Poetry of Psychoanalysis and Joel Faflak's Romantic Psychoanalysis: The Burden of the Mystery.*
68. (London: MacMillan, n.d.), 240.
69. S. Y. Tan, D. Shigaki, "Jean-Martin Charcot (1825–1893): Pathologist who Shaped Modern Neurology," *Singapore Medical Journal* 48 (2007): 383–84.
70. Charcot's "Sur la claudication intermittente" [1858] is in *Comptes Rendus des Séances et Mémoires de la Société de Biologie* (Paris) 1858, 5:225.
71. P. Olivier and André Halipré, "Claudication intermittente chez un homme hystérique atteint de pouls lent permanent," *La Normandie Médicale* 11 (1896): 21–28 (plate on 23).
72. For a technical and semantic history of this medical condition, see M. Condorelli and G. Brevetti, "Intermittent Claudication: An Historical Perspective," *European Heart Journal Supplements* (2002) 4 (Supplement B), B2–B7. This article points out that, as a technical term, intermittent claudication is a misnomer.
73. Joseph Babinski, "Sur le réflexe cutané plantaire dans certains affections organiques du système nerveux central," *Comptes rendus hebdomadaires des séances de la Societé de biologie* [Paris] 48 (1896): 207–8.
74. Wilhelm Erb, "Über das *intermittierende Hinken* und andere nervöse Störungen in Folge von Gefässerkrankungen," *Deutsche Zeitschrift für Nervenheilkunde* 13 (1898): 1–77.
75. Halipré, *La Paralysie pseudo-bulbaire d'origine cérébrale* (Paris: G. Steinheil, 1894).
76. Philadelphia: P. Blakiston, Son, & Co. The Infirmary was in Philadelphia.
77. SE 1. For links to Freud and Osler, see L. D. Longo and S. Aswal, "William Osler, Sigmund Freud, and the Evolution of Ideas Concerning Cerebral Palsy," *Journal of the History of Neuroscience* 2 (1993): 255–82.

78. See Shell, *Polio and Its Aftermath*.
79. Herman Determann, "'Intermittierendes Hinken': eines Armes, der Zunge und der Beine (Dyskinesia intermittens angiosclerotica)," *Deutsche Zeitschrift für Nervenheilkunde* 29 (1905): 152–62.
80. *Neurologische Zentralblatt* 28 (1908): 754.
81. See Lorenzo Bellettini, "Freud's Contribution to Arthur Schnitzler's Prose Style," *Rocky Mountain Review* (fall 2007): 1–27.
82. *Internationale Kinische Rundschau* 3 (1889).
83. SE 2:35.
84. SE 2:148. See Peggy Phelan, "Immobile Legs, Stalled Words: Psychoanalysis and Moving Deaths," in *Mourning Sex: Performing Public Memories* (London: Routledge, 1997).
85. Fragments of an Analysis of a Case of Hysteria [1905 (1901)], SE 7:101–2.
86. Freud, SE 7:102.
87. Felix Deutsch, "A Footnote to Freud's 'Fragment of an Analysis of a Case of Hysteria,'" reprinted in Charles Bernheimer and Claire Kahane, *In Dora's Case* (New York: Columbia University Press, 1985), 41.
88. P. 64.
89. Chicago: University of Chicago Press.
90. Freud, SE 7:16–17, n.2.
91. *Faust*, "Auerbach's Cellar."
92. Also mentioned in *Faust*.
93. Gn 32.32.
94. Correspondence, Freud to Fliess, May 1900.
95. Freud, *The Interpretation of Dreams* (1900), SE 4–5:424.
96. SE 2.
97. Freud, *The Complete Letters of Sigmund Freud to Wilhelm Fliess 1887–1904*, ed. and trans. Jeffrey Moussaieff Masson (Cambridge, MA, and London: Belknap Press of Harvard University Press), 268. All three children were born in 1855/1856.
98. Marianne Krull, *Freud und sein Vater: d. Entstehung d. Psychoanalyse und Freuds ungelöste Vaterbindung*, intro. Helm Stierlin (Munich: Beck, 1979); trans. by Arnold J. Pomerans, pref. Helm Stierlin (New York: W. W. Norton, 1986).
99. Opus 62, vol. 1, no. 5 (1837)
100. See Sybille Schmitz, *Warum Kinder stottern: Ein kindgerechter, psychosomatischer Zugang. Ein einfühlsames Bilderbuch für Eltern und Kinde*, illus. Martina Vierthaler (Munich: Gruppenpaedag, 2010): "Wenn dann noch das Angstgefühl dazukommt, wird es chaotisch im Mund, und das Wort hüpft und hinkt heraus."
101. SE 18:338.
102. *Al maquamat* by Abu Muhammad al Qasim ibn Ali al-Hariri of Basra by Abu Muhammad al Qasim ibn Ali al-Hariri of Basra.
103. German trans. by Friedrich Rückert.
104. English trans. David Wyatt; wyattdaglobalnet.co.uk.
105. *Sprachheilkunde: Vorlesungen über die Störungen der Sprache mit besonderer Berücksichtigung der Therapie* (Berlin: Kornfeld, 1912), 393.

Cited in Mabel Stevens, "Why Classwork is of Limited Value in the Treatment of Stuttering," *The Pedagogical Seminary: An International Record of Educational Literature, Institutions, and Progress*, ed. Granville Stanley Hall, vol. 24 (1917), 47.

106. For voice and piano. In Acht Lieder mit Klavierbegleitung aus dem "Liebesfrühling."

107. Carl Loewe, *Selbstbiographie*, ed. C. H. Bitter (Berlin: W. Müller, 1870), 31, 351.

108. Set to music by Johann Karl Gottfried Loewe (1796–1869) in his *Hinkende Jamben* op. 62, Heft 1 no. 5 (1837) and by Franz Ippisch (1883–1958), in his "Ein Liebchen hatt' ich" (1918) in his *Acht Lieder mit Klavierbegleitung aus dem "Liebesfrühling" von Friedrich Rückert für hohe Stimme*.

109. "Wigmore Hall Song Competition Final" (10 September 2009); reported in *Opera Britannia* (http://www.opera-britannia.com; accessed 25 September 2012).

5. WALKIE TALKIES

1. *American Journal of Psychology* 24 (July 1913): 305–59; and 24 (October 1913): 508–19.

2. "Kinesthetic Rhythms: Participation in Performance," in *Rhythms: Essays in French Literature, Thought and Culture*, ed. Elizabeth Lindley and Laura McMahon (New York: Peter Lang, 2008).

3. For this phrase, see www.silentera.com.

4. Phono-Cinéma-Théâtre Sound Films produced "Le Duel d'Hamlet" (1900) and "Tich et ses 'Big Boots'" (1900). British Phono-Cinéma-Théâtre Sound Films had "The Lambeth Cake Walk" (1901). Gaumont (British) Chronophone Films put out "Strolling Home with Angelina" (1906), "The Waltz Must Change to a March" (1906), and "We All Walked into the Shop" (1906). Warwick Cinephone Sound Films had "The Galloping Major" (1909) and "The Waltz Must Turn to a March" (1909). U.K. Kinoplastikon Sound Films had "Persian Dance: Eightpence a Mile." De Forest Phonofilm Sound Films did "Tramp Tramp Tramp, The Boys Are Marching" (1926).

5. U.K. Kinoplastikon Sound Films had "Syncopation and Song" (1927).

6. On Berlin's song per se, see Jeffrey Magee, "'Everybody's Step': Irving Berlin, Jazz, and Broadway in the 1920s," *Journal of the American Musicological Society* 59.3 (2006). Compare Berlin's "They Were All Out of Step but Jim" (1918).

7. See "A World Court of Eminent Musicians Discuss 'The Ten Great Masterpieces,'" *Etude* (March 1924): 150.

8. Here quoted from *Brief Introduction to the Skill of Musick*, 13th ed. (1697), 19.

9. *OED*, sv "Goodness," 2a and 5.

10. In much the same way, doctors in this period believed that massage with peanut oil would treat paralytic polio.

11. *The Wizard of Oz* by Noel Langley, Florence Ryerson, and Edgar Allen Woolf. Cutting Continuity Script. Taken From Printer's Dupe. Last revised 15 March 1939. Based on the book by Frank Baum.

12. See the discussion of Dickenson's "After great pain" in Shell, *Polio and Its Aftermath* (Cambridge, MA: Harvard University Press, 2006).

13. Thomas H. Johnson, ed., *The Poems of Emily Dickinson: Including Variant Readings Critically Compared with All Known Manuscripts* (Cambridge, MA: Harvard University Press, 1955), "How many times these low feet staggered—," # 187.

14. *Dickinson*, Johnson, ed., "After great pain a formal feeling comes—", # 341.

15. Cristianne Miller, "Dowering All the Word," *Proceedings of the Modern Language Association* 104.6 [program 456] (November 1989), 1087. See also Michael Cherlin, "Thoughts on Poetry and Music, on Rhythms in Emily Dickinson's 'The World Feels Dusty' and Aaron Copland's Setting of It," *Intégral* 5 (1991): 55–75.

16. *Dickinson*, Johnson, ed., # 7.

17. *Dickinson*, Johnson, ed., # 328.

18. James C. Bulman and J. M. Nosworthy, "Timon" or "The Comedy of Timon." MS 52 in the Dyce Collection at the Victoria and Albert Museum and a *Source for Shakespeare's "Timon of Athens"* (Oxford: Oxford University Press, 1980); spelling modernized.

19. 4 October 1939: 24/3. S.C.R. = Signal Corp Radio.

20. "The walkie-lookie (a new NBC handheld camera, which was promptly dubbed a creepie-peepie) did for the visual audience what the roving candid microphone had done for radio listeners" (*Life* [magazine] [21 July 1952], 18).

21. *OED*, sv "Walkman."

22. In *Looney Tunes Golden Collection*, DVD box-set, Warner Brothers 2005, vol. 3.

23. *The Squawkin' Hawk* (1942) was "the first cartoon Henery Hawk appeared in. In this film he was a young hawk whose mother was trying to get him to eat a worm because he was too young to go after chickens. But Henery was stubborn and he goes after chickens behind her back."

24. I discuss the latter cartoon in Shell, "Animals that Talk," *differences* 15 (2004): 84–107.

25. Also *OED*.

26. That is, "anatomie mouvante."

27. See Rosemarie Wildermuth, *Die mechanische Ente: Geschichten, Gedichte und Berichte von Menschen und ihren Erfindungen* (Munich: Ellermann, 1974).

28. Vaucanson, "Le mecanisme du fluteur automate," Paris, 1738. Reproduced in *l'Encyclopédie*, ed. d'Alembert and Diderot, sv "Androgine." See also André Doyon and Lucien Liagre, *Jacques Vaucanson: Mécanicien de génie* (Paris: P.U.F., 1966).

29. Diogenes Laertius, *Lives and Opinions of the Eminent Philosophers*, "Diogenes of Sinope," 6.40–42.

30. *Plato and a Platypus Walk Into a Bar—: Understanding Philosophy Through Jokes* (New York: Abrams, 2006).

31. Thomas Cathcart and Daniel M. Klein, *Kant and the Platypus: Essays on Language and Cognition* [*Kant e l'ornitorinco*], trans. Alastair McEwen (London: Secker & Warburg), see esp. chap. 4.

32. Robert McKimson Jr., *"I Say, I Say . . . Son!": A Tribute to Legendary Animators Bob, Chuck, and Tom McKimson*, intro. Darrell Van Citters, foreword John Kricfalusi (Solana Beach, CA: Santa Monica Press, 2012).

33. John Camden Hotten, *Dictionary of Slang*, 2d ed. (London: n.p., 1860), 227: "*Stems*, the legs."

34. *Penny Cyclopædia of the Society for the Diffusion of Useful Knowledge* (1842), 24.154/1: "Speaking-pipes, or tubes to convey the voice from one place to another."

35. Many early silent films had already depicted the cure of deafness and muteness. In such silent films as *Rimrock Jones* (1919) and *The Big Little Person* (1919), curing muteness and deafness was already the essential subject. One finds the same in *The Silent Voice* (1915) and *The Man Who Played God* (1922)—both based on Jules Eckert Goodman's play *The Silent Voice*, in which a concert pianist goes deaf. The theme was long-lived enough so that the film *Sincerely Yours* (1955), likewise based on Goodman's stageplay, was a popular film.

36. This movie is an adaptation of the play by Moss Hart and George S. Kaufman.

37. One of its main sources was *Once in a Lifetime*.

38. When she is leaving, Freddy Eynsford-Hill asks her if she is going to walk across the park, to which she famously replies, "Walk! Not bloody likely. [Sensation] I am going in a taxi." It is not so much *what* Eliza Dolittle says to Freddy Eynsford-Hill at this middle point (act 3) of Shaw's *Pygmalion*—that it is unlikely that she will go for a walk—that causes the sensation among the interlocutors. It is the way she talks. Eliza drops her upper-class accent and/or returns to her traditional Cockney accent and/or uses the perhaps mildly offensive term *bloody*. In other words, Eliza for the moment cannot quite talk the walk. That is the reason that, in the wake of the success of Shaw's play, using the word *bloody* came to be called "pygmalion." (For the adjective *pygmalion*, see OED, sv "Pygmalion," B2.)

39. OED, sv "Dub," v^5.

40. There is an irony in these films: the actors who play the "best-spoken" women are themselves often dummies. The real Debbie Reynolds, whom film audiences believed to be the actual voice-woman Kathy Selden in *Singin' in the Rain*, does not actually do the singing for Lina: Jean Hagen does. Similarly, the real Audrey Hepburn, who plays Eliza Doolittle in the film version of *My Fair Lady* (1964), does not do her own singing: Marni Nixon does. The "theme" of voice change and illusion in cinematography was often thus reproduced in "production." My own favorite examples of such dubbing concern two polio survivors who could not walk or could not walk well. Opera singer Eileen Farrell did the singing for Eleanor Parker, who portrays the opera-singer Marjorie Lawrence felled by polio in *Interrupted Melody*

(1955). Peg La Centra did the singing for the polio (survivor) Ida Lupino in two films: *The Man I Love* (1946), in which Lupino plays the singer Petey Brown, and *Escape Me Never* (1947), in which Lupino plays Gemma Smith.

41. It also points to Moses's painting Aaron's toes red with the blood of a ram. Some persons might almost conclude that there are two "Moseses" [sic] in opposition with each other: the one who supposes and the one who knowses; others, in discussing this "nursery rhyme" per se, point to Leviticus 22–24, where the "dummy" Moses, using the blood of a ram, paints red the toes of his "ventriloquist" brother Aaron.

42. Sinatra said, "I've always thought Lewis was one of only about four or five great artists in this century."

43. Newspaper reports at the time had it that the mobster cut off a piece of Lewis's tongue.

44. Cohn, *The Joker Is Wild: The Story of Joe E. Lewis*, 47.

45. On James Stewart's stuttering, see Benson Bobrick, *Knotted Tongues: Stuttering in History and a Quest for the Cure* (New York: Simon and Shuster, 1995); and Jhan Robbins, *Everybody's Man: A Biography of Jimmy Stewart* (New York: G. P. Putnam's Sons, 1985).

46. Double-exposure was a preferred photographic method of the twentieth-century ballerina Elizabeth Twistington. Dance therapy did not cure her paralysis—which landed her for decades in an iron lung. This artist of bodily motion expressed through still photography the choreographies of stillness. Tanaquil LeClerq, Georges Balanchine's wife, did something like the same. After dancing in Ravel's *La Valse*—a ballet based loosely on Edgar Allan Poe's story *Masque of the Red Death* in which Balanchine himself play-acted the part of Polio—LeClerq actually contracted polio itself and ended up in an iron lung. Whence she wrote a book intended as choreography for her pet cat, Mourka, which Balanchine himself taught to dance for her. Mourka the Cat, thereafter, danced for the entirely stilled human ballerina. Her prosthetic animal soul.

47. *OED*, sv "Totter," n^1, 2.

48. The quotation is from E. A. Solinas. 14 June 2006 review of DVD collection *The James Stewart Hollywood Legend Collection (Vertigo / Rear Window / Harvey / Winchester '73 / Destry Rides Again)*, as listed at http://www.amazon.com/Stewart-Hollywood-Collection-Vertigo-Winchester/dp/B00023P4RY.

49. *OED*, sv "Tot," n^4, 1a, defines *tot* as "a very small . . . child"—like the young girl (in a wheelchair) included in the opening scene of *Rear Window*; see Marc Shell, *Polio and Its Aftermath*, esp. 159.

50. For the etymological link between *tottering* and *stuttering*, see esp. "Stand," in Hensleigh Wedgewood, *A Dictionary of English Etymology* (London: Trübner & Co., 1865), 3:309–10.

51. *Rear Window* 00.11.57.

52. *Rear Window* 00.02.33.

53. *Pedeconference* is not (yet) an entry in the *OED*. However, its use is common. Thus Aaron Sorkin, a scriptwriter for the television show *The West Wing*, writes in his script for the "Two Cathedrals" episode (directed by

Thomas Schlamme), apparently writes "C. J. strides through the hall. Sam spots her and *walks* after her. They *pedeconference* as they *talk*" [emphasis mine]; http://communicationsoffice.tripod.com/2-22.txt.

6. MARCHING AND HEILING IN *THE GREAT DICTATOR* (1940)

1. Johann Caspar Lavater, *Essays on Physiognomy*, trans. Henry Hunter, 3 vols. (London: n.p., 1789–98), 3: 260.

2. Christopher Rivers, *Face Value: Physiognomical Thought and the Legible Body in Marivaux, Lavater, Balzac, Gautier, and Zola* (Madison: University of Wisconsin Press, 1994).

3. See also Phorkian Heinrich Clias, *An Elementary Course of Gymnastic Exercises* (1823), who suggests that walking "well executed, evinces not only the force of the body, but . . . the moral character of the individual," and that walking "contributes . . . in presenting to the attentive physiologist, the distinguishing features of the predominating ideas, as well as those of the constitution, or of the physical and moral temperament" (qtd. in Bennett, "'Devious Feet'").

4. TMP 4.1.

5. Cf. Pericles of Tyre's praise of his wife Thaisa's "pace like Juno" (PER 5.1).

6. Alexander Walker, "Character of the French," *Blackwood's Edinburgh Magazine* (1829).

7. See Marcel Mauss's "Techniques of the Body" (1935).

8. Ovid, *Metamorphoses*, 3: 528–29.

9. J. Michael Walton, *Greek Sense of Theatre: Tragedy Reviewed*, 2d ed. (London: Methuen and Co. Ltd., 1996), 130.

10. "But Agave was foaming at the mouth, / eyes rolling in their sockets, her mind not set / on what she ought to think—she didn't listen—/ she was possessed, in a Bacchic frenzy. / She seized his left arm, below the elbow, / pushed her foot against the poor man's ribs, / then tore his shoulder out. The strength she had—/ it was not her own. The god put power / into those hands of hers" (Euripides, *Bacchae*, 1391–99; trans. Ian Johnston).

11. London: Methuen & Co.; p. 441. Cf. "It seemed to him that suspended in the air before him he saw his own brain pulsating to the rhythm of an impenetrable mystery." See Catherine Phillips Morales, "A Study of Rhythm in Conrad's 'The Secret Agent,'" PhD diss. (Texas Tech University, 1974).

12. Hamburg: Classen, 1960.

13. Elias Canetti, *Crowds and Power*, trans. Carol Stewart (London: Gollancz, 1962).

14. See above, esp. Tate, "Numme Feete."

15. Trans. Carol Stewart (London: Victor Gollancz, 1962).

16. Andrew Rosenberg and Julia Hirschberg, "Acoustic/Prosodic and Lexical Correlates of Charismatic Speech," *INTERSPEECH* (September 2005).

17. Chaplin spent hours studying films of Hitler to perfect an imitation of his speaking style. He would eventually do this with a combination of nonsense syllables and isolated German words.

18. Quoted in David Jablonsky, *Churchill and Hitler: Essays on the Political-Military Direction of Total War* (Portland, OR: F. Cass, 1994), 146. See also Robert G. L. Waite, *The Psychopathic God: Adolf Hitler* (New York: Basic Books, 1977), 35; and Joachim C. Fest, *Das Gesicht des Dritten Reiches, Profile einer totalitären Herrschaft ([1963?];* translated into English as *The Face of the Third Reich [1970]*), 84.

19. Some say that Erik Jan Hanussen coached Hitler on the use of hand movements; see the movies *Hanussen* (dir. O. W. Fischer, 1955), *Hanussen* (dir. István Szabó, 1988), and *Invincible* (dir. Werner Herzog, 2001), and Mel Gordon's book *Hanussen: Hitler's Jewish Clairvoyant* (Los Angeles: Feral House, 2001).

20. Paul Devrient, in memoir written after the war, claims to have trained Hitler early in his career in the art of effective speaking. See Werner Maser, ed., *Mein Schüler Hitler: Das Tagebuch seines Lehrers Paul Devrient* (Paffenhofen, Germany: Ilmgau Verlag, 1975). See also Bertolt Brecht, *Auftieg des Artuo Ui* (written in 1941), often compared with Chaplin's movie *The Great Dictator*. At the performance of Arturo Ui at the Minerva Theatre in Chichester, UK, Henry Goodman, who plays Arturo Ui (=Adolf Hitler) "introduces recognisable [sic] elements—rigid goose-steps, defensive arm postures, jabbing fingers, an explosive fury—that shift him by degrees from harmless figure of fun to glinting, fully fledged Führer" (*The Telegraph*, 12 July 2012; http://www.telegraph.co.uk/).

21. Denis Judd, *King George VI* (London: Michael Joseph Ltd., 1982): "[Lionel] Logue's approach was not purely psychological and many of his patients had been reassured that their difficulties could be partly caused by incorrect breathing."

22. Based on the historical drama written by David Seidler et al., *The King's Speech: How One Man Saved the British Monarchy* (Toronto: Penguin, 2010).

23. F. W. Lambertson, "Hitler, the Orator: A Study in Mob Psychology," *The Quarterly Journal of Speech* 28 (1942): 134–42.

24. Gilles Deleuze, *Cinema [I]: The Movement-Image*, trans. Hugh Tomlinson and Robert Galeta (Minneapolis: University Of Minnesota Press, 1986).

25. New York: Harcourt, 2007.

26. *Günter Grass*, "To Be Continued," in *Art and Humanist Ideals: Contemporary Perspectives*, ed. William Kelley (South Yarra, Victoria, Australia: MacMillian Publishers, 2003), 198.

27. Kleist, *On the Marionette Theater*: "Yet he did believe this last trace of human volition could be removed from the marionettes and their dance transferred entirely to the realm of mechanical forces, even produced, as I had suggested, by turning a handle" (trans. Idris Parry).

28. London: Leadenhall Press, 1891.

29. Worcester, Massachusetts.

30. Ellis R. Ephraim (composer) and Rida Johnson Young (lyricist) (New York: M. Witmark & Sons).

31. Discussed in Dan Kamin and Scott Eyman, *The Comedy of Charlie Chaplin: Artistry in Motion* (Plymouth, England: Scarecrow, 2008), 164.

32. The documentary movie *Unknown Chaplin* (Kevin Brownlow and David Gill, 1983), include a 1929 clip from a home movie in which Chaplin, acting out the part of Julius Caesar, dances with a globe. Chaplin choreographed the entire scene himself.

33. Helen Bushby, "Chaplin Colour Footage Unearthed," *BBC News: World Edition* (online edition), 16 May 2002. Hynkel there more distinctly goose-steps in the dance with Mrs. Napolini.

34. Weber and Weber, *Mechanik der Menschlichen Gehverkzeuge* [Mechanics of the human walking apparatus]: *Eine anatomisch-physiologische Untersuchung* (Göttingen, Germany: Dieterichischen Buchhandlung, 1836).

35. Christian Wilhelm Braune (son of Ernst Heinrich Weber), together with his colleague Otto Fisher, in *Der Gang des Menschen* (1895–1904), which introduced the methods of gait analysis still used today.

36. Prince of Anhalt-Dessau.

37. "Doom of *Goose-Step* Sought by Nazi Military Officials," *The Baltimore Sun*, 6 June 1937, 19.

38. *OED*, sv "Goose-step."

39. Marcel Mauss, *Sociology and Psychology: Essays* (London: Routledge and Kegan Paul, 1979), 114–15. On the goose-step, see also Mary Mosher Flesher, "Repetitive Order and the Human Walking Apparatus: Prussian Military Science Versus the Webers [Wilhelm and Eduard] Locomotion Research," *Annals of Science* 54.5 (1997): 463–87.

40. Episode 14, 1970.

41. Henri Bergson, *Laughter: An Essay on the Meaning of the Comic*, trans. Cloudesley Brereton and Fred Rothwell (New York: Macmillan, 1911), pt. 4.

42. "The balance or goose-step introduced for their practice excites a fever of disgust" (11 February 1806), in *Life of General Sir Robert Wilson . . . from autobiographical memoirs, journals, narratives, correspondence, &c.*, ed. Herbert Randolph (London: J. Murray, 1862), 1:308; and George Orwell, *The Lion and the Unicorn* (London: Secker and Warburg, 1941), i.ii.21: "The goose-step . . . is one of the most horrible sights in the world."

43. Mark S. Nixon, Tieniu Tan, and Rama Chellappa, *Human Identification Based on Gait* (New York: Springer, 2006), 53. For some other reference in this section, I am indebted to Tim Ingold, "Culture on the Ground: The World Perceived Through the Feet," *Journal of Material Culture* 9.3 (2004): 315–40.

44. George Orwell, *Why I Write* (1946). Consider Upton Sinclair's *Goosestep: A Study of American Education* (Pasadena, CA: self-published, 1923). See Lois P. Jones's poem "Goose-Step" (2008), which begins with the statement from Orwell that the goose step is horrible: "He loves to goosestep in her parking lot, / fluorescent light casting the stage / for Dachau." Fleda Brown (a judge for the poetry contest) comments: "A tightly controlled, dense poem that in its language evokes the goose-step itself."

45. Producers Distributing Corp.

46. Volker Klotz, "Cancan contra Stechschritt: Antimilitarismus mit Ruckfalles in der Operette" (Vienna: Brandstätter, 1989); also in *Österreich und der Grosse Krieg, 1914–1918: die andere Seite der Geschichte C.*, ed. Klaus Amann and Hubert Lengauer (Brandstätter: n.p., 1989).

47. Richard Ullerston, John Purvey, Jerome Barlow, William Tyndale, and William Roy, *A Compendious Olde Treatyse, Shewynge Howe that we Oughte to Haue ye scripture in Englysshe*, ed. 1863 (Antwerp: J. Hoochstraten, 1530), 52.

48. Chaplin had sound (effects) and sung a macaronic Italianate nonsense song in *Modern Times* (1936).

49. *The Great Dictator*, HD, 1.47.20.

50. Ibid., 1.37.14.

51. Ibid., 1.29.05

52. Said Hitler: "I made it the salute of the Party long after the Duce had adopted it" (*Hitler's Table Talk* [*Tischgespräche*] 3 January 1942, in Hugh Redwald Trevor-Roper, ed., *Hitler's Table Talk 1941–1944*, trans. Norman Cameron and R. H. Stevens [London: Weidenfeld and Nicolson, 1953]).

53. Some say that Erik Jan Hanussen coached Hitler on the use of hand movements; see the movies *Hanussen* (dir. O. W. Fischer, 1955), *Hanussen* (dir. István Szabó, 1988), and *Invincible* (dir. Werner Herzog, 2001), and Mel Gordon's book *Hanussen: Hitler's Jewish Clairvoyant* (Los Angeles: Feral House, 2001).

54. Paul Devrient, who in his memoir written after the war, claims to have trained Hitler early in his career in the art of effective speaking. See Werner Maser, ed., *Mein Schüler Hitler: Das Tagebuch seines Lehrers Paul Devrient* (Paffenhofen, Germany: Ilmgau Verlag, 1975). See also Bertolt Brecht, *Artuo Ui*.

55. *The Great Dictator*, HD, 0.15.30.

56. Robert Cole, "Anglo-American Anti-fascist Film Propaganda in a Time of Neutrality: *The Great Dictator*, 1940," *Historical Journal of Film, Radio and Television* 21.2 (2001): 137–52.

57. On the prosodic significance of the Italian-like nonsense song in *Modern Times*, see Pedro De Alcantara, *Integrated Practice: Coordination, Rhythm & Sound* (Oxford: Oxford University Press, 2011), 6.

58. Discussed in Robert Stam and Toby Miller, eds., *Film Theory: An Introduction* (Berkeley and Los Angeles: University of California Press, 2000), 49.

59. David Bordwell, *The Cinema of Eisenstein* (Cambridge, MA: Harvard University Press, 1993).

60. Christian Metz, *Film Language: A Semiotics of the Cinema*, trans. Michael Taylor (New York: Oxford University Press, 1974), 34. The original French-language book is called: *Essais sur la signification au cinéma*.

61. Quoted by William Sandys, *Specimens of Macaronic Poetry*, ed. by William Sandys (London: Richard Beckley, 1831), ix; from John Mason Good and Alexander Geddes, *Memoirs of the Life and the Writings of the Reverend Alexander Geddes* (London: n.p., 1803), 236.

62. Charles Anthon, *A System of Latin Prosody and Metre: From the Best Authorities, Ancient and Modern* (New York: Harper & Brothers, 1842), 11.

63. Alan T. Gaylord, ed., *Essays on the Art of Chaucer's Verse* (New York: Routledge, 2001), 124.
64. *OED*, sv "Foot," n. II.3; cf. *pedestal*.
65. *The Great Dictator*, HD, 2.05.16.
66. These lines also appear in Chaplin's *My Autobiography* (New York: Simon and Schuster, 1964), 433: "Greed has poisoned men's souls . . . , has goose-stepped us into misery and bloodshed."
67. *Wycliffite Bible* (early version), 1 COR 14:11.
68. Holmes, *Autocrat*, 269.
69. Robert C. Reimer, "Does Laughter Make the Crime Disappear?: An Analysis of Cinematic Images of Hitler and the Nazis, 1940–2007." Consider, among other films mentioned above: *To Be Or Not To Be* (dir. Ernst Lubitsch, 1942), and *The Producers* (dir. Mel Brooks, 1968).
70. Warner Brothers.
71. RKO Radio.
72. For Vaucanson's duck, see Figure 5.1, in Chapter 5 (A late representation of Jacques Vaucanson's automaton "Digesting Duck" [1739]).
73. *The Great Dictator*, HD, 1.50.41.
74. The composer Horst Wessel had originally had the line thus: "SA marschiert mit *ruhig*, festem Schritt" [The storm troopers march with *quiet*, steady step].
75. Augustine of Hippo, *City of God*, trans. Marcus Dods, book 14. chap. 24.
76. There were two recordings: RCA Victor Records and Bluebird; see the novel by Herman Wouk, *War and Remembrance* (Boston: Little, Brown & Company: 1978).
77. RKO Pictures.
78. Ziemer, *Education for Death: The Making of the Nazi* (New York: Oxford University Press, 1941); a feature-length movie also based on Ziemer's book is *Hitler's Children* (1943).
79. See Ziemer's "Our Education Failure in Germany," in *The American Mercury* (June 1946), 726–33, in which he criticizes the United States for "not using motion pictures for re-education in Germany" (733).
80. For a relevant image of goose-steppers, see *The Great Dictator*, HD, 0.9.19.
81. Charles Ives, *Memos*, ed. John Kirkpatrick (New York: W. W. Norton and Company, Inc., 1972), 140.
82. Wes D. Gehring, *Forties Film Funnymen: The Decade's Great Comedians at Work in the Shadow of War*, foreword Anthony Slide (New York: McFarland, 2010), 18.
83. *Theory of Walking* was apparently meant to be a part of that project.
84. Desiderius Erasmus, *Paraphrase of Erasmus vpon the Newe Testament*, trans. Miles Coverdale et al., vol. 2 (London: n.p., 1549), col. iii. f. vii^v.
85. "I suspect that the first printed version of the song was subtitled 'The Lexington March'" (J. A. Leo Lemay, "The American Origins of *Yankee Doodle*," *William and Mary Quarterly* 33.3 [1976], 436).

86. *OED*, sv "Doodle," n¹ (1629 and 1764). See also German *Dudeltopf* ["fool," "noodle"].
87. *OED*, sv "Doodle," v² (1816 and 1847–78). See also James Orchard Halliwell-Phillips, *Dictionary of Archaic and Provincial Words* (London: J. R. Smith, 1847–78): "*Doodle-sack*, 'a bag-pipe.'"
88. *OED*, sv "Macaroni," etymology.
89. *OED*, sv "Macaroni," 8, 9.
90. See Marc Shell, "'Prized His Mouth Open': Mark Twain's *The Jumping Frog of Calaveras County*: In English, Then in French, Then Clawed Back into Civilized Language Once More by Patient, Unremunerated Toil," in *American Babel: Literature of the United States from Abnaki to Zuni*, ed. Marc Shell (Cambridge, MA: Harvard University Press, 2002), 491–520.
91. Sinclair, *Catalogue*, no. 122. In Charles Ives, set of *Five Takeoffs for Piano* (1906–7).
92. Henry Cowell and Sidney Cowell, *Charles Ives and His Music* (New York: Oxford University Press, 1955), 15.
93. Laurence Wallach, "The New England Education of Charles Ives," PhD diss. (Columbia University, 1973), 50.
94. J. Ryan Garber, "The Influence of George Ives on His Son Charles" (1995); http://www.ryangarber.com/ives.html#8.
95. Jan Swafford, *Charles Ives: A Life with Music* (New York: W. W. Norton, 1996), 251–52.
96. Sinclair, *Catalogue*, no. 5.
97. Charles Ives, *Essays Before a Sonata* (New York: Knickerbocker Press, 1920).
98. Cowell and Cowell, *Charles Ives*, 21.
99. Sinclair, *Catalogue*, no. 206, in Charles Ives, *114 Songs* (Redding, CT: C. E. Ives, 1922). For what Charles says (as reported here), see Ives, *Memos*, 142.
100. Sinclair, *Catalogue*, no. 383; in Ives, *114 Songs*.
101. Charles Ives, *Walking: Song for Voice & Piano*; Sinclair, *Catalogue*, no. 383. On this song, see Kevin O. Kelly, "The Songs of Charles Ives and the Cultural Contexts of Death," PhD diss. (University of North Carolina at Chapel Hill, 1988), 476–84.
102. Charles Ives, "Postface" [so-called], in *114 Songs*.
103. Martha Davis, Dianne Dulicai, and Ildiko Viczian, "Hitler's Movement Signature," *TDR* 36.2 (Summer 1992): 152–72.
104. See Werner von Axster Heüdtlass's Nazi propaganda pamphlet, *Ein Volk, Ein Reich, Ein Führer* [One people, one reich, one führer] (1938), which quotes Hitler as saying, "Im Anfang war das Wort / München 1920." This pamphlet is in Western Michigan University Library Special Collections.
105. Quoted in Catherine Drinker Bowen, *Miracle at Philadelphia* (Boston: Little Brown & Co., 1966), 291–92.
106. *Quebec Gazette* (8 May 1788).

7. KNOCK-KNEED AND TONGUE-TIED IN *THE KING'S SPEECH* (2010)

1. *The King's Speech*, DVD, 0.52.
2. Head-of-page title in Hector Berlioz, *Memoirs*, annot. and rev. Ernest Newman (New York: Tudor Publishing, 1932), 269.
3. 31 October 1925.
4. *The King's Speech*, DVD, 1.40.
5. Confirmed by the author in correspondence with Elliott (2 July 2013), who is editor of *Research in Post-Compulsory Education* and a professor at the University of Worcester (UK).
6. *The King's Speech*, DVD, 0.52.
7. London: Arthur Barker, 1934.
8. Ibid.
9. Quoted by Shell, *Stutter*, 188.
10. Merle Oberon was seriously injured.
11. For this speculation, see Karol Kulik, *Alexander Korda: The Man Who Could Work Miracles* [1975] (London: Virgin Books, 1990), 197. Korda was the film's producer.
12. " . . . like his father and all his brothers except David [the Prince of Wales and future King Edward VIII], Bertie suffered from knock knees [called genu valgum by doctors]. In an attempt to correct this defect, a system of splints had been devised which Bertie wore during the day and, for a while, also at night.—The experiment proved to be a painful one for the wearer, though the Prince bore it stoically" (Peter Gordon and Denis Lawton, *Royal Education: Past, Present, and Future* [London: Frank Cass, 1999], 187).
13. *St. George's Hospital Reports* 9 (1879): 614: "Knock-knee . . . treated by the long-continued application of splints."
14. Shakespeare, H 2.1.
15. OED, sv "knock knee."
16. *OED*, sv. "knock," v, 1; "To strike with a sounding blow."
17. London: MacMillan and Co.
18. 5.
19. Ibid.
20. Saintsbury, *The Earlier English Renaissance* (Edinburgh: William Blackwood & Sons, 1901), 5:271.
21. *The King's Speech*, DVD, 26.
22. Vincent Brome, *Aneurin Bevan: A Biography* (London: Longmans, Green, 1953). For his uncle: Michael Foot, *Aneurin Bevan: A Biography—Volume 1: 1897-1945* (London: Macgibbon & Kee, 1962).
23. John Campbell, *Nye Bevan: A Biography* (London: Hodder & Stoughton, 1994).
24. *Westminster Gazette* [London] (7 December 1898), 4/1.
25. See Benson Bobrick, *Knotted Tongues: Stuttering in History and the Quest for a Cure* (New York: Simon & Schuster, 1995).
26. *London Daily Mail* (20 December 2010).

27. This is Firth's view as documented in the movie *The King's Speech: The Man Behind the King's Speech* (ITN Productions, 2011).
28. Mozart, Köchel 492.
29. Sanja Perovic, *Untamable Time: A Literary and Historical Panorama of the French Revolutionary Calendar* (1792–1805) (Stanford: Stanford University Press, 2004), 270.
30. *The King's Speech*, DVD, 27.
31. Todd Martens, "The Sound of Silence: Alexandre Desplat on the Music that 'Just Floats' Throughout *The King's Speech*," *Pop & Hiss* (26 November 2010).
32. Quoted in Lisa Zhito "Alexandre Desplat Brings *The King's Speech* to Life," *MusicWorld* (17 June 2011).
33. Beethoven, opus 92.
34. Berlioz, "Étude critique des symphonies de Beethoven," #7, in Berlioz, *A Travers Chants* (Paris: Michel Lévy Frères, 1862).
35. New York: Charles Scribner's Sons, 1898, 227.
36. Hector Berlioz, *The Memoirs of Hector Berlioz*, trans. David Cairns, 104.
37. Berlioz, opus 18.
38. Berlioz, opus 16.
39. The review of 23 November 1934 is reported in G. A. Osborne, "Berlioz," in *Proceedings of the Royal Musician Association* 5–6 (1878–79): 68. Berlioz himself reports the review in *The Memoirs of Hector Berlioz*, 226.
40. See Louis Vincent Guillouard, *Les Origines de la clameur de haro* (Paris: [E. Bourges], 1872). See also *OED*, s.v. "Harrow | haro, *int.*"
41. *The King's Speech*, DVD, 1.43.
42. Ibid., 1.07.
43. Beethoven, opus 73.
44. Mozart, Köchel 622.
45. Johann Friedrich Schink, "Musikalische Akademie von Stadler," *Litterarische Fragmente* (Graz: Widmanstätten, 1785).
46. Beethoven's concerto received the name "Emperor" from its English publisher Johann Baptist Cramer. On King George as the last emperor, see Peter Townsend, *The Last Emperor* (London: Weidenfeld and Nicolson, 1975).
47. Beethoven, opus 67.
48. Ego sum rex Romanus et supra grammaticam.
49. *Caesar non est supra grammaticos*. That is how Immanuel Kant puts the matter in his "What Is Enlightenment?" in *On History*, ed. Lewis White Beck, trans. Lewis White Beck, Robert E. Anchor, and Emil L. Fackenheim, 1st ed. (Indianapolis, IN: Bobbs-Merrill, 1963), 8.
50. Molière, *Femmes savantes* 2.6.465–66; trans. Charles Heron Wall. At the time, French *grammaire* was pronounced as *grand'mère*.
51. *OED*, sv "Grammar," 1a. Cf. B. Jonson, *English Grammar* (1637), in Works (London: n.p., 164[?]), vol. 3.
52. *The King's Speech*, DVD, 0.46.
53. Reported in *The Pittsburgh Press* (23 April 1939).

8. SIGN LANGUAGES

1. John Bulwer, *Chirologia, or, The Naturall Language of the Hand*, composed of the speaking motions, and discoursing gestures thereof. Whereunto is added, *Chironomia, or, The Art of Manual Rhetoricke*, consisting of the naturall expressions, digested by art in the hand.... With TYPES, OR CHYROGRAMS, a long-wish'd for illustration of this argument [by J. B., Gent. Philochirosophus] (London: Henry Twyford, 1644).

2. Charlotte Gray, *Reluctant Genius: Alexander Graham Bell and the Passion for Invention* (New York: Arcade Publishing, 2006), 9.

3. "The Twitching Finger of the Telegraph: Gregory Whitehead, Lost and Found Sound," *All Things Considered* (National Public Radio, 23 April 1999).

4. Grosz and Wright, *Let Your Fingers Do the Walking*, Aviva # 6000 (1977), LP.

5. 45 RPM, Capitol #P-4127, 1975.

6. 45 RPM. Promo Record.

7. COL 660328 2.

8. A track in his *International Harvesters*, CD, 2011.

9. http://adage.com.

10. *OED*.

11. George Grote, *History of Greece* (London: John Murray, 1847), IV. ii.xxix.114.

12. John Bulwer (1644).

13. Thomas Blount, *Glossographia* (1656).

14. Rabelais, *Works*, trans. Thomas Urquhart and Pierre Anthony Motteux, third book, Xix.

15. Chicago: University of Chicago, 1992.

16. i.vi.36.

17. See Hammerstein, *Diabolus in musica*, 7.

18. *Der vollkommene Capellmeister* (Hamburg: n.p., 1739), pt. II, chap. 6 §22, 23; cited http://www.bach-cantatas.com/BWV138-D3.htm.

19. BWV-846 to BMV-893.

20. BMV-138.

21. Bach wrote this cantata (BMV-138) for the fifteenth Sunday after Trinity. For that day the church readings include Galatians 5:25–6:10—Paul's caution to "walk in the Spirit": *si vivimus spiritu spiritu et ambulemus* (5:25).

22. Thomas Braatz, in "Cantata BWV 138: 'Warum betrübst du dich, mein Hertz?', discussions part 3," http://www.bach-cantatas.com/BWV138-D3.htm. Cf. Richard Troeger, *Playing Bach on the Keyboard: A Practical Guide* (Swavesey, Cambridge: Amadeus Press, 2003).

23. Braatz, "Cantata BWV 138."

24. Dorothy Miles, *Bright Memory* (Doncaster, England: British Deaf History Society, 1998).

25. Rachel Sutton-Spence, "Dorothy Miles," *European Cultural Heritage Online* (ECHO), http://www.let.kun.nl/sign-lang/echo/docs (December 2003).

26. It is likely that Miles had polio, not meningitis as referenced in the epigraph; see below on Miles's work at the Salk Institute. "Most cases reported prior to July 1 1958 of non-paralytic poliomyelitis are now reported as 'viral or aseptic meningitis' in accordance with instructions from Washington," reported the Los Angeles County Health Authority, and the confusion of nomenclatures was typically for most jurisdictions. "As a result, the number of cases of meningitis diagnosed went from near zero to many thousands while polio came down equivalently" (Janine Roberts, "How a Continuing Polio Epidemic Is Being Hidden," in *Fear of the Invisible* [Impact Investigative Media Productions, 2008]).

27. Bulwer, *Chirologia*, 203.

28. Anon., "The Chirogymnast, or Finger Exercises," in *Magazine of Science and Schools of Art* (1845) 6:278: "The Chirogymnast . . . ought . . . to cause the different parts of the hand to acquire . . . dexterity."

29. Aristotle, *Parva Naturalia*, 436a–37a, and *Analytica Posteriora*, 81a, 87b.

30. Plato, *Cratylus*, 422e–23a, in *Plato in Twelve Volumes*, vol. 12, trans. Harold N. Fowler (Cambridge, MA: Harvard University Press; London, William Heinemann Ltd., 1921).

31. Aristotle, *Poetics*, 54b.

32. Ovid, *Metamorphoses*, bk. 4.

33. Coauthored with Howard Poizner and Ursula Bellugi (Cambridge, MA: MIT Press, 1987).

34. See Edward Bellugi and Ursula Klima, "Poetry and Song in a Language Without Sound," in *The Signs of Language* (Cambridge, MA: Harvard University Press, 1979), chap. 14; on Dorothy Miles, 350–52.

35. Marvin Harris, *Our Kind: Who We Are, Where We Came From, Where We Are Going* (New York: Harper & Row, 1989).

36. Penny Boyes Braem and Rachel Sutton-Spence, eds., *The Hands Are the Head of the Mouth: The Mouth as Articulator in Sign Languages* (Hamburg: Signum, 2001).

37. See Marc Shell, *Stutter* (Cambridge, MA: Harvard University Press, 2005).

38. Manabi Miyagi, Masafumi Nishida, Yasuo Horiuchi, and Akira Ichikawa, "Investigation on Effect of Prosody in Finger Braille," Lecture Notes in Computer Science 4061 (2006).

39. Charlotte Baker and Carol Padden, "Focusing on the Nonmanual Components of American Sign Language," *Understanding Language Through Sign Language Research*, ed. Patricia Siple (San Francisco: Academic Press, 1978), 25–57.

40. Linda Lupton, *Aspects of Rhythm in American Sign Language: A Comparative Study of Native and Non-native Signers* (Ann Arbor, MI: U.M.I Research Press, 1993).

41. Paul Scott, *British Sign Language Poetry*, with transcript [DVD] (Coleford, England: Forest Books, 2006). The signs vary, of course, within sign

languages and especially from one language to another (for example, British Sign Language to American Sign Language, and vice versa).

42. "I like to feel that I am like Dylan Thomas. I was born in Wales but I don't know any Welsh. He and I are the same in that" (poetry performance at CSUN, 8 August 1980); Sutton Spence, "Dorothy Miles."

43. Based on Dylan Thomas's *Under Milkwood: A Play for Voices* (New York: New Directions, 1954).

44. Dorothy Miles and Louie J. Fant, *Sign-language Theatre and Deaf Theatre: New Definitions and Directions*, Center on Deafness publication series, issue 2 (Northridge: California State University Northridge Center on Deafness, 1976).

45. She said at the time, "I really believe that sign language adds something to English and the combination is richer and more exciting than English alone."

46. Dorothy Miles, interview on the subject of the San Francisco Community Programme, *Deaf Perspectives* (1976): In another interview (1976), Miles commented on some of her poems that were written specifically for sign language. That is to say that they were written so that they could combine English language and sign language together. "Because I grew up as a hearing person I remember English as my first language and a combination of the two I find is a very strong way of expressing myself."

47. Dorothy Miles, interview with Greg Brooks, on *Deaf Focus*, a Theta Cable Special (Los Angeles, 1975).

48. Dorothy Miles, *Gestures: Poetry in Sign Language* (Northridge, CA: Joyce Motion Picture Co. 1976).

49. See Dorothy Miles, *Bright Memory: The Poetry of Dorothy Miles*, ed. Don Read [recorded 1985] (Feltham, Middlesex, England: British Deaf Historical Society, 1998),

50. Paul Scott, "Three Queens," in *Paul Scott's BSL Poetry* [DVD] (Coleford, England: Forest Books, 2006).

51. Paul Scott, "The Tortoise and the Hare" (2003), online: http://www.let.ru.nl/sign-lang/echo/; see Rachel Sutton-Spence and Donna Jo Napoli, "Anthropomorphism in Sign Languages: A Look at Poetry and Storytelling with a Focus on British Sign Language," *Sign Language Studies* 10.4 (summer 2010): 456.

52. George John Romanes, *Darwin, and After Darwin: An Exposition of the Darwinian Theory and a Discussion of Post-Darwinian Questions* [1893] (Cambridge: Cambridge University Press, 2011), 1:182.

53. On the "basic asymmetry between the body and the hands," see "Hand as Event," in Irit Meir, Carol Padden, Mark Aronoff, and Wendy Sandler, "Re-Thinking Sign Language Verb Classes: The Body as Subject," sandlersignlab.haifa.ac.il/; and Karl J. Franklin, review of Edna Andrew's *Markedness Theory: The Union of Asymmetry and Semiosis in Language*, in *Notes on Linguistics* 56 (1992): 51–54.

54. "The Tortoise," in Ogden Nash's *Carnival of the Animal Poems* (1949).

55. John Napier, "The Antiquity of Human Walking," in *Human Variations and Origins: Readings from the Scientific American,* ed. W. S. Laughlin and R. H. Osborne (San Francisco: Freeman, 1967), 117.

56. See John Devine, "The Versatility of Human Locomotion," *American Anthropologist* 87 (1985): 550–70. Also Hitoshi Watanabe, "Running, Creeping and Climbing: A New Ecological and Evolutionary Perspective on Human Evolution," *Mankind* [TAJA: *The Australian Journal of Anthropology*] 8 (1971): 1–13.

57. The palaeo-social anthropologist Wiktor Stoczkowski provides a short overview of the relevant history (*Explaining Human Origins: Myth, Imagination and Conjecture,* trans. Mary Turton [Cambridge: Cambridge University Press, 2002], esp. 73–74).

58. See Samuel Dowse Robbins, *Dictionary of Speech Pathology and Therapy,* 2d ed. (Cambridge, MA: Sci-Art Publishers, 1963), 67. See too William Alexander Newman, *Illustrated Medical Dictionary,* 12th ed. (Philadelphia, PA: Saunders, 1923), 622/1, sv "Logopedia, logopedics."

59. For *paed,* see *Royal Charter: Wihtred [King] of Kent, to St. Mary's Church, Lyminge,* eighth century AD [Peter H. Sawyer, *Annotated List,* number 19], in Henry Sweet, *The Oldest English Texts* (London: N. Trübner & Co., 1885), 428: "Terminos, id est, bereueg et meguines paed et stretleg."

60. OED, sv "Path," n^1.

61. Hans Kuhn, "Anlautend *p-* im Germanischen," *Zeitschrift für Mundartforschung* 28.4 (1961), 14. Cf. OED, sv "Path."

62. Ogden and Richards, *The Meaning of Meaning: A Study of the Influence of Language upon Thought and of the Science of Symbolism* (1923; reprint, New York: Mariner Books, 1989).

63. Rodney Koeneke, *Empires of the Mind: I. A. Richards and Basic English in China, 1929–1979.* Finally, in works like *The General Basic English Dictionary* and *Times of India Guide to Basic English,* Richards and Ogden developed their most internationally influential project—the Basic English program for the development of an international language based with an 850-word vocabulary.

64. *Duke Ellington and His Orchestra,* Band Call, LP World Record Club (1954); Collection Selechonek.

65. See bandleader's Ray Anthony's version of the song recorded for Capitol Records (1952). A single rpm record, titled "The Bunny Hop," includes "The Bunny Hop" and "Bunny Hop Boogie" by Ray Anthony, "Bunny Hop Mambo" by Duke Ellington, and "The Bunny Hop" by Cliffie Stone (Capitol EAP 1–605; in Collection Selechonek).

66. John Updike, *Collected Poems 1953–1993* (New York: Alfred A. Knopf, 1993), 226–27.

9. POSTAMBLE AND EPILOGUE

1. John Wolf, "The Printer's Advertisement to the Gentleman Reader," in Gabriel Harvey, *Pierce's Supererogation; or, A New Praise of the Old Ass* (London: John Wolfe, 1593).

2. Hawkins's song is partly a response to the *Suzie Q*, a dance-walk of the 1930s, and to the song-talk *Doin' the Suzie Q* (78 rpm, Decca, 1935), from Lil Hardin Armstrong (Louis Armstrong's wife). Hawkins's song became a "smash hit" in the 1960s when it was covered by Credence Clearwater Revival in 1968.

3. For example: Artsy fartsy, argy-bargy, backpack, bedspread, bedstead, blackjack, blue flu, boogie-woogie, brain drain, chill pill, Chilly Willie (the cartoon penguin), Chitty Chitty Bang Bang (movie title), chrome dome, chug-a-lug, city kitty (CB jargon), county Mountie (CB jargon), Cox and Box (an operetta by Sir Arthur Sullivan), creepie-peepie (hand-held TV camera), demisemiquaver, Dennis the Menace, dilly-dally, Ditch Witch, double trouble, downtown, dream team, fancy-schmancy, fat cat, fender-bender, fine line, flower power, Flub-a-dub, frat rat, freight rate, Frito Bandito, fuddy-duddy, funny money, gaggin' wagon, gator freighter, gritz blitz, ground round, hanky-panky, harum-scarum, head shed, heebie-jeebie(s), helter-skelter, hemidemisemiquaver, herky-jerky, hexaflexagon, higgledy piggledy, hipper-dipper, hobnob, hobson-jobson, hocus-pocus, hoity-toity, hokey-cokey, hokey-pokey, holy moly, honey-bunny, hootchie-kootchie, hotch-potch, hot shot, Hubble-bubble, hugger-mugger, Humpty Dumpty, hurdy-gurdy, hurly-burly, hurry-scurry, ill will, itsy-bitsy, jet set, legal beagle, legal eagle, local yokel, lovey-dovey, unch bunch, mean machine, mellow yellow, middle fiddle, motor voter, Mr. Green Jeans, mud-blood, mumbo-jumbo, namby-pamby, near beer, night flight, night fright, night light, nitty-gritty, okey-dokey, Ollie's Trollies, Pall Mall, pell-mell, phony baloney, Pick-Quick, picnic, piggly-wiggly, pooper-scooper, pop top, powwow, quick trick, ragin' Cajun, razzle-dazzle, red lead, repple-depple, Rikki-Tikki-Tavi, Rin-Tin-Tin, roach coach, rock 'em sock 'em, rock jock, roly-poly, rope-a-dope, rough tough cream puff, rub-a-dub, schlock rock, shock jock, slick chick, slim Jim, snail mail, soap-on-a-rope, Spruce Goose, Steady Eddie, Stormin' Norman, stun gun, sump pump, super-duper, sweetmeat, teeny-weeny, Tex-Mex, tie-dye, tzitzit, tooti-fruiti, town clown (CB jargon), Transistor Sister, virgin sturgeon, walkie-talkie, Watusi Luci, white flight, white knight, willy-nilly, wingding, and so forth.

4. This term I borrow from my friend Scott Newstrom/Newstok.

5. *OED* 2a. See L.C.S., "*Recueil de travaux* . . . and . . . *Dictionnaire*," *Contemporary Review* (London) 10 (1869), 160: "Doublets, i.e., double and divergent derivations from a common root, as, for example, *raison* and *ration*." See also Walter W. Skeat, *Etymological Dictionary* (1881), 175: "Thus *dole* is a doublet of *deal*." The French word *doublet* as such was apparently first used by Nicholas Catherinot; see the short pamphlet by Auguste Brachet, *Dictionnaire des Doublets, ou Doubles Formes de la Langue Française* (Paris: Librairie A. Franck, 1871).

6. For the French at work, see *Letters and Papers Illustrative of the Wars of the English in France, dir Master of the Rolls* (London: Longman, Green, Longman, Roberts, and Green, 1861–64), 2: 444. "For elles youre partie adverse and the saide duc might not godely have founden the moyens and the weyes to have communed to geder to conclude thaire confederacy. There are

many other examples: fit and proper, save and except, goods and chattels, to have and to hold, breaking and entering, keep and maintain, deem and consider, maintenance and upkeep, final and conclusive, null and void, fit and proper, hue and cry, free and clear, aid and abet, mind and memory, goods and chattels, peace and quiet, had and received, will and testament, and pain and penalties."

7. For a fuller discussion of the use of Latin, French, and English in medieval and modern law, see David Mellinkoff, *The Language of the Law* (Boston and Toronto: Little, Brown and Company, 1963), chaps. 6–9.

8. Frenchmen *perspire* and Englishmen *sweat*.

9. Porky's very name is already a "doublet": *porc* is the French for *pig*, which term is English.

10. *OED*, sv "Hue-and-cry."

11. John Earle, *The Philology of the English Tongue*, 5th edition (Oxford: Clarendon Press, 1892), "Bilingualism of the King's English," 83–89; see also Oliver Farrar Emerson, "Professor Earle's Doctrine of Bilingualism," *MLN* 8 (November 1893): col. 404.

12. Oliver Farrar Emerson, "Earle," 404.

13. Ibid., 405.

14. Earle, "King's English."

15. Frederic William Farrar, *Families of Speech* iii (1873), 88. "In the perfect the second letter is often reduplicated, as in *Rabab*."

16. *Penny Cyclopedia* 13 (1839), 314/1.

17. For other *-alk* words, see above.

18. Consider, too, how *teetolly* is a reduplicated form of *totally* and how *hodmandod* reduplicates *dodman*, referring to a shell-snail and figuratively applied to a deformed person. See Thomas Killigew, *The Parson's Wedding* (London, 1663), V.iv; in W. Carew Hazlitt revision of Robert Dodsley's *A Select Collection of Old English Plays* (London: Reeves and Turner, 1874–76), XIV.525. *Flowers of Literature for 1807* (London: n.p., 1808), 278: "His head was thrice broader than his body, which ... accident had made such a hodmandod one of the greatest philosophers of this age."

19. Ablaut reduplication involves "Vowel permutation; systematic passage of the root vowel into others in derivation, as in s*i*ng, s*a*ng, s*o*ng, s*u*ng." *Ablaut* has been used as such for a long time. Thus Ebenezer Thomson in his *Select Monuments of the Doctrine and Worship of the Catholic Church in England Before the Norman Conquest* (London: Lumley, 1849)—sometimes favorite reading where I was being educated as a young man—"As if it took its meaning from 'roar'; which in reality is the *ablaut*-form of 'rear.'" See Thomson, *Monuments*, xxxi.

20. See the list above, and also Jila Ghomeshi, Ray Jackendoff, Nicole Rosen, and Kevin Russell, "Contrastive Focus Reduplication in English (the *salad-salad* paper)" (forthcoming).

21. In differentiated reduplication, the first and second terms, although they are the same words, sound different. This is, in some ways, parallel to synonymy, but it is not synonymy, and it is rarely if ever dealt with in treatises in philology, as if the subject were beneath investigation or beside

the point. *Duplication* involves sounding out the "proper" pronunciation of a word and then slightly varying it. Examples would include: arsy versy, bibble-babble, bingle-bangle, bribble-brabble, chip-chop, clipper-clapper, clitter-clatter, clush-clash, crick-crack, cringle-crangle, crinkle-crankle, criss-cross, curly-murly, curly-wurly, dibble-dabble, dindle-dandle, draggle-draggle, drip-drop, feery-fary, fible-fable, fingle-fangle, finter-fanter, fix-fax, [flaunt-a-flaunt], flip-flap, flip-flop, flant-tant, fluster-bluster, gew-gaw, gibble-gabble, giff-gaff, hinch-pinch, hardy-dardy, higgle-haggle, hoddy-noddy, hoity-toity, hotch-potch, hudder-mudder, huddle-muddle, huff-snuff, hugger-mugger, hurly-burly, hurry-burry, jim-jam, jingle-jangle, killer-diller, knicky-knackers, kim-kam, flim-flam, kit-cat, knit-knot, mingle-mangle, mish-mash, mixty-maxty, namby-pamby, niddle-noddle, nig-nog, mizmaze, [mome], pishery-pashery, pitter-patter, prink-prank, prittle-prattle, prinkum-prankum, repple-depple, ribble-rabble, rimble-ramble, rick-rack, rumpy-pumpy, scribble-scrabble, scritch-scratch, scrip-srap, shiffle-shuffle, shilly-shally, super-duper, see-saw, swing-swang, swish-swash, teeter-totter, tingle-tangle, tinkle-tankel, titter-totter, tew-taw, tig-tag, tip-top, tittle-tattle, tory-rory, trim-tram, trit-torit, trinkum-trankum, tow-row, triff-traff, trish-trash, trush-trash, tum-tum, twittle-twattle, twiddle-twaddle, twingle-twangle, tuzzy-muzzy, whim-wham, wig-wag, wishy-washy, wringle-wrangle, and zig-zag. There are also the longer ones, like nievie-nievie-nick-nack.

22. The technical term *reduplication* might apply. It means twice repeating the same word in order to make up a new word from the two repeated ones. This often involves the "repetition of a syllable or letter, *esp*. in the case of verbal forms (chiefly the perfect tense) in Greek and other Indo-European languages." Standard examples would include the city name *Sansanah* (in Canaan). Reduplication is also exemplified in the Greek *akékoa* from *akouó*, *égagon* from *agó*. (Here one might want also to consider reduplication under its OED definition as "A word-form produced by repetition of a syllable: Tartaros is taken to be the reduplication of the 'tar' in 'tarik'" (William Gladstone, *Juventus Mundi* [1868] vol. xiii [1869], 489). There are more than 1,800 in modern English alone—excluding nursery talk and slang, tunes and refrains, interjections and exotic loanwords (Nils Thun, "Reduplicative Words in English: A Study of Formations of the Types 'Tick-tick', 'Hurly-burly', and 'Shilly-shally'" [1963], ix).

23. BDN International, *Dispatches*, 31 January 2011; http://www.bdn-intl.com/SameSameButDifferent.php; accessed 31 January 2011.

24. Examples of "copy-reduplication," where one of the two words' repeated sounds and/or is exactly the same as the other, as for *same-same* and *talkee-talkee*, are many: beri-beri, boo-boo, clever-clever, din-din, gee-gee, goody-goody, hush-hush, go-go, gong-gong, lap-lap, [lomi-lomi], never-never, night-night, paw-paw, phut-phut, rah-rah, ringat-ringat, shush-shush, pretty-pretty, strum-strum, unk-unk, and wakey-wakey.

25. See Ray D. Kent and Giulana Miolo, "Phonetic Abilities in the First Year of Life," in *Handbook of Child Language,* ed. P. Fletcher and B. MacWhinney (London: Blackwell, 1995), 25. Roman Jakobson, *Child Language, Aphasia and Phonological Universals* (The Hague: Mouton, 1968) argues

that this first year of phonological development is completely unrelated to later language development because infants' very earliest vocalizations do not show an effect of language environment; cf. F. J. Koopmans-Beinum and J. M. van der Stelt, "Early Stages in the Development of Speech Movements," in *Precursors of Early Speech,* ed. B. Lindblom and R. Zetterström (Basingstoke, England: Macmillan Press, 1986), 37–50.

26. "Ablaut reduplication and prosodic well-formedness in English: the criss-crossing of phonetics and phonology." This is the html version of the file: http://englishwww.humnet.ucla.edu/faculty/minkova/EnglishAblaut_Reduplication.pdf.

27. One etymology has it that *hocus pocus* derives from the Latin *hoc est corpus,* which has it that, in the mysterious Catholic transubstantiation, the wafer is transformed into the body of God.

28. Other etymologies include: *"avar k'davar"* (Hebrew: it will be according to what is spoken). Moira Yip, "Reduplication as Alliteration and Rhyme," *GLOT International* 1999 (ROA 377–02100) and "Segmental Unmarkedness Versus Input Preservation in Reduplication," in *Segmental Phonology in Optimality Theory,* ed. Linda Lombardi (Cambridge: Cambridge University Press, 2004). See Max Müller, "*Die Reim- und Ablautkomposita des Englischen,*" PhD thesis (University of Strasbourg, 1909).

29. See Müller.

30. Thomas Blount, Glossographia, or, A dictionary, interpreting all such hard words, whether Hebrew, Greek, Latin, Italian, Spanish, French, Teutonick, Belgick, British or Saxon, as are now used in our refined English Tongue (London: Humphrey Moseley ... and George Sawbridge, 1656): "Reduplication ... is a figure in Rhetoric, when the same word that ends one part of a verse or sentence, is repeated in that which follows."

31. *Athenaeum* 2981 (1884): 765: "There are laws of cæsuric effect in blank verse."

32. Compare the Danish-language phrase *Kongen leve kongen er død* ("The king lives, the king is dead"). The original of the English formula is the fifteenth-century French, "Le roi est mort, vive le roi."

33. Shakespeare, *Richard II* 3.2.3.

34. The Royal Council (1272) puts it thus: "The throne shall never be empty; the country shall never be without a monarch." Cf. Ernst Kantorowicz, *The King's Two Bodies* (1957), 411–12.

35. OED, sv "epana-."

36. Puttenham, *English Poesy* (1589), iii.xix.167. "*Epanalepsis,* or the echo sound."

37. Shell, *The End of Kinship: Measure for Measure, Incest, and the Ideal of Universal Siblinghood* (Stanford: Stanford University Press, 1988), esp. chaps. "Taliation I" and "Taliation II."

38. Thus *whittie-whattie* means "vague or undecided talk or statement; indecision, shilly-shallying; a frivolous excuse." *Bribble-brabble* is "usually identified with *brabbelen* to confuse, stammer, jabber." *Prattle-prattle* suggests "trivial, worthless, or idle talk; also, light, easy, familiar conversation, small talk; chatter, tittle-tattle; childish prattle." *Tittle-tattle* indicates "talk,

chatter, prattle; *esp.* empty or trifling talk about trivial matters, petty gossip." The list would go on to include *dilly-dally and twittle-twattle*: "idle talk, chatter, babble."

39. *Mansfield News* [newspaper] (Mansfield, OH: 27 June 1921), 9/3.

40. Cf. *balk*, *chalk*, and *stalk* and maybe also *caulk*. These "alk" words had their postvocalic (in this case, following the "a") "l" dropped in Middle English. Related may be *stalk* and *lurk* (cf. *lour*).

41. Compare the title of Geoffrey R. Skoll's book: *Walk the Walk and Talk the Talk: An Ethnography of a Drug Abuse Treatment Facility* (Philadelphia, PA: Temple University Press, 1992).

42. Herb Gardner writes in his play *A Thousand Clowns* (New York: Random House, 1962), "I get up, I go, I lie a little, I peddle a little, I watch the rules, I talk the talk" (3.77).

43. Joseph A. Walker, *Tribal Harangue: A Domestic Comedy* (1969) (electronic text), 40. Likewise Skip Gates writes in his *Intimate Critique* (1993), "The first chapter . . . contains an extended recreation of the African-American ritual of signifying, which is also known as 'talking that talk', 'the dozens', 'nasty talk', and so on" (Henry Louis Gates, "What's in a Name?: Some Meanings of Blackness," in *The Intimate Critique*, ed., Diane P. Freedman, Olivia Frey, and Francis Murphy Zauhar [Durham, NC: Duke University Press, 1993], 144).

44. See Skip Gates's understanding of the phrase "talking the talk," in *The Signifying Monkey: A Theory of African-American Literary Criticism* (New York: Oxford University Press, 1988).

45. *POW* [Prisoner of War] magazine (March 2002), 72/1.

46. *Rolling Stone* magazine (28 November 1991), 9/2.

47. According to *Rolling Stone* (1991), Rob Tyner was the "lead singer of the influential Detroit band MC5," and MC5 was "the preeminent political band during the late Sixties and early Seventies" ("MC5's Rob Tyner Dies," *Rolling Stone* [31 October 1991], issue 616). MC5 was the house band for the White Panther Party. For background, see David Carson, *Grit, Noise, and Revolution: The Birth of Detroit Rock 'n' Roll* (Ann Arbor: University of Michigan Press, 2005).

48. Mike Mosher, "FREE!—The Political Economy of the White Panthers—Should the widely-read text of The White Panther State/meant be classified by historians among artists' manifestoes, comparable to those of Berlin Dadaists or Italian Futurists?" *Bad Subjects* 42 (March 1999). The ellipsis replaces these words: "in their cover of John Lee Hooker's *The Motor City is Burning* (1968), written about the African-American riots (or rebellion) of the previous year, the MC5's lead singer Rob Tyner shouted out 'I'm a white boy but I can be bad, too!'"

49. *New York Times* (29 May 1972) 17/4.

50. So the *Mansfield News* (1921), quoted above, gets it pretty much in the spirit of Arthur Miller's dramatic character Willy Loman in *Death of a Salesman*: "Although he has no gilded medals upon his bosom, Howard Herring of the North American Watch company, walks the walk, and talks the talk, of a hero today" (*Mansfield* [Ohio] *News* [27 June 1921], 9/3).

51. Van Morrison, *The Lost Tapes* (album), 1997: "Walk & Talk Lyrics."
52. In *Enlightenment* (album).
53. The movie was directed by Peter Locke in 1971. Park Records.
54. In the CD *Modern Terms* 2006.
55. Dylan, "Ain't Walkin', Just Talkin.'"
56. Joyce Wilson, "Of the Sonnet and Paradoxical Beauties: An Interview with Rafael Campo," *Poetry Porch* 3; http://www.poetryporch.com. Rafael Campo is at Harvard Medical School and has published several volumes of poetry and essays.
57. "La voix, la respiration, la démarche sont identiques" (Balzac, "Théorie de la démarche," first published in the journal *L'Europe littéraire* [1833], later as part of Balzac's collection of essays, *Pathologie de la vie sociale* [Pathology of social life] [1839]).
58. *Independent* (London), tabloid ed., review sect., 17 February 2004, 2/3.
59. See Viggo Hjørnager Pedersen, *Ugly Ducklings?: Studies in the English Translations of Hans Christian Andersen's Tales and Stories* (Odense: University Press of Southern Denmark, 2004).
60. Walter Benjamin, *The Arcades Project*, ed. and trans. Howard Eiland and Kevin McLaughlin (Cambridge, MA: Harvard University Press, 1999). See also Benjamin's "Die Wiederkeht des Flâneur" (1929), about Franz Hessel's *Spazieren in Berlin* (Vienna and Leipzig: Dr. Hans Epstein Verlag, 1929). On this "review" by Benjamin, see Benjamin's correspondence with Gershom Scholem, in *Correspondence of Walter Benjamin: 1910–1940*, ed. Gershom Scholem and Theodor Adorno (Chicago: University of Chicago Press, 1993). For a critical overview of Benjamin's readings of Poe and Baudelaire, see Martina Lauster, "Walter Benjamin's Myth of the Flaneur," *Modern Language Review* 102.1 (January 2007).
61. *The Practice of Everyday Life*, trans. Steven Rendall (Berkeley and Los Angeles: University of California Press, 1984), 98.
62. de Certeau, *Practice*, 101.
63. See too Michael Sheringham, "Everyday Rhythms, Everyday Writing: [Jacques] Réda with Deleuze and Guattari," which largely concerns the flâneur Réda's "Le Pied Furtif de l'hérétique," in his *Les Ruines de Paris* (1977); and Angelika Wellman, ed., *Der Spaziergang: Ein Literarisches Lesebuch* (anthology) (Hildesheim: Olms, 1992).
64. Marcel Mauss, "Techniques of the Body (1935)," in *Techniques, Technology and Civilisation*, ed. Nathan Schlanger (New York: Durkheim, 2006).
65. Jan N. Bremmer, "Walking, Standing and Sitting in Ancient Greek Culture," in *A Cultural History of Gesture*, ed. Bremmer and Herman Roodenburg (Oxford: Polity Press, 1992), 15–35.
66. Erving Goffman, *Relations in Public: Microstudies of the Public Order* (London: Allen Lane, 1971), 6–7.
67. Pseudo-Aristotle, *Problems* 11.902b.
68. R. Camicioli, D. Howieson, S. Lehman, and J. Kaye, "Talking While Walking: The Effect of a Dual Task in Aging and Alzheimer's Disease," *Neurology* 48.4 (1997): 955–58.

69. O. Beauchet, V. Dubost, G. Allali, R. Gonthier, F. R. Hermann, and R. W. Kressig, "'Faster Counting While Walking' as a Predictor of Falls in Older Adults," *Age and Ageing* 36.4 (1 July 2007): 418–23.

70. This is the title of a letter from Bastiaan R. Bloem, Yvette A. M. Grimbergen, Monique Cramer, and Vibeke V. Valkenburg of the Department of Neurology, Leiden University Medical Centre, Leiden, The Netherlands, to *Annals of Neurology* 48.2 (2001): 268.

71. Ruth M. Tappen, Kathryn E. Roach, E. Brooks Applegate, and Paula Stowell, "Effect of a Combined Walking and Conversation Intervention on Functional Mobility of Nursing Home Residents with Alzheimer Disease." Consulted at *NIH Public Access*: Author Manuscript; http://www.pubmedcentral.nih.gov/articlerender.fcgi?artid=1950269.

72. Joe Verghese, Gail Kuslansky, Roee Holtzer, Mindy Katz, Xiaonan Xue, Herman Buschke, and Marco Pahor, "Walking While Talking: Effect of Task Prioritization in the Elderly," *Archives of Physical Medicine and Rehabilitation* 88.1 (January 2007): 50–53.

73. A. Santi, P. Servos, E. Vatikiotis-Bateson, T. Kuratate, and K. G. Munhall, "Perceiving Biological Motion: Dissociating Talking from Walking," *Journal of Cognitive Neuroscience* (January 2008).

74. Dr. Michael Barilan (Sackler Faculty of Medicine, Tel Aviv University), personal correspondence with Marc Shell, 4 January 2007.

75. Horace Walpole, *The Castle of Otranto: A Gothic Story* (1765), in *Works of Horace Walpole, Earl of Orford* (London: G. G. and J. Robinson, Paternoster-Row, and J. Edwards, Pall-Mall, 1798), 2:31. Robert B. Hamm, "*Hamlet* and Horace Walpole's *The Castle of Otranto*," *Studies in English Literature [SEL]* 49 (2009): 667–92.

76. Ed. 1812. sig. D4^v.

77. See above.

78. Henry Aldrich, *Artis logicæ rudimenta, accessit solutio Sophismatum in usum juventutis academicae* [1750] (Oxford: J. H. Parker, 1837). For the earlier edition of Aldrich's *Artis logicae compendium* (Oxford: E. Theatro Sheldoniano, 1691), see Early English Books, 1641–1700, # 996:1. The reference is to Diogenes of Sinope.

79. *OED*.

80. See the CD *Talking Feet: Solo Southern Dance* (2007), with Mike Seeger.

81. Charles Lyell, letter to Charles Darwin, 6 September 1938. In Charles Darwin, *Correspondence*, ed. Frederick Burkhardt (Cambridge: Cambridge University Press, 1986), 2:101.

82. "Present Condition of Ireland," *Christian Examiner and Religious Miscellany* (Boston), 4th series 45.10 (July 1848), 133.

83. Letter of 19 August 1785, in *The Papers of Thomas Jefferson*, ed. Julian P. Boyd, Charles T. Cullen, John Catanzariti, Barbara B. Oberg et al. (Princeton, NJ: Princeton University Press, 1950-), 8:406–8.

84. See Richard Serra and Maria Anna Tappeiner's DVD, *Richard Serra— Sehen ist Denken Richard Serra—Thinking on Your Feet* (Berlin: Absolut-Medien, 2007); Absolut Medien Series, Document 929.

85. See John Rajchman, "Serra's Abstract Thinking," in *Richard Serra Sculpture: Forty Years*, ed. Kynaston McShine and Lynne Cooke (New York: MoMA; London: Thames and Hudson, 2007), 63–64.
86. Lynne Cooke, "Thinking on Your Feet: Richard Serra's Sculptures in Landscape," in *Richard Serra Sculpture*, 80.
87. Cambridge, MA: Harvard University Press, 1986, 10.
88. Both in manuscript form at Christ Church Library, Oxford. See Henry Aldrich, *Selected Anthems and Motet Recompositions*, ed. Robert Shay, Recent Researches in the Music of the Baroque Era (Madison, WI: A-R Editions, 1998), 85.
89. *Summulae logicales magistri Petri Hispani* [Logical matters of Master Peter of Spain], thirteenth century.
90. Among the many Oxford-educated persons who made editions of Aldrich's work is John Wesley, the founder of Methodism.
91. See Carroll's "Vivisection as a Sign of the times" [a letter to the editor of *Pall Mall Gazette*] (10 February 1875), in chap. 4 of Stuart Dodgson Collingwood's *Life and Letters of Lewis Carroll* (London: T. F. Unwin, 1898).
92. *Artis logicae rudimenta*, ed. Henry Longueville Mansell, 4th ed. (London: Rivingtons, 1862), 140–41.
93. Aristotle, *Physics*, VI, pt. 9; trans. R. P. Hardie and R. K. Gaye.
94. Simplicius, *On Aristotle's Physics 6*, trans. David Konstan (Ithaca, NY: Cornell University Press, 1989).
95. "Zeno contends that reason contradicts the evidence of the senses. Diogenes replies that the evidence of the senses contradicts that of reason" (Mansel, "Note in Aldrich, ed. Mansel, *Rudimenta* [Oxford: William Graham: Whittaker and Co. London, 1852], 142).
96. Favorinus of Arles notes that Zeno was Parmenides's favorite student; Diogenes Laertius, *Lives*, "Life of Parmenides."
97. "This paradox still perplexes even those who know that it is possible to find the sum of an infinite series of numbers forming a geometrical progression whose common ratio is less than 1, and whose terms consequently become smaller and smaller and thus 'converge' on some limiting value" (Alfred Hooper, *Makers of Mathematics* [New York: Random House, 1948], 237).
98. Kevin Brown, "Zeno and the Paradox of Motion," in *Reflections on Relativity* (lulu.com, 2011), 252–59, claims that the paradox is a "'Rorschach image' onto which people . . . project their most fundamental phenomenological concerns."
99. Georg Wilhelm Friedrich Hegel's *Logic* (1812–17) and Bertrand Russell's *Principia Mathematica* (1910).
100. Roger Dunkle, "Swift-Footed Achilles," *The Classical World* 90.4 (March–April 1997): 227–34.
101. For Achilles's death by means of a poisoned-arrow in the heel, see Ovid, *Metamorphosis* 12:580–619.
102. Lewis Carroll, "What the Tortoise Said to Achilles," in the philosophical journal *Mind* 4.14 (April 1895): 278–80; my emphasis.

103. Frederic William Maitland, *The Life and Letters of Leslie Stephen* (New York: Putnam: London, Duckworth, 1906), 366. Stephen was father of both Virginia Woolf and Vanessa Belt.

104. [Pseudo-]Plutarch, *Lives of the Ten Orators*, trans. Charles Barcroft, in *Plutarch's Morals*, with various translators (London: R. Bentley, 1690). See also Shell, *Islandology*, forthcoming.

105. Richard H. Immerman, *The CIA in Guatemala: The Foreign Policy of Intervention* (Austin: University of Texas Press, 1982), 102.

106. Thomas Dekker (probably with Thomas Middleton), *The Honest Whore*, First Part (1604), V.ii. sig. K4^v.

107. For Canetti, see above.

108. Balzac, *Théorie de la démarche et autres texts*, ed. Jacques Bonnet (Paris: Pandora/Le Milieu, 1978), x.

109. Erwin W. Straus, "The Upright Posture," *Psychiatric Quarterly* 26.1–4 (October 1952): 529–61.

110. On the prosody of the "dying fall," see George Saintsbury's remarks on the ending couplet of Alfred Lord Tennyson's poem "Ode on the Death of the Duke of Wellington" (1852): "And in the vast cathedral leave him, / God accept him, Christ receive him." In Saintsbury, *A History of English Prosody from the Twelfth Century to the Present* (London: MacMillan and Company, 1910), 3: 206. For the reference to Twelfth Night, see above.

111. On Wilhelm and Eduard Weber in this context, see Brian L. Davis, Maunak V. Rana, and Ari Levine, "Human Gait and Joint Mechanics: Is the Pendulum Swinging Back to Passive Mechanics?" in *Classics in Movement Science*, ed. Mark Latash and Vladimir M. Zatsiorksy (Champaign, IL: Human Kinetics, 2001), 87.

112. John Napier, *The Roots of Mankind* (Washington, DC: Smithsonian Institution Press, 1970), 165.

113. Merleau-Ponty, *Éloge de la Philosophie* (Paris: Édition Gallimard, 1953), 58/59; translation in *In Praise of Philosophy and Other Essays*, trans. John Wild, James Edie, and John O'Neill (Evanston, IL: Northwestern University Press, 1963). According to Friedrich Diez, the etymology of the French *boiteux* connects its meaning with the ham knee joint (*boiste*). For the link with Freud, see also Lucien Israël, *Boiter n'est pas pécher* (Paris: Denoël, 1989); *boiter* is the French word often used to translate the German *hinken*.

114. Merleau-Ponty, *Éloge*, 61. Cf. Richard Shusterman, "The Silent, Limping Body of Philosophy," in Shusterman, *Body Consciousness: A Philosophy of Mindfulness and Somaesthetics* (Cambridge: Cambridge University Press, 2008), 152.

INDEX

Abravaya, Ido, 49
"Achilles and the Tortoise," 143–45, 203nn95–98
acting, 18–19
Adorno, Theodor, 48, 103–4
Aldrich, Henry, 142, 143
Alexander, Henry, 52
ambling, 78–80
Ammons, A. R., 72, 80
Andersen, Hans Christian, 38
animals: animal-feet and verse-feet, 20, 102; canine walkies, 22–23; galloping verse, 23–24, 129; Hamlet's, crawl, forked tongue, 58–59; politics of walking and, 101, 146; talking and walking, 157n153; tortoise parables, 129–30, 130f, 132, 143–45; walkie talkies and, 92–93. See also ducks and drakes
animated cartoons, 88–89, 92–94, 109
Anthon, Charles, 108
Apollinaire, Guillaume, 24, 25f, 32
Aristotle, 20, 127, 143
art to walk through, 143
Ascham, Roger, 27, 28
Ashbery, John, 73
automatons, 93, 94f

Bach, Johann Sebastian, 51–52, 126, 166n96, 192n21
Baines, Andrew Cuthbert, 47
Balzac, Honoré de, 1, 30, 31, 100, 111, 114, 139
Barilan, Michael, 141
Baum, L. Frank, 91
Beethoven, Ludwig van, 119–20, 121, 191n46
Bell, Alexander Graham, 52, 123–26
Bell, Alexander Melville, 37–38, 161n229
Benjamin, Walter, 13, 140

Bergson, Henri, 105–6
Berlin, Irving, 88
Berlioz, Hector, 116, 119–21
Bible: a barber speaks, 109; "in the beginning," 4, 41–49; Jacob's limping, 83–84; reduplication, 136; sons killed by fathers, 66, 173n58, 174n60; translation variations, 43–44, 47, 66, 83; walking is what "counts," 138; "walk in the spirit," 126, 192n21. See also Moses
blank verse, 62, 170n25
Bradley, A. C., 68
breathing and breath, 45–46, 48–49, 62, 136. See also caesura; stutter and stutterers
Bulwer, John, 123, 125, 126, 127, 192n1
bumming, 76–78
Byron, George Gordon, 23, 39, 74, 79

caesura, 11–14, 56, 61, 103, 117, 136, 199nn31–34. See also breathing; stutter
calligrams, 25f, 32–33
calligraphy, 22, 32–35, 34f, 35f–37f
Campione, Thomas, 21, 28
Campo, Rafael, 139
Canetti, Elias, 101, 102, 146
Carroll, Lewis, 58, 143, 144–45
Celan, Paul, 45
cerebral palsy, 81
Certeau, Michel de, 140
Chaplin, Charles: The Great Dictator, 102–3, 104, 106–9, 186nn32–33, 188n66; Hitler's speech and voice, 102, 111, 184n17; Modern Times, 108, 187n48
Charcot, Jean-Martin, 80–81
Chiang Yee, 33, 34f
chirology, 125–26. See also sign language

Churchill, Winston, 106, 116, 118
cinematography, 88–99, 108. *See also* talkies
claudication, 63, 147, 173n48
Claudius, 65, 117
Coleridge, Samuel Taylor, 14, 18, 76, 78
comedy and humor, 3, 97, 102, 104–6, 108–10, 136, 139, 142
comma, 62, 136, 170n23
Conrad, Joseph, 12, 101
Coppola, Francis Ford, 99
crab walk, 63–64, 77, 172n35
crowds and movement, 101–15

dancing, 9, 23, 30–36, 60, 67, 69, 74, 102, 104, 106; tap films and dancers, 15–16
Daniel, Samuel, 20, 21
Dardot, Liliane, 6f
Demosthenes, 145
de Quincy, Thomas, 30, 77, 78
Determann, Herman August, 81
Dickinson, Emily, 91
dilation, 27, 73, 79
Diogenes of Sinope, 93, 143–44, 203nn95–98
disabled/disability: biblical beginnings and, 48–49; blind English poet, 42; club-footed lord, 23, 39, 74, 79; deafness, 119, 123; in *Hamlet*, 57, 58–59, 64–65; inability to join crowds, 101; philosophy limps, 147; psychogenic pedal limping, 80–81; sign language, 125–32; silent films, 95–97, 182n35; talk and limp/halt, 3, 10, 28, 53, 55, 65, 85–87, 97–99, 117, 139, 190n12; walking/talking cures, 72–73. *See also* lame metrics; polio; stutter
double exposure, 98, 183n46
doublets, 133–34, 196n5. *See also* reduplication
Dryden, John, 27
dubbing (voice), 95, 96, 182n40
ducks and drakes: anatine quacks, 109–11, 139; "Digesting Duck," 93, 94f; "duck test" of Wonderland, 145–46; as Hitler, 109–10; stone skipping, 39, 162nn240–41; talking and walking like, 139; *The Ugly Duckling*, 140f. *See also* animals; goose-stepping
duplication and ablaut duplication, 135, 197n19, 197n21
Dylan, Bob, 54, 138–39
dyskinesia, 81

Earle, John, 134
education, purpose of, 130–32
Education for Death: The Making of a Nazi (1943), 110–11
Eisenstein, Sergei, 108
Elliott, Geoffrey, 117
em-dash, 65, 91, 145
Emerson, Ralph Waldo, 1, 11, 91
epanalepsis, 136, 199n36
epizeuxis, 69–70
Euripides, 101, 184n10

feet/foot: animal-feet and verse-feet, 20, 102; definitions, 9, 10–11, 15; limping feet poems, 86–87; missing foot/metrical pun, 145; pedestrian, 73–76; podium, 108–9; prosthetics, 27; Pyrrhic, 61; structure of, 126; "think on your feet," 142–43
films, silent, 94–97, 182n35. *See also* talkies
Finch, Annie, 19
fingers, walking and talking, 52, 123–26, 124f–125f
Firth, Colin, 118–19
Fleming, Abraham, 65
Florio, John, 22
forked tongue, 58–59, 83
French Revolution, 30, 75, 112
Freud, Sigmund, 7, 58, 72–73, 81–84, 86, 87
Frith, John, 65

Gassendi, Pierre, 5
Gauguin, Paul, 16, 17f
Gaylord, Alan T., 108
Geddes, Alexander, 108
George VI (1936–52), 103, 106, 109, 116–22, 190n12
Gilbert, Roger, 74
god/God: walking voice, 41–49, 66
Goffman, Erving, 141
Goldstein, K., 81
goose-stepping, 102, 103–6, 107, 109–11, 186n42, 186n44
grammar and grammarians, 9, 121, 134–35
gramophone advertisement, 45, 122
Grass, Günther, 64, 103–4
Graves, Robert, 117
gravity, 146–47
Gutzmann, Hermann, 87

Hacker, Marilyn, 19
Hacket, John, 67
Hadot, Pierre, 141

Index

halt/haltingly, 65, 87, 170n25. *See also* disabled/disability
Handel, George Frideric, 46–47, 50, 51, 164n45, 164n56
hand rhetoric/hand talking, 10, 123–26
Hart, James D., 22
Harvey, Gabriel, 24
Hazlitt, William, 18, 73, 74, 76, 77–78, 177n43
Hebrew-language scholars, 43, 44
Hegel, Georg Wilhelm, 4, 13
Henry, Matthew, 138
Heyrman, Hugo, 32
Hilmi, Ahmed, 36f
hink/hinking, 80–87
Hipponax of Ephesus, 26
Hitchcock, Alfred, 97–99
Hitler, Adolf, 102–3, 106–7, 118, 185n20, 187n52
Hobbes, Thomas, 5
Hölderlin, Friedrich, 13, 18
hopping, 78–80
Huloet, Richard, 62
hypnosis, 82
hysteria, 58–59, 80–85, 97–99

ischiorrhopgic (back broken) verse, 18, 26
Ives, Charles, 111, 113–14

Jarvis, Robin, 74–75
jazz, 22, 46, 50, 52, 133; list of, 52
Jeffer, Robinson, 27
Jefferson, Thomas, 142
Johnson, Samuel, 78

Kahlo, Frida, 28–30, 29f
Kant, Immanuel, 30, 121, 191n49; as a walker, 30, 146, 159n192
Kaspar, Johann, 100
kinesiology and prosody, 20–22
The King's Speech (2010), 103, 109, 116–22
Kleist, Heinrich von, 104, 185n27
Klima, Edward S., 128
"knock-kneed," 117–18, 190nn12–13
K'uei Hsing, 32–33

La Marseillaise, 111
Lamb, Charles, 73
lame metrics, 22, 24–30, 78, 79, 86–87, 107, 117. *See also* disabled/disability
language: bone, hamlet, shank, 174n66; fencing terminology, 69; logopedia, 142; *pæd-* and *ped* conflation, 131; pen as mighty, 33, 161n218; rhyme, 28; rhythm, 50–51; scansion, 10–11, 21–22; sign language, 128–29, 193n41; stay/stayed/paralyzed, 66–67, 174nn60–61; "straight" meanings, 3, 130–31; walking style and, 140–41; walking voice, 41–49. *See also* reduplication; speech and/or language therapists
Let's Make Love (1960), 3, 102, 139
Levin, Harry, 36–40
Lewis, Joe E., 96–97, 183n42
limping iambics, 85–87
Lin Yutang, 33
"Lipsian hop," 78
Liu Qi, 32
Loewe, Johann Karl Gottfried, 87
logopedia, 142
Logue, Lionel George, 103, 117, 118–22, 185n21
Lully, Jean-Baptiste, 54
Lyell, Charles, 142

macaronics, 108, 112
Maitland, F. W., 145
Mansel, Henry Longueville, 144
marching and marching bands, 111–15
Mason, John, 61
Matheson, Johann, 126
Mauro, Robert, 14
Mauss, Marcel, 19, 100–101, 105, 140
McNeil, William, 101–2
Merleau-Ponty, Maurice, 147
Meschonnic, Henri, 8
metaphor, 24–30, 139–40. *See also* animals
Metz, Christian, 108
Miles, Dorothy, 127–29, 193n26, 194n42, 194nn45–46
Miller, Tim, 9
Milton, John, 28, 37, 42, 43, 64, 158n183, 162n2, 173n45
mobility, 62–63, 97–99, 171n25
montage, 108
Monteverdi, Claudio, 49, 50–59
Monty Python's Flying Circus, 105, 112
Moses (the lame stutterer), 3, 8–9, 32, 43–44, 45–46, 84, 96, 183n41
Mosher, Mike, 138, 200n48
motion pictures. *See* talkies
Mourgues, Michael, 11
Mozart, Wolfgang Amadeus, 56, 119, 121
Munk, Edward, 39
Musa, Hassan, 35–36, 37f
music and musical notation: archaic link to talking, walking, dancing, 48–49; "let your fingers do the walking" songs, 123–24; pause signals, 12,

59–62, 65–67, 172n31; pedal aspect of syncopation, 88–89; popular, big band, etc., 10, 19–20, 31–32, 52–54, 56, 111, 132, 133, 138; rhythmic structure of a foot, 126; shofar, 44–48. *See also* walking bass; jazz
Muybridge, Edward, 24, 98
My Fair Lady (1956, 1964), 96

Nadel, Arno, 47–48
Nakagawa, Soen, 34, 35f
Napier, John, 130, 146
Nashe, Thomas, 20–21, 23
Nazis, 102, 114, 116. *See also* goose-stepping
neurology, 70, 73, 80–81, 125–26, 141–42
Nietzsche, Friedrich, 3, 31, 67
nursery rhymes, 17–18, 39, 109–10, 162n241, 183n41
Nyman, Michael, 55

O'Brien, Mark, 14
Oedipus, 3, 16–17, 139
Offenbach, Jacques, 106, 111, 130
Orbison, Roy, 53–54
Ovid, 20, 93, 101, 127, 155n123

Palmer, Thomas, 75
paralysis, 58, 66–67, 80, 97–99, 107, 141, 183n46
Parnell, Thomas, 26
The Passionate Pilgrim (1599), 65
Patterson, Richard, 145–46
pedagogy, 131
pedal: definitions, 19, 149n3, 154n107
pedeconference, 99, 183n53
pedestrian, 73–76
philosophers and theorists: philosophy as limping, 147; a stuttering or a walking, 139; as walkers, 4, 11, 28, 30, 75–76, 91, 131, 141, 159n192
Plato, 4, 93, 127, 131
platypus, 93
Playford, John, 88
poets and poetry: lame metrics, 24–30; poetry of walking, 4–5, 9, 11, 17–21, 31; poets who walk, 18–19, 42, 72, 76–78, 162n3
polio, 14, 28, 29f, 53, 81, 99, 106, 127, 141
Poole, Joshua, 20
prosody and rhythm and meter: beat, 11, 14–17, 24; galloping verse, 23–24; kinesiology and, 20–22; "knock-kneed," 117–18; macaronics, 108, 112; of music and language, 50–51;

the "pause," 12, 59–62, 65–67, 172n31; pedestrian dance, 74–75; politics of rhythm, 101, 102, 146; Pyrrhic foot and, 22, 61; development of civilization (list of literature), 7; of sign language, 128–29; structure of a foot, 126; stuttering, 120–21; swimming and, 38–40; understandings of (various), 7–9
psychoanalysis, 53–54, 72–73, 80
Purcell, Henry, 53, 54–56, 168n136, 169n138
Puttenham, George, 13, 21, 22, 23, 24, 26, 69, 175n71
Pygmalion, play and films (1916, 1938), 93, 96, 107, 122, 182n38
Pyrrhic, frozen, paused, 12, 22, 60–62, 65–67, 143, 144, 145, 172n31

reduplication (and twoblets), 133–36, 197nn18–19, 198n22, 198n24, 199n38, 199nn26–30; ablaut duplication, 135, 197n19; examples of, 196n3, 196n6
Reeves, David Wallis, 113–14
rheology, 8, 39–40
riddle of the Sphinx, 15, 16
Rückert, Friedrich (trans.): *Hinkende Jamben*, 85–87
Ruff, Jacob, 44

Safadi, Yasin, 34
Saintsbury, George, 9, 39, 117–18; "falling cadence," 146, 204n110
saunter: definitions, 4, 149n7
Sayers, Dorothy Leigh, 24
scansion and breathing, 9–11, 16, 61. *See also* breathing and breath; caesura
Schlegel, August Wilhelm, 18
Schnitzler, Arthur, 82
Schoenberg, Arnold, 47–48, 49, 165n65
Schwabsky, Barry, 18
Scott, Paul, 129–30, 130f
Scott, Walter, 79, 141
Seidler, David, 118–19
Sempill, Robert, 39
Serra, Richard, 142–43
Shaftesbury, Lord, 79
Shakespeare, William: 14, 23, 27–28, 64–65, 68, 70–71, 74, 127, 136, 139, 146; *The Tempest*, 63, 71, 100, 121–22, 162n8; trippingly, 57, 61–62, 69–70, 80
–*Hamlet*: claudication (crab, ham, pork), 63–65; crawling Hamlet, 49, 57–59; dying, 146; Hamlet's soliloquy, 103, 117, 119; meaning of

Index

"mobled," 62–63, 171–72nn26–27; one leg up, 132; the play within the play, 57, 60–62; Pyrrhus/Hamlet, frozen, paused, 12, 60–62, 65–67, 143, 144, 145, 172n31; scansion, 10; stuttering, 120; "threes" in/"triplex," 68–71; uncaesaric invertibility, 136; use of goose-quills, 33; "will he, nill he," 65–67
shofar (musical horn), 44–48, 66, 164n38, 174n62
Sidney, Philip, 13
sign language, 125–32, 193n41
Singin' in the Rain (1952), 95–96
slips of the tongue, 80, 83–85
Solnit, Rebecca, 4–5
solvitur ambulando, 143–45
Songs from Milk Wood, 129
Sophocles, 13, 16–17, 139
speech and/or language therapists, 103, 118–21, 130–31, 141, 185nn21–22
Spenser, Edmund, 22, 24, 26, 158n167
Spitzer, Michael, 13
Steele, Joshua, 9–10
Steiner, Rudolf, 13–14
Stella, Frank, 143
Stewart, Jimmy, 97–99
Stewart, John "Walking," 75–76, 79
Stewart, Susan, 17
Stoker, Gill, 18–19
stones, skipping of, 39–40, 162n240, 162n245
The Story of Joe E. Lewis (Cohn), 96–97, 183n42
Strauss, Erwin W., 57
stutter and stutterers: allied with irregular gait, 26; as chattering, shivering, freezing, 54–55; hexameter and, 13; missing foot/metrical pun, 145; music as stuttering, 119–21; Porky Pig, 61; recitation for, 37, 103, 117, 118, 161n229; reduplicate words, 135; stumblers and, 87, 117; "teeters on the edge," 146. *See also* caesura; Chaplin, Charles; disabled/disability; *Wizard of Oz* (1939); *individual stutterers*
swimming, 14, 36–38

talkies, 88–99, 102–3, 104, 106–9, 182n35
talking cures, 30, 59, 72, 80–85, 87
Talk the talk: meanings of, 137–38, 200nn41–43
Tarlton, Richard, 70
Tatter, John D., 76
Thoreau, Henry David, 4, 11, 91

"The Tortoise and the Hare," 129–30, 130f, 143
translation, 28, 43–44, 47, 59, 66
trippingly, 15, 57, 61–62, 69–70, 80, 83, 132
Twain, Mark, 11, 112–13
"The Two Gold Coins," 85–86
Tyner, Rob, 138, 200n48
Tynyanov, Yuri, 108

Van Gogh, Vincent, 16
Vaucanson, Jacques, 93, 94f
Vergil: *Aeneid*, 10, 28, 59–60, 63, 170n19
vertigo of walking, 2, 147
Vidor, Charles, 96–97

walk and gait, character revealed in, 20, 100–103, 140–41, 184n3
Walker, Alexander, 100
Walker, J. A., 137
Walker, Obadiah, 26
walkie-lookie (creepie-peepie), 92, 181n20, 196n3
walkie-talkies, 92–94, 135
walking bass, 46, 49–54, 114, 127, 166nn81–82
walking: definitions, etymologies, 14, 60, 83, 146, 170n21; observational study of, 104–5
walking meditation *(cankama)*, 3–4
walking on talking, 3–6, 6f
walking poems. *See* poets and poetry
Walk the walk: meanings of, 137–39, 200nn41–43
Walky Talky Hawky (1946), 88–89, 92–94, 181n23
Wang Xizhi, 33–34
Warshauer, Meira, 47
Warton, Thomas, 79
Waterman, William, 64–65
Weber brothers, W. E. and E., 104–5, 146
Wessel, Horst, 110, 112
White, Richard Grant, 60
Whitman, Walt, 60
Williamson, George, 78
Wizard of Oz (1939), 89–91, 96
Wordsworth, William, 18, 27, 58, 72, 73, 76–78, 79, 80, 178n54

"Yankee Doodle" ("The Lexington March"), 112, 114–15
Yellow Pages, 123–24, 124f–125f

Zeno of Elea, paradox of, 143–45, 203nn95–98
Zhu Yunming, 34

VERBAL ARTS :: STUDIES IN POETICS
SERIES EDITORS :: Lazar Fleishman & Haun Saussy

Kiene Brillenburg Wurth, *Between Page and Screen: Remaking Literature Through Cinema and Cyberspace*

Jacob Edmond, *A Common Strangeness: Contemporary Poetry, Cross-Cultural Encounter, Comparative Literature*

Christophe Wall-Romana, *Cinepoetry: Imaginary Cinemas in French Poetry*

Marc Shell, *Talking the Walk & Walking the Talk: A Rhetoric of Rhythm*

Ryan Netzley, *Lyric Apocalypse: Milton, Marvell, and the Nature of Events*

Ilya Kliger and Boris Maslov (eds.), *Persistent Forms: Explorations in Historical Poetics*. Foreword by Eric Hayot

Ross Chambers, *An Atmospherics of the City: Baudelaire and the Poetics of Noise*

www.ingramcontent.com/pod-product-compliance
Lightning Source LLC
Chambersburg PA
CBHW020109020526
44112CB00033B/1103